THE CONSTITUTION OF CHINA

This book on China's constitution and its tradition of constitutionalism is one of the first in the English language and as such provides a much needed overview of China's constitutional history and present arrangements. The nine chapters are divided into three parts. The first part (chapters one and two) deals with China's constitutional history, its indigenous and Confucian antecedents, as well as the turbulent century that led up to the 1982 Constitution and the new order that this ushered in. The second chapter deals with the distinctive features of its current constitution. The second part of the book (chapters three through six) introduces the institutional structure defined in the current constitution – the relationships between the Central government and the regions, the role of the Party and the People's Congress, the meaning of the socialist rule of law, and the independence of the judiciary. The third part of the book (chapters seven through nine) discusses the major developments in human rights and their deficiencies – the protection offered to life, liberty, property and equality and, at the same time, the currently dormant areas of political and religious freedom. The book concludes with a chapter looking forward to the future of the People's Congress and Chinese constitutionalism. In sum, the book offers a readable account of the salient features of Chinese constitutional developments in all major areas.

Constitutional Systems of the World
General Editors: Peter Leyland and Andrew Harding
Associate Editors: Benjamin L Berger, Gregoire Webber

In the era of globalisation, issues of constitutional law and good govern-ance are being seen increasingly as vital issues in all types of society. Since the end of the Cold War, there have been dramatic developments in demo-cratic and legal reform, and post-conflict societies are also in the throes of reconstructing their governance systems. Even societies already firmly based on constitutional governance and the rule of law have undergone constitutional change and experimentation with new forms of governance; and their constitutional systems are increasingly subjected to comparative analysis and transplantation. Constitutional texts for practically every coun-try in the world are now easily available on the Internet. However, texts which enable one to understand the true context, purposes, interpretation and incidents of a constitutional system are much harder to locate, and are often extremely detailed and descriptive. This series seeks to provide schol-ars and students with accessible introductions to the constitutional systems of the world, supplying both a road map for the novice and, at the same time, a deeper understanding of the key historical, political and legal events that have shaped the constitutional landscape of each country. Each book in this series deals with a single country or a group of countries with a com-mon constitutional history, and each author is an expert in their field.

Published volumes

The Constitution of the United Kingdom
The Constitution of the United States
The Constitution of Vietnam
The Constitution of South Africa
The Constitution of Japan
The Constitution of Germany
The Constitution of Finland
The Constitution of Australia
The Constitutional System of Thailand
The Constitution of the Russian Federation
The Constitution of the Republic of Austria

Link to series website
http://www.hartpub.co.uk/series/csw

The Constitution of China

A Contextual Analysis

Qianfan Zhang

·H A R T·
PUBLISHING

OXFORD AND PORTLAND, OREGON
2012

Published in the United Kingdom by Hart Publishing Ltd
16C Worcester Place, Oxford, OX1 2JW
Telephone: +44 (0)1865 517530
Fax: +44 (0)1865 510710
Email: mail@hartpub.co.uk
Website: http://www.hartpub.co.uk

Published in North America (US and Canada) by
Hart Publishing
c/o International Specialized Book Services
920 NE 58th Avenue, Suite 300
Portland, OR 97213-3786
USA
Tel: +1 (503) 287-3093 or toll-free: 1-800-944-6190
Fax: +1 (503) 280-8832
Email: orders@isbs.com
Website: http://www.isbs.com

© Qianfan Zhang 2012

Qianfan Zhang has asserted his right under the Copyright, Designs and Patents Act 1988 to
be identified as the author of this work.

British Library Cataloguing in Publication Data
Data Available

ISBN: 978-1-84113-740-7

Typeset by Hope Services Ltd, Abingdon
Printed and bound in Great Britain by
TJ International Ltd, Padstow, Cornwall

Preface

This book aims to produce a readable narrative and analysis of Chinese constitutional developments in all major areas. It contains nine chapters that can be roughly divided into three parts. The first part (chapters one and two) deals with China's constitutional history and the distinctive features of the current constitution. The second part (chapters three through six) introduces the institutional structure defined in the current constitution, and the third part (chapters seven through nine) discusses the major developments in human rights and their deficiencies.

In the course of writing this book, I received much help and support for which I am grateful. I first thank Professor Andrew Harding for inviting me to write the book and providing me with the opportunity to think through some of the Chinese constitutional problems in a different language. I thank Andrew, Professor Benjamin Berger and the Hart editor Ms Lisa Gourd, for spending much time editing the manuscript and making it a better book, and Ms Putachad Leyland for her wonderful design of the cover and the Hart Publishing team for their elegant and efficient handling of the manuscript. I thank Professor Jeremy Webber for graciously sponsoring my visit to the beautiful University of Victoria between September 2009 and January 2011, during which the main body of this book was completed. I thank Dean Donna Greschner, Associate Deans Cheryl Crane, Heather Raven and Elizabeth Adjin-Tettey, and former Dean Andrew Petter, who made my visit possible and my teaching experience at UVic Law Faculty both enjoyable and rewarding. Last but far from least, I thank my wife, Maria Xiaoyang Wei, who shared much happy time with me during our Victoria visit.

This book is dedicated to my friend and colleague, Professor Cai Dingjian (1955–2010), who fought tirelessly for China's constitutionalism till the very end of his life.

Table of Contents

Glossary of Terms

Pinyin	Original Chinese	Translation
bairi weixin	百日维新	Hundred Days Reform
beifa	北伐	Northern Expedition
bumen guizhang	部门规章	departmental rule
buwei	部委	ministries and commissions
chengshi fangwo chaiqian guanli tiaoli	城市房屋拆迁管理条例	Regulation on Management of Urban House Demolition
Chiang Ching-kuo	蒋经国	
Chiang Kai-shek	蒋介石	
zhanguo shidai	战国时代	Warring States Period
Cixi	慈禧太后	Empress Dowager
cunmin weiyuanhui	村民委员会	villagers' committees
dangzhang	党章	Charter of the Chinese Communist Party (CCP)
dangzhi	党治	rule of the party
dezhi	德治	rule of virtue
defang guizhang	地方规章	local rule
difangxing fagui	地方性法规	local regulations
dijishi	地级市	Prefecture-level cities
duli pinglun	独立评论	Independence Review
fa	法	law
fagongwei	法工委	Legal Affairs Commission (LAC)
fagui shencha beian shi	法规审查备案室	Office for Regulatory Review and Records
falü	法律	laws
falü weiyuanhui	法律委员会	Legislative Committee
falü yiju	法律依据	legal grounds

fazhi	法治	rule of law
gaige kaifang	改革开放	open-door reform
gonggong zhishi fenzi	公共知识分子	public intellectuals
gongqingtuan	共青团	Communist Youth League
Guangxu	光绪	Emperor Guangxu
guifanxing wenjian,	规范性文件	normative documents with binding force
guojia zhuxi	国家主席	State President
guomindang	国民党	Nationalist Party
guowuyuan	国务院	State Council
guoying jingji	国营经济	state-operated economy
hanzu	汉族	Han ethnicity
hongtou wenjian	红头文件	red tape
Hu Shih	胡适	
Hu Yaobang	胡耀邦	
huanzheng yumin	还政于民	return political power to the people
jiandu	监督	supervision
jiaoda shi	较大市	relatively large cities
jiating lianchan chengbao zerenzhi	家庭联产承包责任制	household responsibility system
jiceng qunzhong zizhi zuzhi	基层群众自治组织	grassroots mass self-organisations
jigou jingjian	机构精简	institutional streamlining
jijian	纪检	Discipline Inspection Commission
jingji tequ	经济特区	Special Economic Zone (SEZ)
jiti sanbu	集体散步	collective walk
jundui guojia hua	军队国家化	nationalisation of the military
junzheng	军政	military politics
Kang Youwei	康有为	
Liang Qichao	梁启超	
liangxing weixian	良性违宪	benign violation
liansheng zizhi	联省自治	provincial autonomy
lifa yuan	立法院	Legislative Council

lingdao	领导	lead; leader
liufa	六法	Six Basic Laws
liusi shijian	六四事件	Tiananmen Protests
luan shoufei	乱收费	unauthorised fees
mangliu	盲流	blind migrations
manzu	满族	Manchu ethnicity
Mao Zedong	毛泽东	
minzhu dangpai	民主党派	democratic parties
minzhu jizhong zhi	民主集中制	democratic centralism
minzu quyu zizhi	民族区域自治	nationality regional autonomy
minzu	民族	Nation; race; the collective
nanfang dushi bao	南方都市报	South Metropolitan Daily
nongmin gong	农民工	peasant workers
qian guize	潜规则	latent rules
Qin Shihuang	秦始皇	The First Emperor
qinding xianfa dagang	钦定宪法大纲	Outline of Imperial Constitution
qu	区	district
ren	仁	humanity
renmin	人民	people
renmin daibiao dahui	人民代表大会	People's Congress
renmin gongshe	人民公社	People's Commune
renmin minzhu zhuanzheng	人民民主专政	people's democratic dictatorship
renmin tuanti	人民团体	People's organisation
rujia hua	儒家化	Confucianisation
sange daibiao	三个代表	the 'three represents'
sangong xiaofei	三公消费	three public expenditures
sanmin zhuyi	三民主义	The Three People's Principles
sanse xianfa	三色宪法	tricolour constitution
shangyou zhengce, xiayou duice	上有政策、下有对策	For every national policy made above, there are local countermeasures from below

shaoshu minzu zizhiqu	少数民族自治区	ethnic autonomous region
shehui hexie	社会和谐	social harmony
shehui zhuyi	社会主义	socialism
sheng	省	province
sheng guan xian	省管县	direct provincial control over counties
shi	市	city
shijiu xintiao	十九信条	Doctrine of Nineteen Articles
shiyijie sanzhong quanhui	十一届三中全会	Third Plenum of the 11th Congress
shourong qiansong	收容遣送	Custody and Repatriation (CR)
Sirenbang	四人帮	Gang of Four
sixiang jiben yuanze	四项基本原则	Four Cardinal Principles
Sun Yat-sen	孙中山	
Sun Zhigang	孙志刚	
tebie xingzheng qu	特别行政区	Special Administrative Region (SAR)
tiandao	天道	Way of Heaven
tongyi zhanxian	统一战线	United Front
Wei Yuan	魏源	
weiwen	维稳	maintenance of stability
weiyuanzhang huiyi	委员长会议	Session of Chairpersons (of the NPCSC)
Wen Jiabao	温家宝	
Wuchangqiyi	武昌起义	WuchangUprising
wuquan xianfa	五权宪法	five-power constitution
wuwu xiancao	五五宪草	Draft Constitution of May Fifth
xian	县	county
Xi'an shibian	西安事变	Xi'an Incident
xianfa	宪法	constitutional law
xianfa sifa hua	宪法司法化	constitutional judicialisation
xiangpi tuzhang	橡皮图章	rubber stamp
xiang	乡	township

xianzheng	宪政	constitutional politics
Xiaogang cun	小岗村	Xiaogang Village
xingzheng	行政	administrative
xingzheng fagui	行政法规	administrative regulations
xingzheng fuyi	行政复议	administrative reconsideration
xingzheng susong	行政诉讼	administrative litigation
xinwenhua yundong	新文化运动	New Culture Movement
xunzheng	训政	tutelage politics
yangwu yundong	洋务运动	Westernisation Movement
yi,	义	righteousness
yidao qie	一刀切	cutting uniformly with one knife
yide zhiguo	以德治国	governing the state with virtue
yifa zhiguo	依法治国	governing the state according to law
yifu liangyuan	一府两院	one government and two chambers
yiguo liangzhi	一国两制	onecountry, two systems
Yuan Shikai	袁世凯	
zhen	镇	town
zhengzhi ju	政治局	Politburo
zhengzhi xieshang huiyi	政治协商会议	Political Consultative Committee (PCC)
zhixiashi	直辖市	municipality
zhonggong zhongyang	中共中央	Central Committee of the CCP
zhongguo tese	中国特色	Chinese characteristics
zhonghua minguo	中华民国	Republic of China (ROC)
zhongti xiyong	中体西用	Chinese scholarship as the foundation, Western scholarship for application
zhongyang junwen	中央军委	Central Military Commission (CMC)
zhongyang renmin zhengfu	中央人民政府	Central People's Government
zhuxi tuan	主席团	Presidium
zizhengyuan	资政院	Consultative Council
zonggang	总纲	General Principles

zuigao renmin fayuan	最高人民法院	Supreme People's Court (SPC)
zuigao renmin jianchayuan	最高人民检察院	Supreme People's Procuratorate (SPP)
zuqun	族群	ethnic group
zuzhi bu	组织部	Organisation Department

Table of Acronyms

ALL	Administrative Litigation Law
APL	Administrative Penalty Law
ARL	Administrative Reconsideration Law
CCP	Chinese Communist Party
CMC	Central Military Commission
DPP	Democratic Progressive Party (of Taiwan)
HKBL	Hong Kong Basic Law
LAC	Legislative Affairs Committee
LAO	Legislative Affairs Office
LL	Law on Legislation
LPC	Local People's Congress
LPCSC	Local People's Congress Standing Committee
LPG	Local People's Government
NAR	nationality autonomous region
NPC	National People's Congress
NPCC	National Political Consultative Committee
OLVC	Organic Law on the Villagers' Committees
PLA	People's Liberation Army
PRC	People's Republic of China
PSB	public security bureau
PSC	Politburo Standing Committee
ROC	Republic of China
SAPP	State Administration of Press and Publications
SAR	Special Administrative Region
SEZ	Special Economic Zone
SPC	Supreme People's Court
SPP	Supreme People's Procuratorate

Table of Cases

China

Hong Kong

United States

Table of Legislation

Constitutions of China

National Law of China

Administrative Legislation of China

Local Legislation of China

1

A Century of Turmoil: An Overview of China's Constitutional Reform and Revolutions

INTRODUCTION: THE DAWN OF A CONSTITUTIONAL MOMENT – CONSTITUTIONAL ELEMENTS IN THE ANCIENT REGIME AND THEIR LIMITATIONS – Confucian *Li* as a Social Constitution? – Imperial Constitutional Reforms under Western Influence – Lessons to be Learned: The Dilemma of Constitutional Reform in an Authoritarian State – THE FIRST REPUBLIC: THE NATIONALIST REVOLUTION OF 1911 – The Clash of Regimes within the First Republic – An Interlude for Warlords: The Provincial Autonomy Movement and the Experiment with Federalism – The Northern Expedition, Reunification and the Ascendance of Party Rule – Limitations in the Nationalist One-Party Monopoly – WHY REVOLUTIONS FAIL TO BRING ABOUT CONSTITUTIONALISM

I. INTRODUCTION: THE DAWN OF A CONSTITUTIONAL MOMENT

IT WAS THE last day of April 1895. In a mansion outside the inner Capital city, Kang Youwei (康有为), who shortly became China's most influential constitutional entrepreneur, gathered more than a thousand Confucian scholars (举人, juren) participating in the annual imperial examination and prepared to petition the Emperor against signing the Treaty of Shimonoseki with Japan. In most Chinese minds, Japan was but a tiny, peripheral, barbarian island (蕞尔岛, zui'erdao); but to their surprise and humiliation, this 'barbarian' island had eliminated China's entire fleet in a decisive battle on a single day in 1894 and forced its giant neighbour to relinquish sovereignty over Taiwan and the Liaodong peninsula. To be sure, the Sino-Japanese War was not the only humiliating defeat from which China suffered in the nineteenth century; as early as 1840, China had lost the first Opium War to Great Britain, to which China ceded Hong Kong, and had since been defeated in a series of battles by the Western powers and signed a number of unequal treaties. But this time the damage was done by a tiny island that had historically relied on China for its language and cultural heritage and, like China, had undergone centuries of seclusion, until the Meiji Reformation of 1868. What had lent this island such magical power as to defeat an empire many times its size? What did China lack that had enabled Japan to attain such great achievements within such a short period? Ever since the very first defeat, Chinese intellectuals had been searching for ways to strengthen their country. First they saw the immediate necessity of building sturdier warships and more powerful cannons; next they realised the need to establish modern industry as the basis for military power.[1] For almost half a century, they had been preoccupied with the Westernisation Movement (洋务运动, *yangwu yundong*), which introduced new science, technologies and manufacturing to revitalise the ancient country, but the sad fact that the giant fleet they had studiously built for decades disappeared in a single day before a seemingly tiny rival could not have failed to shock them and raise a far-reaching question: what else had been missing?

The nineteenth-century Chinese were nationalists, proud of their cultural tradition, but they were not blind chauvinists who refuses to learn from their rivals. In fact, Japan had become an object of admiration and imitation for the ordinary Chinese; it had been admired not only for its economic and military achievements but also for its achievements in legal and institutional reforms. During merely two decades following the Meiji Reformation, Japan transplanted the entire body of civil, criminal and administrative law from Western legal systems, before it eventually succeeded in adopting the Meiji Constitution in 1889.[2] Constitutional reformers like Kang Youwei and his prominent disciple, Liang Qichao (梁启超), could not fail to seize the chance and make Japan a persuasive

---

[1] See JD Spence, *The Search for Modern China* (New York, WW Norton, 1990) 143–51.

[2] See R Benedict, *The Chrysanthemum and the Sword: Patterns of Japanese Culture* (New York, Mariner Books, 2006) 27–97; and S Matsui, *The Constitution of Japan: A Contextual Analysis* (Oxford, Hart Publishing, 2011) ch1.

case for their own constitutional cause: Japan succeeded because it was a stronger military power, but it was able to build up a strong military and economy only because it had undertaken constitutional and legal reforms as the necessary institutional precondition to its success. It was precisely the lack of a constitution and, together with it, a parliamentary system and rule of law that ultimately accounted for China's failures. It thus became widely accepted that if China was to part with its disgraceful recent past and join the world as a major power, as Japan had successfully done, the most urgent thing was not to build more warships and set up more factories but to prepare for constitutional reforms that would essentially replace the institutional structure of the ancient Chinese state. And this was precisely what Kang and Liang proposed in their petition to the Emperor: strength through institutional reform (变法图强, *bianfa tuqiang*).[3] While the petition ultimately failed to prevent the Emperor from signing the Treaty (just as the many other official petitions on the matter had), the scholarly gathering that day symbolised the first organised constitutional movement in modern China initiated from below.

The impact of the civic constitutional movement proved to be far-reaching. In the span of several years civic associations sprang up across China, and private newspapers thrived. As early as August 1896, Kang and Liang established in Shanghai an influential newspaper, *Current Affairs* (时务报), which soon became the major mouthpiece for constitutional reforms. During the next two years, over 300 associations and news agencies were established across China. Under the persistent influence of this reformist enlightenment, Emperor Guangxu (光绪) finally issued an edict on 11 June 1898, declaring the inauguration of constitutional reform. The next 100 days saw the introduction of China's 'New Deal' (百日维新, *bairi weixin*). The Emperor, following the teachings of Kang and Liang, issued over a hundred directives covering a wide range of initiatives from the right to petition to freedom of the press; from

---

[3] Scholars have recently questioned whether Kang actually presented the petition to the Council of Censors (都察院, *ducha yuan*) as he claimed in his autobiography, but there has been no doubt that he drafted the petition and held the assembly in his mansion. See Mao Haijian, 'Additional Examinations of "Public Petition" I' (2005) 3 *Studies in Modern History* 1; and Mao Haijian, 'Additional Examinations of "Public Petition" II' (2005) 4 *Studies in Modern History* 1. Cf Fang Deling, 'Kang Youwei and the Public Petition: Questioning Additional Examinations of "Public Petition" II' (2007) 1 *Studies in Modern History* 111.

educational reforms to streamlining of bureaucratic structures; from centralisation of finance to modernisation of the army; and above all, the repeal of special privileges enjoyed by the small minority ruling class, the *Manchu* ethnic group (满族), which had managed to maintain dominance over the *Han* (汉族) population for nearly 300 years. Although the imperial edicts fell short of bringing onto the agenda the more grandiose issues of constitutional monarchy and the establishment of a parliament, these reforms seemed to lay a political and legal foundation for the sustainable modernisation of China, just as they had for Japan.

Unfortunately, the reformist momentum was not sustained for long before it was stalled by the threatened underlying *status quo*. On 21 September, the Empress Dowager (慈禧, Cixi, Emperor Guangxu's mother) took over control, put the Emperor under house arrest, repealed all reform measures and executed the 'six gentlemen' – high officials in the reform camp. Kang and Liang managed to flee to Japan and continued to try to muster support for constitutional monarchy overseas. Despite this seemingly fatal conservative backlash, the domestic constitutional movement did not simply fail, since the intellectual elites after 1894 had generally agreed that constitutional reform was necessary for China's modernisation. Shocked by both China's weakness when faced with Western intruders, who overtook the capital and ransacked the imperial Yuanming Park in 1900, and particularly by the Japanese defeat of the Russian fleet in 1904, even the Dowager realised the inevitability of reform and revived the process of constitutional drafting by sending several high-ranking officials overseas to study the constitutional systems of Western countries.[4] An Outline of the Imperial Constitution (《钦定宪法大纲, *qinding xianfa dagang*) was finally promulgated in 1908. Despite its many defects, even vices, it is commonly regarded as the first written constitution in Chinese history and as a convenient point of departure for China's modern constitutional movement.

---

[4] The Qing officials visited a dozen countries, including the United States, the United Kingdom, France, Germany and Japan. Eventually, Germany's Bismarck Constitution (1871) and Japan's Meiji Constitution (1889), both authoritarian constitutions that vested substantive power in the monarch, were selected as blueprints for the Outline, since they were deemed more 'fitting' for China's conditions than the others. See Jing Zhiren, *China's Constitutional History* (Taipei, Lianjing Press, 1984) 134–43.

I shall begin the book with a brief introduction to China's constitutional history, since it not only provides the reader with an important historical perspective and explains why we are where we are now, but also illustrates the basic dilemma that China faces in modernising its constitution and embracing constitutionalism. Some of the historical themes simply recur in a transitional society like China. For example, it is difficult to ascertain why the ruling regime has any interest in fulfilling the promises it made in the Constitution by sharing its powers and making itself accountable to the people, when it has managed to concentrate all powers in its own hands; those within the ruling circle can derive tremendous personal profit from the traditional system, and power-sharing means they will lose at least some of their means for making personal profit. The lessons China learned (or should have learned) from the imperial and Nationalist failures should shed some light on how to transcend China's constitutional predicaments today.

With that in mind, I divide this chapter into several periods, beginning with a short account of indigenous resources for constitutionalism in China. The Confucian concept of *li* (礼, sometimes translated as 'rites' or 'propriety') can be fairly characterised as a social constitution that had governed traditional Chinese society for over 2000 years, but when China was confronted by the Western powers as early as the seventeenth century, the incompatibilities of *li* with modern society became obvious and eventually led to the demise of the traditional institutions. The chapter will then deal with the efforts to modernise these institutions, and it will end with an explanation of the institutional and cultural causes for the repeated failures to establish a stable constitutional state.

II. CONSTITUTIONAL ELEMENTS IN THE ANCIENT REGIME AND THEIR LIMITATIONS

A. Confucian *Li* as a Social Constitution?

That China's constitutional movement did not begin until near the end of the nineteenth century does not imply, of course, that pre-modern China had no conception of constitution or fundamental laws. It is true that the word corresponding nowadays to 'constitution' (宪, *xian*) meant in ancient times no more than laws or edicts in their ordinary senses[5] and was made to designate a constitution only when China imported such meaning from Japan at the turn of the twentieth century. But the Confucian cultural tradition that dominated China for over 2000 was certainly versed in strong normative language and took for granted a few moral precepts as the 'Way of Heaven' (天道, *tiandao*), the application of which to the human world constituted the 'Way of Man' (人道, *rendao*). The most fundamental precepts at the core of Confucianism are humanity (仁, *ren*) and righteousness (义, *yi*), around which an elaborate body of rules on rites, ceremonies, etiquette and other aspects of human behaviour were developed. This body of rules was specific, complex and all-inclusive, covering matters ranging from local festivals to state ceremonies; from specific procedures of marriage to the minute rituals for mourning the dead; from the manner in which children must treat their parents to the education programme for producing social elites. Taken together, they formed a vast normative system of 'propriety' (*li*),[6] which, as its etymology suggests, was a set of customs, conventions and procedures to be practised in daily life for the purposes of cultivating moral virtue, directing and containing human passions, preserving a well-ordered society, and bringing the social lives of ordinary men and women into accord with the basic principles of humanity and righteousness.

According to the *Book of Rites* (礼记, *liji*), a comprehensive collection of rules and their exegesis, *li* was supposed to serve as the basis of every human law and govern every moral aspect of human relationships. It furnished 'the means of determining (the observance towards) relatives, as near and remote; of settling points which may cause suspicion or doubt; of distinguishing where there should be agreement, and where difference; and of making clear what is right and what is wrong'.[7] Similarly, the great Confucian scholar Xunzi (荀子) accorded supreme importance to propriety when he remarked that it 'deals with the great distinction of society through rules and is the unifying principle of gen-

---

[5] According to the first Chinese utilitarian, Mozi (~ 478–376 bc), for example, 'the ancient sage kings promulgated the constitution (*xian*) and issued edicts (*ling*) to define rewards and punishment, with the purpose of encouraging virtues and deterring violence.' See 'Against Fatalism I', Mozi 35: 3, 5.

[6] These rules were collected in a dense *Book of Rites*. See J Legge (ed), *The Sacred Books of China*, vols 27 and 28 (Oxford, Clarendon Press, 1885).

[7] See *Book of Rites* (ibid) vol 27, ch 1, 'Summary of the Rules of *Li*', 63.

eral classes of things'.[8] Its chief function was to maintain the proper distinction of different classes of people by treating people differently according to their moral, social and familial status and to lay down for each separate instructions of proper conduct:

> The ancient kings invented the rules of proper conduct (*li*) and justice (*yi*) for men in order to divide them; causing them to have the classes of noble and base, the disparity between the aged and the young, and the distinction between the wise and the stupid, the able and the powerless; and to cause men to assume their duties and each one to get his proper position.[9]

Although rules of propriety, established and maintained by human beings, were never characterised as natural law, neither can they be characterised as ordinary human laws. For several reasons, Confucians had consistently accorded *li* with a status higher than the rules and conventions formally enforced by particular states or societies. Indeed, *li* as higher law was supposedly taken by the legendary sage-kings from the eternal operations of Heaven, giving rise to the durability if not eternity of its binding force.[10] Of course, not every rule of propriety carried supreme significance; the bulk of specific rules played only minor roles, but they served to realise the core Confucian values of humanity and righteousness, which supposedly defined the very essence of being human. These features make the Confucian system of propriety similar to a modern constitution, marked essentially as it was by its supremacy, durability and the hierarchical structure of norms. Thus, although *li* was manmade (as distinguished from natural) law, it did contain those fundamental precepts that imitate the laws of nature. It had been the fundamental law of the land, supposedly 'framed' as it were by the legendary sage-kings that had governed Chinese society until the early twentieth century.

From this perspective, the traditional debate between rule of virtue (德治, *dezhi*) and rule of law (法治, *fazhi*) was a mischaracterisation.[11]

---

[8] *Xunzi*, ch 1, 'An Encouragement to Study' in *The Works of Hsuntze*, HH Dubs (trans) (Taipei, Cheng-wen Publisher, 1966) 37.

[9] Ibid, ch 4, 'On Honor and Shame', 65.

[10] '*Li* is that which the ancient kings inherited from the Way of Heaven, in order to govern the human passion': *Book of Rites* (above n 6) vol 27, ch 9, 'The Evolution of *Li*', 383.

[11] See, for example, *Collection of Papers on the Discussions of the Rule of Law and Rule of Man Problem* (Beijing, Social Science Literature Press, 2003).

This debate was initiated between Confucians and classical Legalists during the Warring States Period (战国时代, *zhanguo shidai*) (475–221 BC), which ended with a massive persecution of the Confucians by the First Emperor (秦始皇, *Qin Shihuang*), who succeeded in vanquishing the warring states and establishing a united China with military power gained through practising Legalist policies. The debate carried on through a large part of Chinese history, however, after the Confucian doctrine managed to regain orthodoxy after the quick fall of the Qin dynasty. The debate was revived once again in the early twentieth century, when *li*, as the moral tradition that had reigned over China for two millennia, was held responsible for the country's weaknesses and failure in confronting Western powers, and was to be replaced by Western political and legal traditions, which were introduced to China together with modern science, artillery and opium. But truly fatal blows against the Confucian tradition arrived only after the Communist takeover in 1949, and its demise culminated in the great devastation of the Cultural Revolution (1966–76) initiated by Mao Zedong (毛泽东), who exhibited a clear personal Legalist inclination when he launched an ideological campaign 'against Lin Biao and Confucius' (批林批孔, *pilin pikong*). The moral and cultural vacuum left after the destruction prepared the way for the reintroduction of the Western conception of the rule of law, the Chinese variant of which became codified in the Constitution in 2004. Yet these vicissitudes of law, virtue and *li* constituted parts of political fights for governing principles, and suggested little, if anything, of the nature of the concepts themselves.

To be sure, *li* differs from law in important aspects, but in essence the two concepts belong to the same type of social norms. They differ in scope of coverage: *li* covered almost the whole of human social life, while *law* in China's Warring States was limited to penal regulations; yet many of these laws had been transcribed from *li* through a process of so-called 'Confucianisation' (儒家化, *rujia hua*) of laws since the early Han dynasty.[12] Far from being its antagonist, *li* had been the very source and justification of law in imperial China, just as moral or customary principles were the foundation of modern Western laws. *Li* and law also differ in the modes of implementation: while laws relies on compulsory enforcement by the state, the uncodified parts of *li* were enforced only

---

[12] See Qu Tongzu, *Chinese Society and Chinese Law* (Beijing, Zhonghua Books, 1981) 328–46.

through social mechanisms, without the direct aid of the state. Social enforcement could be defective, but that did not abrogate *li* of theoretical or practical binding effect. Partly for this reason, Confucians like Xunzi had always advocated social distinctions and a hierarchical structure in which the parents were to dominate over the children, husbands over wives, the nobles over the common and the superiors over the inferiors, in order to enforce rules of propriety that they believed to be quintessential to a good social order.[13] In contrast, the Legalists, usually ascending from inferior ranks against the status quo, advocated for the equal application of laws to all classes. These social differences were a valid ground for rival policy platforms, but not for making *li* and law fundamentally different governing mechanisms. In other words, there were tensions between them, just as there are tensions between the modern laws of a state and its constitution, but these tensions hardly negate the fact that *li* was not only one type of social norm but the ultimate source from which imperial laws and edicts derived. It was, virtually, a 'constitution' for pre-modern China.[14]

In substance, of course, Confucian *li* was anything but a modern liberal constitution. It was centred on humanity and righteousness, precepts that still govern the world today, but it was clothed in a terribly dogmatic straightjacket, as traditional doctrines usually were. That straightjacket not only deprived individuals of any space for free development but also inculcated a stiflingly intolerant inclination, with lasting influence even today, to readily identify one doctrine as the sole and absolute truth. It prevented *li* itself from evolving over the centuries, during which it grew into an ossified mummy governing a stagnant society. When Confucian *li* was blamed for China's weaknesses and unending failures and was systematically attacked around the time of the May Fourth Movement (五四运动, *wusi yundong*) in 1919, it was to be cast aside altogether and replaced by another orthodoxy, this time imported from the West, and the dogmatic tradition was to perpetuate itself – although that banner was flown by Marxists.

---

[13] A good social order means 'a king should behave like a king, a minister like a minister, a father like a father, and a son like a son': *Analects*, 12: 11.

[14] Zhang Qianfan, 'Between the Natural Law and Ordinary Law: A Constitutional Analysis of *Li*' (2001) 2001 *Law Review of China University of Politics and Law* 336.

B. Imperial Constitutional Reforms under Western Influence

The Opium Wars of 1840 and 1860 marked the beginning of modern China and initiated a cascade of movements that ultimately toppled the theretofore dominant Confucian cultural and political tradition. This is not to say that China had been governed under *li* without interruptions; near the end of almost every dynasty, when courts became hopelessly corrupt and law enforcement was relaxed to the point of bankruptcy, the moral principles implied in *li* obviously fell into disuse. But when society regained its legal order and moral vigour in a new dynasty, everything would be restored to its normal position as dictated by *li*. The only exception was perhaps the Yuan dynasty (1578–1665), during which China was ruled by the Mongols under Genghis Khan and Kublai Khan, who defied the Confucian tradition after they ascended to the throne and maintained their relatively egalitarian nomadic way of life. But to their sorrow, their reign lasted for a mere 87 years, one of the shortest in Chinese history. The rulers of the last dynasty, the Qing (1644–1911), were also a minority (Manchus from northern China) but learned a lesson from their predecessors and completely abandoned their customs, baptising themselves in Confucian culture. Take a look at the Dowager's painting and calligraphy, you cannot fail to be impressed that these were the products of a well-educated Confucian woman. And that made the obvious difference: their dynasty lasted for 267 years, three times as long as that of the barbarous Mongols, and it was brought to an end only by a challenge that China had never met before.

The long record of successful Chinese cultural dominance inspired feelings of confidence, contentedness and pride among pre-modern Chinese. Unlike their contemporary counterparts, they were immensely proud of their cultural tradition, embodied in the unchanging *li*, perhaps even more proud than Americans are of their 200-year-old Constitution. And they felt this way for good reasons. Take a look at China's poetry, literature, arts, the elaborate social etiquette and bureaucratic structure, even its relatively weak scientific inventions. It can hardly be denied that it was a sophisticated civilisation that enabled high personal achievements. The rules in *li* are largely anachronistic today, but even a modern person cannot fail to be struck by the comprehensive design of the education programme and the civility (even some romance) of the marriage ceremony that took place at dusk. It was true that *li* was anything but egalitarian and could be repressive, and perhaps only a small minority of ruling elites had the leisure to practice the full panoply of its rules anyway, the vast majority of population being at all times kept in ignorance and illiteracy;[15] but when its critics imputed to it every failure and backwardness from which China had suffered, as if *li* were monstrous enough to 'devour personality' (礼教吃人, *lijiao chiren*), a now famous quip from a radical novelist,[16] they were simply exaggerating its vice, having determined to make it a scapegoat. At the very least, the conservative ruling elites were deeply convinced that *li* was the very core of Chinese civilisation that made it superior to any foreign civilisation, and the excessive pride they took in their cultural heritage cost them much time in finding the root cause for China's weaknesses and failures.

When China received the first blows from the Western powers, hardly anyone related them to cultural or institutional problems. Initially, intellectuals, both in and out of office, thought the Western powers were just other Mongolian-type barbarians, only this time from the sea and with superior weaponry. Once China had learnt and mastered military techniques from these 'barbarians', then it would be able grow strong enough to bring the same 'barbarians' to its feet (以夷制夷, *yiyi zhiyi*). An influential reformist thinker, Wei Yuan (魏源, 1794–1857), who edited a 50-volume *Geographic Records of Sea Countries* (海国图志, *haiguo tuzhi*) within two years after China's defeat in the first Opium War, explained famously that the purpose of this comprehensive multi-volume work was 'learning from the advantageous techniques of the barbarians in order to subdue the barbarians'. Even though the book did touch upon Western legal and political institutions, the crux of these 'advantageous techniques', he summarised, was 'warships, gunpowder and methods of maintaining and training soldiers'.[17] A few prospective thinkers did advocate the learning of Western constitutional systems, but their opinions failed to attract sufficient attention among officials and intellectuals. It was not until the Sino-Japanese War that Chinese were convinced that

---

[15] It was estimated that as many as 99 per cent of the population were illiterate by the time the first Constitutional Outline was enacted in 1908: Jing Zhiren (above n 4) 134.

[16] See Lu Xun's influential short story, originally published in *New Youth* in 1918: *Diary of a Madman and Other Stories* (Honolulu, University of Hawaii Press, 1990).

[17] See Wei Yuan, *Illustrative Records of Maritime States* (Beijing, Zhonghua Books, 1976) 208.

they needed to learn from the West not only the hard science of making more powerful weapons and stronger industry but also the 'soft science' of designing a modern legal and constitutional framework, which was critical for the overall modernisation of this ancient civilisation. National arrogance not only impeded the modernisation efforts and caused China to lag far behind Japan during the first confrontation with Western civilisation, but continues to play a role even today in resisting constitutional reforms inspired by Western models.

Since the very beginning, Chinese officials and mainstream intellectuals were primarily concerned with how to preserve the core of Chinese culture while allowing the peripheries to change as expedience required, with the result being a compromise between native and foreign elements. In 1898 a mixed notion of lasting influence was forged: Chinese scholarship being the foundation, Western scholarship being the application (中体西用, *zhongti xiyong*),[18] which was shortly developed into a systematic theory in an influential pamphlet by Zhang Zhidong (张之洞), *On Encouragement of Learning* (劝学篇, *quanxue pian*), which essentially argued that the core of Confucian moral teachings should remain untouched, while arts, techniques, even laws and the legal system, could be Westernised.[19] And one can still see the same mentality today, when such notions of Western origin as 'market economy' and 'rule of law' are prefixed by 'socialist' (社会主义, *shehui zhuyi*) in Chinese constitutional amendments, and even the notion of 'socialist road' is modified by 'Chinese characteristics' (中国特色, *zhongguo tese*) to distinguish it from other (say, the more orthodox Soviet or North Korean) types of socialism. In retrospect, under the mixed theory of Chinese foundation with Western applications, the space for imperial constitutional reform was quite considerable, since all of the 'superstructures' beyond the moral core could be changed. Presumably, even the political system was amenable to democratic transformation.

Ideological constraints retarded but fell short of stalling sorely needed constitutional reform. What ultimately halted the reform was the threatened interests of the status quo, whose powers would be

---

[18] Sun Jianai, 'Imperial Memorial for Reopening Peking University' in Shen Tongsheng (ed), *Main Collections of Guangxu's Policies*, vol 22 (Yangzhou, Jiangsu Guangling Ancient Books Printing Press, 1991).

[19] See Zhang Zhidong, 'On Encouraging Learning' in Yuan Shuyi, Sun Huafeng and Li Bingxin (eds), *Complete Works of Zhang Zhidong*, vol 12 (Shijiazhuang, Hebei People's Press, 1998) 9767.

impaired and privileges be repealed had the reform gone through as planned. This led to, as we have seen, the abortion of the 'Hundred Days Reform'. Even though the Dowager restored the reform after a forced evacuation from the capital and promulgated the Outline of Imperial Constitution in 1908, the constitutional reform went nowhere in substance. Copied from Japan's authoritarian Meiji Constitution and opening with a pompous, self-perpetuating clause ('The Great Qing will perpetuate for ten thousand generations, and be loved and respected forever'), the Outline itself was a paragon of despotic monarchy with substantive supreme power, a model so familiar to Chinese political tradition, as opposed to the British model of constitutional monarchy with nominal supremacy. Things worsened when the Qing came to 'reform' the bureaucratic structure. While the early rulers of the Qing dynasty, conscious of their own predicament as a minority regime, maintained a balance of opportunities by designing a dual leadership mechanism for each province and major department – one reserved for the Manchu minority and the other for the Han majority – the reform ostensibly made race an irrelevant issue but in effect allowed the Manchu minority to dominate the cabinet by a two-thirds majority; it was aptly nicknamed the 'cabinet of imperial siblings' (亲贵内阁, *qingui neige*).[20] These unpopular measures necessarily alienated the majority Han population even further and paved the way for deeper social crisis when the unwise minority regime indulged itself in dangerous victories.

Before long, a mutiny broke out, putting an abrupt end to the disappointing imperial reform. On 10 October1911, now celebrated annually in Taiwan as the national holiday for the Republic of China, revolutionaries initiated an uprising in Wuchang (武昌起义, *wuchang qiyi*). The imperial house panicked and, under the imminent political pressure, quickly promulgated the Doctrine of Nineteen Articles (十九信条, *shijiu xintiao*) as a new constitutional document. Contrary to the earlier Outline, the Doctrine envisioned a constitutional monarchy borrowed from the British model. Although the Qing regime was still supposed to be everlasting (Article 1), and the Emperor maintained sacred, inviolable dignity (Article 2), his powers were limited to those laid out in this constitutional document (Article 3) and were reduced in substance to no more than that of the nominal State President in China today.[21] The text of the

---

[20] Jing Zhiren (above n 4) 146–47.
[21] See below ch 5.

Doctrine itself was discussed and decided by the Consultative Council (资政院, *zizhengyuan*); the Emperor simply promulgated it (Article 5), and the power of amendment belonged to the Congress (国会, *guohui*). The Congress was also to elect the Prime Minister and other ministers upon his recommendation, and imperial members were excluded from these positions for incompatibility; the Emperor was, again, simply to affirm the appointments (Article 8). He was the commander-in-chief, but domestic forces had to be deployed under special conditions decided by the Congress (Article 10). The Congress was to decide not only the annual budget for the state but also remuneration for the imperial house (Articles 14 and 15); and the imperial regulation governing its own operation had to be compatible with the Constitution (Article 16). Had this 'soft' Doctrine been put into practice, China would have embarked on the gradualist British approach and avoided a century of revolutionary tumult. Unfortunately, the rescue came too late; the long deprived and oppressed populace, having lost its last bit of confidence in the regime and having little patience with anything like a mild reform, found much more appeal in the revolutionary rhetoric of Dr Sun Yat-sen (孙中山), who vowed to 'drive out the Manchu convicts' (驱除鞑虏, *quchu dalu*). And that summon rang the death-knell of China's last dynasty.

C. Lessons to be Learned: The Dilemma of Constitutional Reform in an Authoritarian State

The failure of the imperial constitutional reforms, beginning with the Hundred Days Reform, proved to be ominous for China's next century. Far from a single incident of bad luck, it portended that progressive reform in an authoritarian state was almost doomed to fail. A reform, by definition, is to make changes within the existing political framework rather than outside it; while a revolution aims to forcefully wipe out current institutions together with the persons filling its offices, a reform seeks rather to cope with the current institutions and use the channels they provide to remedy existing wrongs. Reformist strategies usually result in a gradualist approach that is not only less costly to society as a whole but often optimal to all major factions having regard to their long-term interests, including the ruling class, whose legitimacy may be recognised by other groups as long as it is willing to go along with a reform that will accommodate their interests and maintain a minimal degree of confidence in the existing regime. Thus, it seems to be in the best interest of an enlightened ruler to do everything to promote reform, if only to avoid a revolution that is likely to break out once the oppressed groups have lost hope that the existing regime can do any good for their concerns. And this was precisely the argument that some of the high officials in the Qing dynasty used to dissuade the court from resisting reform before the rising pressure of revolution gathered both domestically and from overseas under the leadership of Sun Yat-sen, among others.[22] Unfortunately this seemingly persuasive argument failed to work for several reasons.

First and foremost, in contrast to Tocqueville's thesis that an enlightened despot, like Louis XVI of France, may adopt certain salutary reforms on his own initiative, only to be overwhelmed by the 'rising expectation' of the populace,[23] most authoritarian regimes are naturally opposed to any change of the status quo. Although reform is premised on recognising the legitimacy of the ruling regime and stops short of tossing the regime completely out of office, it nevertheless usually requires it to relinquish some of its privileges and, more often than not, the political power necessary to maintain the privileges, thus directly running counter to at least the short-term interests of the regime and everyone under its patronage. This was most obvious for the Manchu notables of the Qing regime, a small minority that reigned over the dominant Han population for nearly three centuries, during which it monopolised the maintenance of army and enjoyed numerous political, legal and judicial privileges.[24] This privileged ruling clique was instinctively opposed to any social, and particularly political, reform that tended to diminish its ability to maintain its own privileges. In fact, the cabinet reform near the end of the Qing dynasty indicated that a reform might not only fail to achieve its original purpose but positively make things worse by relaxing the previous constraints on the ruling regime, thus creating even more opportunities for exploiting social and political resources.

---

[22] See below ch 5.

[23] A de Tocqueville, *The Old Regime and French Revolution*, S Gilbert (trans) (New York, Doubleday, 1955) 169–79.

[24] For the Manchu privileges, see MC Elliott, *The Manchu Way: The Eight Banners and Ethnic Identity in Late Imperial China* (Stanford, Stanford University Press, 2001) 15. The monopoly over the army was given up only during the Taiping Rebellion in the 1860s, when the Manchu army proved to lack sufficient competence in subduing the rebellion and had to rely on the private armies of Zeng Guofan, a high official of Han origin.

Second, it is true that progressive reform usually serves the long-term interest of a regime, but its rulers may simply fail to see such interest and mistakenly adopt myopic measures. It is also true that, unlike a modern authoritarian regime with a democratic façade, whose interest in good governance is discounted by the term of appointments that may often be expressly provided in its constitution (and thus difficult to circumscribe), a traditional hereditary regime should find it easier to perceive its long-term interest in the perpetuity of its reign. But most conservative power-holders in the last dynasty, represented best by the Dowager, were mediocre, blinded by their immediate self-interest and lacking in vision for the future of the alien country over which they ruled. Even if a few top rulers are farsighted enough to propose a progressive reform, it is likely to remain an individual proposal that will fail to arouse enough sympathy among the ruling clique. Above all, a despotic regime is used to commanding by brute force and maintains excessive confidence in its power and capacity to keep everything in order by suppression rather than negotiation. If one can simply retain all goods with such power, what can be the rationale for giving it up? In a democracy majority, votes decide every change, against which neither personal nor institutional impediments can stand in the way – apart from such mechanisms as presidential veto or judicial review, which serve to check against the arbitrary exercise of majoritarian power and may delay the execution of majority will.[25] But an authoritarian regime will come to the same table with its opponents only when it has used up its power, and by that time, the chance may have well passed for reaching a credible agreement that all sides are willing to accept. And this was precisely what happened to the rulers of the last dynasty. Even with the belated beginning of the Hundred Days Reform, it had plenty of chances to reform and thus help to perpetuate itself, but every time, astonishingly, it rejected its own opportunity and forcefully suppressed reform efforts. Indeed, when the chance for change arrived under the banner of 'constitutional reform', it positively manipulated it for the sake of its own privileges and aggravated the discrimination against the dominant population. At last, when the latter resorted to mutiny against a regime in which their confidence had long expired, it suddenly found itself in a

[25] Judicial review may delay the execution of a genuine majority decision for some time but is usually unable to stall it forever. For the American constitutional experience during the New Deal, see M Tushnet, *The Constitution of the United States of America: A Contextual Analysis* (Oxford, Hart Publishing, 2009) 28–35.

feeble position and quickly enacted a progressive constitutional document to save its own fate. But by then it was too late.

Finally, added to the difficulty, if not impossibility, of sustaining constitutional reform in an ordinary authoritarian regime, the Qing reform was further complicated by the very fact of its minority rule, which made it a vulnerable target of nationalist attacks and, at the same time, further diminished its confidence in peaceful reform for the mutual benefits of itself and of the nation as a whole. From the very beginning, when the minority regime was vigorous, powerful, competent and confident enough to keep things in control, the Qing rulers took positive cautions in reconciling the thorny relationship between the Manchu and Han peoples; by the end of the dynasty, the regime had grown increasingly defensive against any proposal that tended to threaten its status quo. The repressive and regressive measures it took against the Han population could only, of course, further degrade its image, fuel more resentment against itself and make the revolutionary cause against the oppression of an incorrigible minority clique even more appealing to the general population. Thus, although Kang and Liang did their utmost to promote constitutional monarchy even during their exile, their moderate reformist appeal was eventually defeated by Sun Yat-sen's radical call for revolution based on the premise that genuine reform was impossible under a corrupted monarchic regime, and constitutionalism was to be realised only by establishing a brand new democratic republic.[26]

Most fundamentally, of course, the Manchu minority rule merely illustrated the conspicuous lack of popular participation in critical decision-making processes in an authoritarian state, where policy conflicts between reformists and conservatives were invariably carried out in the form of court struggles. Since reformists usually represented the more conscientious but politically weaker strain of the ruling regime and pitted themselves against the more powerful conservatives, who represented the status quo under that regime and were ultimately backed up by the state machinery, their reformist cause necessarily failed. If a reform is for the good of the majority people, then the people themselves must stand up and step in to carry out the reform;[27] otherwise, if they are missing in the political arena and stay out as bystanders, having

---

[26] Spence (above n 1) 230–43.
[27] For the issue of popular constitutionalism in democratic states, see LD Kramer, *The People Themselves: Popular Constitutionalism and Judicial Review* (Oxford, Oxford University Press, 2004).

relegated their own cause to certain benevolent elites, then they cannot help but witness the failure of reform. Even the Emperor himself was put under house arrest when he and his reformist mentors failed to bring constitutionalism to China without the people's support. The people were likewise missing when Yuan Shikai (袁世凯) committed numerous treacheries against the Nationalists (国民党, *guomindang*) after the establishment of the First Republic, as well as when the Nationalists embarked on the Northern Expedition and began to slaughter the Communists (共产党, *gongchandang*) soon after its success in 1927.

The repeated failures of China's constitutional reforms (and revolutions) illustrate the same modernisation difficulty experienced by all nations that are unfortunately trapped in authoritarian models of governance: in such cases, a small group of political elites maintains the monopoly of all powers properly belong to the people and is thus capable of exploiting them to its advantage. The authoritarian regime thus creates its own defenders and perpetuators, who will use the entire state machinery at their disposal to protect their own interests against any reform that threatens to disturb the distribution of powers, until the state becomes so corrupt and notorious as to be incapable of lending them any support, by which time a revolution is bound to break out. In the century following from the Hundred Days Reform of 1898, this same pattern simply perpetuated itself. When armoured vehicles marched toward Tiananmen Square amid protesting crowds on the fateful eve of 4 June 1989, it merely recurred in another social and political context.

III. THE FIRST REPUBLIC: THE NATIONALIST REVOLUTION OF 1911

A. The Clash of Regimes within the First Republic

The republican revolution led by Sun Yat-sen and his Nationalist Party ended the imperial rule of more than two millennia and opened a completely new republican epoch in China. Radical as it might seem, however, the 1911 Revolution did not really end the old regime at one stroke. In many ways the Qing regime was defeated more by its own feebleness than by the strength of the Nationalists, a loosely organised alliance of factions that came under the mantle of Sun's 'Three People's Principles'

(三民主义, *sanmin zhuyi*),[28] virtually without its own army. They could have been easily defeated and eliminated by the well-trained army (北洋军, *beiyang jun*) maintained by Yuan Shikai, a shrewd politician and general who had been appointed to the position of Prime Minister near the end of the last dynasty. This able and ambitious man turned out to be an opportunist, however, and changed China's history more than once in his political and military career. He was commonly regarded as the traitor who sold out Kang, Liang and Emperor Guangxu to the Dowager during the Hundred Days Reform, when they solicited his help to initiate a coup against the conservative forces, thus bringing a premature death to the constitutional reform movement.[29] When it became rather obvious that the Qing regime was a lost enterprise, Yuan betrayed his masters once again, this time to facilitate the republican revolution; twelve years later, he was to turn his back against the republican cause, revert to monarchism and claim throne for himself, only to be overwhelmed by rebellious nationwide censure and suffer a melancholy death.[30] At the critical juncture of 1911, Yuan reached a covert agreement with the Nationalists that he would withhold the army if the latter supported him as the president of the new republic. Shortly after the First Republic was established, Sun fulfilled his promise and yielded the presidency to Yuan.

With Yuan Shikai on its side, the Nationalist revolution was able to sustain its initial victory and establish a new republic, but the Republic of China (中华民国, *zhonghua minguo*) was anything but a complete departure from its imperial past. Just as public sentiment in 1911 was at most a mixture of monarchic and democratic elements, with many a loyalist nostalgic about the immediate past, the republican government retained a considerable portion of the old regime. Indeed, the presidency was held by the same man who had been Prime Minister of the last dynasty, and though he was no dogmatic monarchist, he nevertheless inherited the spirit of a power-craving despot from the old regime. The Nationalists, moreover, were equally determined to gain a grip on power, whether simply out of their self-interest or out of firm conviction of what they believed to be a politically correct and morally

---

[28] It stood for people's livelihood (民生, *minsheng*), civil rights (民权, *minquan*) and nationalism (民族, *minzu*). See 'Outline of Founding the Nationalist Government', *Complete Works of Sun Yat-sen*, vol 9 (Beijing, Zhonghua Books, 1986).

[29] See Spence (above n 1) 224–30.

[30] Ibid, 281–88.

superior ideology. A new strain of blood was fused with the old in the same body, as it were, and conflicts were bound to multiply. Political conflicts in themselves, however, are no enemy to institution-building if they are contained in civilised procedures; both the bicameral system and judicial review,[31] two of the Americans' ingenious constitutional inventions with lasting significance, were created out of political conflicts as mechanisms to resolve them. But the constructive use of conflicts does presuppose a common recognition of basic rules of political games to be shared and observed by rival groups, which were simply not there for the Nationalists and Yuan Shikai in the early twentieth century. It was only a matter of time before their joint venture would fracture and fall apart.

In fact, interesting institutional products did emerge from the political struggles of the First Republic's initial phase. Anticipating Yuan's presidency, the Nationalist-dominated Senate, the sole and supreme legislative body, promulgated in a month the first republican constitutional document, the Provisional Constitution (临时约法, *linshi yuefa*). The system it outlined was based on the Westminster parliamentary model in order to restrict presidential power, even though Sun Yat-sen himself had been influenced by the American institutions during his prolonged stay in the United States and was an admirer of the presidential system.

The Provisional Constitution renounced the monarchy by establishing the republican principle in the opening chapter (Article 2): 'The sovereign power of the Republic of China belongs to all citizens.' The governing framework was a mixture of a presidential system and a parliamentary democracy, consisting of a Senate, an interim President, councillors and courts (Article 4). The interim President wielded substantial power, not only as commander-in-chief (Article 31) but also through the appointment and removal of civil officers, although the appointment of councillors and ambassadors required the Senate's consent (Article 34). The Senate could, with a majority of three quarters among the voting members, who must meet the four-fifths quorum, impeach the President for treason (Article 11). The Provisional Constitution also expressly provided for judicial independence and impartiality: 'The independent adjudication of judges is not to be interfered with by the executive' (Article 51).

---

[31] *Marbury v Madison*, 5 US 137 (1803).

The Provisional Constitution was China's first effort to transplant the Western constitutional model wholesale. Despite its hasty drafting and immature structure, which left out such key parliamentary machineries as confidence voting and dismissal of the cabinet, it was a admirable design for a fresh republic that hitherto had experienced only courtly debates and impeachments before an unchallengeable Emperor. It was also among the first experiments worldwide with an institution that mixed presidentialism and parliamentarism, arguably the best arrangement from the contemporary perspective and suitable for a transitional state like China in the early twentieth century. While the presidency resembled imperial supremacy, gratifying the political ambition of such monarchic remnants as Yuan Shikai and persuading them to live with republicanism, an active parliament would facilitate popular engagement and keep the strongmen in check.

That the Provisional Constitution was accepted by both the Nationalists and Yuan Shikai was by itself a remarkable achievement and a good beginning for practising checks and balances. Unfortunately, to manage such a complicated institution requires both experience and moderation, which neither side in the political arena of twentieth-century China could claim. What ought to have been power skirmishes governed by constitutional rules soon turned into unlimited warfare guided by personal ambitions, sometimes aggravated by loopholes in the constitutional text. In June 1912, for example, Yuan Shikai quarrelled with the Nationalists over the appointment of the governor of northeastern China. While the Provisional Constitution required that the appointment be 'countersigned' by the Premier (Article 45), Yuan interpreted the clause as a requirement for the Premier to concur rather than as a description of his right to decide upon independent judgment. When the Premier refused to countersign the appointment, he was accused of 'violating' the constitution and forced to resign.[32] When the Nationalist allies subsequently left out of anger, the new cabinet was composed of Yuan's protégés, and they were soon vetoed by the Senate. The struggles escalated when Yuan sought to hire police to harass the senators, thus creating a dangerous precedent of military interference in domestic politics.

---

[32] Jin Chongji and Hu Shengwu, *Historical Manuscript of the 1911 Revolution*, vol 4, 'The Success and Failures of the Revolution' (Shanghai, Shanghai People's Press, 1991) 327.

The rivalries continued to intensify and eventually reached the climactic point of civil war when Song Jiaoren (宋教仁) was assassinated during his campaign for the premiership in March 1913. A persistent, staunch advocate for parliamentary democracy, who vowed to establish a constitution with a strong cabinet and a weak president, Song orchestrated the reorganisation of Sun Sat-sen's Common League (同盟会, *tongmenghui*), upon which the Nationalist Party was formed, and he was generally recognised as the de facto Nationalist leader. His assassination, widely suspected to be part of Yuan's plot, was tantamount to a declaration of war against the Nationalists and was bound to trigger fierce Nationalist reactions.[33] Seven provinces under Nationalist control declared 'independence' from the central government in Beijing and initiated the 'second revolution', an armed uprising against Yuan. The rebellion was quickly put out, and Sun Yat-sen and the major organisers had to seek asylum in Japan.

The Nationalist failure provided Yuan with the opportunity to arrest and execute several Nationalist activists and to expand his own party's role in the government. Eager to become a permanent rather than 'interim' President, Yuan pushed Congress, now with diminished Nationalist influence, into promulgating the Presidential Election Law, by which the President was to be elected by parliamentary members rather than the electorate in general. On 6 October 1913, a mere two days after that law went into effect, Yuan held a presidential election for the first time in Chinese history. He was duly 'elected' after thousands of military policemen, disguised as 'voluntary citizens', surrounded the poor representatives from 8 am to 10 pm on the election day, until they succeeded in reaching the legally required three-quarter majority vote.[34] The Nationalists managed to fight back by promulgating a Draft Constitution (天坛宪草, *tiantan xiancao*), which overtly adopted Song Jiaoren's strong parliamentary model at the expense of presidential power. Yuan was so offended by the Draft that he ordered, within three days of its publication and without any legal ground, the disbanding of

---

[33] The investigation at the time revealed that the assassination was instigated by the Premier, Zhao Bingjun, who was summoned to the court but managed to get away by claiming illness. Even so, the summons was hailed as 'China's unprecedented judicial achievement in the twentieth century'. See Yuan Weishi, 'The Historical Experience of Political Strategy and Constitutionalism in the Early Republican Period' (2001) 6 *Strategy and Management* 65–75.

[34] Jing Zhiren (above n 4) 270.

the Nationalist Party and the disqualification of the Nationalist members of Congress, resulting in a crippled body that was unable to meet its quorum, as well as the irrevocable break of Yuan's tie with the Nationalists.

B. An Interlude for Warlords: The Provincial Autonomy Movement and the Experiment with Federalism

Yuan Shikai committed political suicide when he cheerfully followed the recommendation of his American adviser, Professor Frank Goodnow, that China would do better by reverting back to monarchy than by putting up with republican chaos. The demise of this grand warlord plunged China straight into a short period of political chaos dominated by a dozen petty warlords, each successively coming into power and enacting a constitution of his own, which was only to be discarded by his successor. Nothing of this period is worthy of elaboration except the ephemeral 'provincial autonomy' (联省自治, *liansheng zizhi*) movements during early 1920s. Since the process of drafting a central constitution was stalled by Yuan's destruction of the Congress and the miring of the entire country in tangled warfare, the warlords of those provinces caught in and devastated by the crossfire desired to adopt provincial constitutions for their own protection and the consolidation of local powers. In fact, some of these warlords were revolutionaries during the Wuchang uprising and established military governments based on local organisational laws, providing for cabinet responsibility and the separation of powers, even before the Provisional Constitution. Among these provinces, Hunan, which was seriously damaged by the 'War to Protect the Constitution' (护法战争, *hufa zhanzheng*) waged by Sun Yat-sen's Nationalist army in the south with the northern warlords, was the most active advocate of provincial autonomy, and initiated the drafting process of a provincial constitution in November 1920. The draft constitution was revised by a review committee of 150 elected members and ratified in a popular referendum by the citizens of that province in December 1921. Both in procedure and in substance, the Hunan Constitution lived up to the contemporary standard. Most notably, it provided for universal suffrage for all men and women within the province and direct election of the governor by citizens, who enjoyed even rights to referendum and popular initiative.

The Hunan experience inspired other (mostly southern) provinces to initiate their own constitution-making processes, even though they failed to promulgate effective constitutions within the short period of time available, and even the Hunan Constitution itself was not practised effectively enough to change the basic structure of warlord domination. Nevertheless, the provincial movements vividly illustrated China's potential for federalism and local democracy at the grassroots level. After the military government of Zhejiang province declared a draft constitution and solicited private drafts in 1922, Zhejiang citizens exhibited such enormous enthusiasm that they proposed over 100 versions, which, in order to facilitate voting in popular referendum, had to be sorted into three categories according to the nature of their designs and labelled with red, yellow and white colours – hence the distinctive name 'tri-colour constitutions' (三色宪法, *sanse xianfa*). The draft constitutions in Zhejiang, Sichuan and Guangdong provinces resembled the Hunan Constitution in that they all provided for extensive civil and political rights, particularly equality of men and women, direct elections of governors and provincial parliaments, and parliamentary democracy with the right to question and even remove the cabinet by vote of no-confidence.

By 1923, the nominal president of the Republic, Li Yuanhong (黎元洪), had returned to Beijing under the auspices of the victorious warlord Cao Kun (曹锟) and reassembled the Congress he had dissolved five years ago. Coveting the presidency himself, Cao soon forced Li to leave the post. He bribed nearly 200 representatives to return to Congress in order to attain a quorum and in October 1923 got himself enough votes to be elected President.[35] The reassembled Congress quickly passed the Constitution of the Republic of China (中华民国宪法, *zhonghua minguo xianfa*), which unfortunately was tinged by the slur of the bought election. Judging from its provisions, however, the 1923 Constitution was the closest that China has ever achieved to a federal constitution. With 13 chapters and 141 articles, the Constitution provided in appearance a unitary framework for the country, proclaiming that 'China will forever remain a united democratic state' (Article 1) but outlined in essence a federal structure. Chapter V of the Constitution explicitly demarcated the boundary between the central and lower powers, which was not to be amended by ordinary central laws or regulations. Article 23 enumerated 15 items that were in the competence of

---

[35]   Ibid, 331.

the central legislature to enact and implement, including defence, diplomacy, citizenship, civil and criminal laws, coins and balances, taxation, postal service and communication, national railways and highways, civil and military appointments, amongst others. Article 24 listed 13 areas in which the national legislature could require implementation by the local governments, whereas Article 25 listed 11 areas of exclusive provincial competence; disputes with regard to the boundaries of central power arising from uncertainties in these Articles were to be adjudicated by the Supreme Court according to the nature of the powers involved, and disputes among provinces were to be resolved by the Senate. Chapter XII on 'local institutions' further authorised provinces to enact 'provincial autonomy laws' (省自治法, *sheng zizhi fa*), provided that they were consistent with the Constitution and national laws; and Article 128 provided for the autonomous areas properly belonging to county legislatures and not to be interfered with by the provincial governments above them.

C. The Northern Expedition, Reunification and the Ascendance of Party Rule

The federalist experiments proved to be short-lived in China, a country governed under a unitary scheme for over two millennia. Sun Yat-sen, had become a frustrated revolutionary seeking refuge in Guangdong province, but he soon broke with Chen Jiongming (陈炯明), his protector and a warlord controlling Guangdong. Their split was over the Northern Expedition (北伐, *beifa*), a military push to drive out all warlords and reunite China under a single regime. For years the Nationalist Party was but a loose coalition of petty bourgeois, who were infinitely better at parliamentary feuds than fighting in the fields, and Sun was tired of having to constantly shift his alliance to one warlord to fight off the others. He was convinced that constitutionalism would be an impossibility in China as long as it was divided among these barbarous warlords, whose sole interest was to protect and expand their own turfs. To realise constitutionalism, the Nationalists had to establish a strong army of their own that would wipe out all warlord resistance and establish a genuine republic under Nationalist leadership. To accomplish that, Sun set out to reorganise the Nationalist Party and strengthen its internal discipline, this time not along liberal Western lines but on the Leninist model that had succeeded in building a party machine strong enough to seize power in Russia in 1917.

In 1924, Sun published an Outline for Founding the Nationalist Government (国民政府建国大纲, *guomin zhengfu jiangguo dagang*), which delineated an elaborate progressive strategy for achieving constitutionalism in three stages: military politics (军政, *junzheng*), tutelage politics (训政, *xunzheng*) and constitutional politics (宪政, *xianzheng*). In Sun's design, constitutionalism was to be preceded by a military phase, during which 'domestic impediments' would be 'wiped out by armed forces' in order to establish a united republic. This would be followed by a second phase, during which the central government under the Nationalist leadership would provide the Chinese people with guidance and training for practising democratic self-governance, beginning at the county level, mainly the exercise of rights to election, initiative, referendum and recall of corrupt or incompetent officials. When the people of a county had learned to exercise these rights after adequate training, it would become a 'county with complete autonomy'; when all the counties within a province had achieved autonomous rule, that province would be deemed as having completed the tutelage stage and entered the 'beginning stage of constitutionalism'; it would then be entitled to popular election of its governor. When over half of the provinces had achieved autonomous rule, the Nationalist Party was supposed to 'return political power to the people' (还政于民, *huanzheng yumin*) and call the national assembly to enact a constitution, which would bring China into the final stage of constitutional politics.

In the same year, Sun Yat-sen adopted the recommendations of his Soviet adviser and completed the reorganisation of the Nationalist Party according to the Leninist model, which was marked by monopolistic dominance by a single ruling party over the government and the entire nation. The very first article of the Organic Law of the Nationalist Government (国民政府组织法, *guomin zhengfu zuzhifa*) dictated that the national government was to be in charge of national affairs under the direction and supervision the Nationalist Party. As explained by Hu Hanmin (胡汉民), a right-wing Nationalist leader and theorist,

> All powers are to be concentrated in this party, [since] only the party can undertake the great task of founding the republic on behalf of the people of the entire nation, and only the party can lead the people of the entire nation to march towards the objective of realizing the three-people's doctrine. . . Neither is there a single (legitimate) party outside this party, nor any

(legitimate) politics outside the party, nor any party outside the politics (dominated by the Nationalist Party).[36]

Under the logic of tutelage, the Nationalist reorganisation initiated China's first experiment with 'rule of the party' (党治, *dangzhi*), as opposed to both the modern rule of law and the ancient rule of virtue. In effect, the government was merely a mouthpiece that would reflect the will of and exercise the powers properly belonging to the party; all major laws and policies were decided by the Nationalist Party before they were passed to the national government for promulgation and implementation. Thus, when the Communists came to amend their party charter before they amended the Constitution and major laws several decades later, they were following the precedent of party rule as pioneered by their Nationalist predecessors.

Sun Yat-sen died the following year, shortly after the reorganisation of his party, which was now ready to embark upon its first stage of constitutionalism. And this task fell naturally on the shoulders of his follower and personal guard, General Chiang Kai-shek (蒋介石). In 1926, Chiang called for the Northern Expedition, which, with the assistance of the Communists under the first cooperation of the two revolutionary parties, quickly drove out most of the warlords and reunited a large part of China by 1927. The cooperation with the Communists was out of both strategic necessity and Sun's ideological sympathy with them, given the Soviet realignment of the Nationalist Party; but each party, aiming to gain exclusive control over the state against all opposition, was inherently opposed to the other. With their common enemies defeated near the end of the Northern Expedition, conflicts inevitably arose when neither party was prepared to share power with the other. The aggressive Communist infiltration of the Nationalist Party during this short-lived cooperation necessarily invited heavy suspicion and reaction on the part of the Nationalists, who soon initiated a movement to 'cleanse the party' (清党, *qingdang*), and the result was the disarming and execution of many Communist members. Having suppressed the Communists and eliminated most warlords, the Nationalists had accomplished their 'military politics' and entered the stage of tutelage politics, the completion of which was supposed to eventually bring constitutionalism to China. Once again, China was by and large under a unitary

---

[36] Quoted in Zhang Guofu, *Constitutional History of the Republic of China* (Beijing, Huawen Press, 1991) 263.

order, this time under a supreme party rather than a supreme person, though both prohibited any challenge to its supremacy and its monopolistic exercise of power.

D. Limitations in the Nationalist One-Party Monopoly

From its political programme, the Nationalist monopoly over power was meant to be more rigorous even than its Communist counterpart; yet in effect, its one-party rule was limited by a number of factors beyond its control at the time. First, the Communists were not eliminated but merely driven underground in the cities and expelled to the remote rural areas; in both cases they remained the major political rival that openly challenged the Nationalists' domination. Second and perhaps more significant, the Nationalist new order was fatally broken by the Japanese invasion from the 1930s to 1945, which greatly emasculated the strength of its army and diverted its focus away from crushing the Communists. In fact, following the Xi'an Incident (西安事变, *Xi'an shibian*) in 1936, Chiang Kai-shek was compelled by public pressure to set aside past feuds and cooperate with the Communists again, this time to fight against the Japanese as the common enemy and save the nation from crisis. Third, although the Nationalist reorganisation aimed to establish a monolithic party under the uniform control of a supreme party leader, the reality was quite the otherwise. After its spiritual leader, Sun Yat-sen, passed away, the party split into at least three major factions – the left, the right and the military faction headed by Chiang Kai-shek. Although Chiang managed to maintain an upper hand as a result of constant national exigencies that demanded a military strongman, he was unable to claim unconditional dominance over other factions and quash intra-party rivalries. In 1931, for example, after placing the right-wing leader Hu Hanmin under house arrest, Chiang was openly condemned by the party's Central Supervision Committee as having committed an 'illegal' act. Under mounting pressures from both the right and the left, particularly from the young college students who frequently took to the streets, Chiang relinquished all official posts, including the chairmanship of the Nationalist Government and commander-in-chief, and he did not resume these positions until the Japanese takeover of the northeast provinces the following year created such national crisis as to demand his return.

The fracturing of the Nationalist Party from within, as well as open challenges from various sources without, helped to reduce the degree of Chiang's personal dominance over the party as well as the party's dominance over the entire country, thus allowing a limited space for dissenting opinions. By the mid-1930s, when the deadline for entering the last stage of constitutional politics as defined in Sun's Outline was approaching and there was obviously no hope of meeting such deadline, serious constitutional debates were held both in and outside the Nationalist Party.

The rationale behind 'tutelage politics', which was supposed to provide legitimacy for the Nationalist monopoly over political power was a natural development of the traditional Confucian doctrine that divided the people into the dichotomy of 'gentlemen' (君子, *junzi*), a small minority of elites with high morals, and 'small men' (小人, *xiaoren*), who constituted the vast majority of the population.; and it had been expressed publicly as early as the imperial constitutional reforms of Liang Qichao.[37] At its core was a distrust of the political capacity of the common people, who were viewed by both the imperial reformers and the Nationalists as ignorant, selfish and myopic; since 'the institutions were yet to be established, and the people were yet to be enlightened', a rush toward constitutionalism would simply fail to achieve its very purpose if the social conditions remained immature. As Hu Hanmin once explained, 'what we care about constitutionalism is not how soon it will begin, but how truthfully it will be implemented.'[38] While the imperial reformers did not bother to solicit the support of the common people, the Nationalists positively subjected the people under their tutelage, insisting that China's constitutionalism was to be realised only through rule of the party, which would not only establish the right type of institutions but also educate the people and equip them with the abilities to run these institutions. The same logic repeats itself over and over throughout Chinese history and finds its contemporary application in discrimination against the basic political, economic and social rights of the peasants, who still constitute the vast majority of China's population today.[39]

---

[37] The story was more complicated than the simplified version presented here. See Qianfan Zhang, 'Propriety, Law and Harmony: A Functional Argument for the Rule of Virtue' in J Tao et al (eds), *Governance for Harmony in Asia and Beyond* (London, Routledge, 2010) 282–314.

[38] Quoted in Jing Zhiren (above n 4) 402.

[39] See below ch 7.

The tutelage logic was premised, however, on the questionable assumption that the ruling party was purely benevolent in pursuing the grandiose constitutional objective and capable of abstaining from selfish abuse of the enormous powers that it had amassed under that logic. Even if constitutionalism did require a revolutionary vanguard to impose its control over the nation during a transitional period, how could anyone guarantee that such imposition would be exploited for the good of the whole nation rather than its own privilege, and only during the period of necessity without being extended to perpetuity? And, leaving aside speculative disputes on human nature, the tutelage logic might well have confused the cause with the result. As a Confucian student once astutely observed, 'nobody learns how to rear a child to get married';[40] rather, one simply learns how to raise children after the marriage brings them about. Certain human abilities are not learned deliberately but rather acquired naturally through practice, without which these abilities will never be acquired. Even though ordinary Chinese were inexperienced in exercising their own rights, the proper remedy was not to further deprive them of the chance of acquiring more experience and improving their political ability but precisely to provide the political institutions through which they would learn by practising the exercise of their rights. As Hu Shih (胡适), a liberal champion who graduated from Columbia University, pointed out, 'One has to get into water in order to learn how to swim, and be equipped with a guitar in order to learn to play guitar.'[41] The constitutional process itself provides the most efficient training for the people to acquire constitutional capacities, the lack of which is not to be used as an excuse for further deprivation of opportunities for institutional training.

Hu Shih and other liberal intellectuals began to exert their influence on Chinese society around 1915, when they initiated the New Culture Movement (新文化运动, *xinwenhua yundong*) against the Confucian orthodoxy and called for a liberation of Chinese personality from the yoke of archaic *li* and Confucian classics. By the late 1920s and 1930s, when the Nationalists had consolidated their control over China, these intellectuals shifted the focus of their critique to the ruling party. Although most of them acknowledged the necessity of the Nationalists,

---

[40] In *Great Learning* (大学, *daxue*) s 3, Wing-tsit Chan (trans), *A Source Book in Chinese Philosophy* (Princeton, Princeton University Press, 1963) 91.

[41] Hu Shih, 'Constitutional Questions' (1932) 1 *Independence Review* 1.

they aimed to persuade the party and the government to found their governance on a solid constitutional ground by separating the state from the party and by paying genuine respect to freedom of thought and speech. As Luo Longji (罗隆基), founder of the left-wing Democratic League (民主同盟, *minzhu tongmeng*), once famously put it, 'The danger of suppressing free speech is much greater than the danger of free speech itself.'[42] The liberal journal that he and Hu Shih co-edited, *New Moon* (新月, *xinyue*), and Hu's influential weekly, *Independent Review* (独立评论, *duli pinglun*), often carried open criticisms of the Nationalist suppressions of basic human rights, sometimes even directed to its highest leaders, whether Sun Yat-sen or Chiang Kai-shek. For example, Hu Shi mocked scathingly:

> The one-party rule has created a situation of absolute despotism, in which thought and speech have completely lost freedom. One is allowed to deny God, but not to criticise Sun Yat-sen; allowed to forsake weekly worship, but obliged to read the Premier [ie, Sun's] Testament and attend the Memorial Week.[43]

For these critical comments, *New Moon* paid the price by being constantly interrupted by government censorship and prohibition; Luo was once arrested, and Hu was forced to resign as President of Peking University. With the vicissitudes of unstable domestic developments, however, open dissent managed to carry on and cohabit with the supposedly monolithic rule of the party. The very fact that Hu Shih was appointed the President of a top public university while remaining what is today called a 'public intellectual' (公共知识分子, *gonggong zhishi fenzi*) who was sharply critical of the existing regime, meant that the Nationalist one-party rule allowed a limited degree of freedom. Even such limited freedom is absent in the contemporary institutional environment of China, however: Luo Longji was persecuted for his opinions, ironically, by a regime he once loyally supported; and Hu Shih's 'double identities' have never been mingled again in one person. As ideologically lenient as China's government is today, a liberal critic of the regime could hardly aspire to holding a key post at a public institution.

Despite controversies, the Nationalist Party did promulgate a Draft Constitution of the Republic of China in 1936, commonly dubbed the

---

[42] Luo Longji, 'To the Suppressors of Free Speech' (1929) 2 *New Moon* 6.

[43] Hu Shih, 'The New Culture Movement and the Nationalist Party' (1929) 2 *New Moon* 7.

Draft Constitution of May Fifth (五五宪草, *wuwu xiancao*), which was to serve as the prototype for the republican constitution a decade later. Founded on Sun Yat-sen's constitutional blueprint as expressed in the Outline, the opening chapter of the Draft Constitution explicitly defined the state to be 'a republic under the Three People's Principles' (Article 1). Chapter IV on the central government was based on Sun's elaborate design for a 'constitution of five powers' (五权宪法, *wuquan xianfa*), lodged in five councils, respectively, of the legislature, executive, judiciary, supervision and civil examination, above which stood a super-intendent President as both the head of the state and chief of the administration (including commander-in-chief), who had the authority to appoint major officers in charge of administration, supervision and examinations without legislative consent (Articles 36–42). Chapter V rejected the federalist design in the 1923 Constitution, adopting instead a unitary structure mixed with localism according to Sun Yat-sen's distinction of 'political power' (政权, *zhengquan*), by which the local people directly control their government, and 'managerial power' (治权, *zhiquan*) to be exercised by the central government on behalf and for the benefit of its people. While the central government was to appoint and remove provincial governors, whose functions included implementation of central laws and supervision of local autonomous rule (Articles 98 and 99), county sheriffs and councillors were to be elected by local electoral assemblies. (Articles 106 and 108).

The constitutional process was halted by the Xi'an Incident and the Japanese takeover of Beijing's Lugou Bridge in July 1937, which signalled Japan's wholesale aggression in China. It did not resume until the Sino-Japanese War ended in 1945, when the Nationalists and Communists held political negotiations in Chongqing and agreed to establish a Political Consultative Committee (政治协商会议, *zhengzhi xieshang huiyi*, hereinafter PCC) composed of members of various parties roughly in proportion to their sizes. The PCC held its first meeting in January 1946 and proposed 12 principles for revising the Draft Constitution, among which were direct election of the Legislative Council (立法院, *lifa yuan*); legislative consent of executive appointments; a cabinet responsibility system in which the Legislative Council could cast a vote of no-confidence; and a federalist structure in which provinces could adopt their own constitutions. The Nationalist Party squarely rejected these proposals at the beginning but accepted, after several rounds of negotiations, the crux of the above amendments, except the cabinet responsibility system.[44] The negotiation and collaboration between the rival political parties resulted in a revised draft constitution more acceptable to the Chinese public in general. Had this draft been submitted to the National Assembly (国民大会, *guomin dahui*) for ratification, China would have had a genuine state constitution rather than a 'constitution' of the Nationalist Party. Unfortunately, the political agreement soon broke down, and the Communists left the PCC with its ally, the Democratic League, refusing to participate in the National Assembly. By May 1946 the skirmishes over the takeover of the northeastern area formerly occupied by the Japanese army had escalated into warfare. Although a ceasefire agreement was reached under an American reconciliation process, the two rival parties eventually failed to come together. Without participation from the left-wing parties, the National Assembly was reduced to a 'Nationalist Assembly', with as many as 85 per cent of the delegates being Nationalists.

Not surprisingly, the 'Nationalist Assembly' adopted a 'Nationalist Constitution', which by and large reverted back to the Draft Constitution of May Fifth, although the role of the party was somewhat diluted and the federalist aspects enhanced by borrowing from the 1923 Constitution. The Constitution went into force in 1947, amid a massive civil war that wrecked the entire country. In less than two years, the Nationalists were defeated and retreated to Taiwan, where the Constitution is still in force today.[45]

IV. WHY REVOLUTIONS FAIL TO BRING ABOUT CONSTITUTIONALISM

The enactment of the Constitution was not to be confused with the beginning of constitutionalism. The time that the Nationalist Party remained on the mainland was too short for them to implement their own Constitution, but it is doubtful whether they would have implemented it even had they been given more time. As soon as they moved to Taiwan, Chiang Kai-shek initiated the Temporary Regulation During Insurgency Mobilisation (动员戡乱临时条款, *dongyuan kanluan linshi tiaokuan*), which was to be effectively imposed for a record period of 38

---

[44] Quoted in Jing Zhiren (above n 4) 455–56.
[45] For Taiwan's constitutional development, see Chen Shin-min, *Introduction to the Constitution* (*xianfa daolun*) (Taipei, Xin Xuelin Press, 2005) chs 1 and 2.

years, during which the Constitution was suspended, the Nationalist dominance over the island went unchallenged and Chiang's paramount position was beyond question. Not until 1987, six decades after the Nationalists united China through the Northern Expedition, were one-party rule and strict censorship of newspapers lifted by his son and heir, President Chiang Ching-kuo (蒋经国), near the end of his life.

The long interlude between the enactment and implementation of the Constitution ended only with the breach of one-party rule and brought serious doubt to the validity of the tutelage logic as part of the revolutionary rhetoric. China's experiences with Nationalist dominance, both on the mainland and on Taiwan, illustrate how the tutelage politics under one-party rule – supposed to be merely a necessary step in the grand march toward constitutionalism – perpetuated the necessity for (and thus the legitimacy of) the permanent dominance of that party. When the Nationalist revolutionaries imposed tutelage over the nation in the name of constitutionalism, they set up a permanent trap within which they comfortably stayed, eventually without even paying lip service to constitutionalism.

A revolution will almost inevitably fail to fulfil its constitutional promises for several reasons. To begin with, unlike reform, which seeks to change the distribution of powers and resources under the existing regime and thus usually fails in confrontation with the powerful status quo, a revolution aims to sweep the status quo aside, usually by violence, and establish a completely new set of institutions. Indeed, as a result of repeated frustrations and failures from which the reform process suffers, revolution breaks out precisely when reform has come to an end, but revolution is no recipe for achieving what reform has failed to achieve. It is true that resistance of the status quo to change needs be somehow removed, but a simple overhaul of the government or even the constitution will not do, since the old status quo will simply be replaced by a new one. Those who used to be marginalised 'revolutionaries', having just succeeded to power, will be even more determined to protect the fruits of their hard-won victory, if only to compensate the losses they have suffered in the violent power struggle, which is likely to be great given the obvious incentive of the old regime to exploit every means at its disposal to maintain itself.

From this perspective the Nationalist Revolution in 1911 was hardly a 'revolution' in comparison to its Communist counterpart, since the former was won without prolonged violence and bloodshed; the Qing regime was simply too feeble to sustain itself and was forced to yield its throne before the mutinies that culminated in the Wuchang Uprising. Finding that the easy victory did not quite bring the fruits they expected, the Nationalists nonetheless ultimately won their victory – but only through radical reorganisation and transformation of their relatively liberal party into an almost totalitarian machinery, which carried out the Northern Expedition to forcibly eliminate the warlords and numerous bloody campaigns to keep that victory from the Communists. By then the fruits of the revolution were secured, but constitutionalism as originally promised was in jeopardy. When the Communists managed to overcome their Nationalist oppressors, the blood they had shed seemed to suffice by itself to legitimise the exclusive exploitation of the spoils.[46] In any event, it was obviously too much to expect that the revolutionary vanguards would willingly quit the power they had fought hard to win, and once revolutionaries establish and consolidate their exclusive control over a state's machineries, no one else is likely to be equipped to force them to quit and return the power to the people.

Besides the lack of incentives, revolutionaries also lack the right temperament for constitutionalism. This is because revolutions ordinarily break out in authoritarian states, where the populace is accustomed to imperious command and slavish obedience, suppression of dissent, reckless abuse of power, coups and covert manoeuvrings, and everything else that comes with self-affirming, self-perpetuating absolute power. Unlike liberal democracies in which grievances are openly expressed in public debates and persuasions and expediently addressed by peaceful replacement of governments and gradual adjustment of policies through the electoral process, authoritarian states breed revolutions by adamantly resisting the accommodations that are necessary to pacify opposing interests. Meanwhile, such states fail to provide any occasion for their people to educate themselves with the spirit of moderation, tolerance and independent deliberation, so that whole generations grow up in a cultural deficit of collective reasoning capacity.

In retrospect, China was fortunate to experience a relatively brief period of revolution, during which the as yet moderate Nationalist Party

---

[46] It used to be an oft quoted motto that 'the blood of the martyrs should not be shed in vain', implying that 'capitalist roaders' should not be permitted to lead the Communist cause astray. With the Communist ideology long decayed, however, the rationale has been twisted to imply that the ruling party should not share its power with anyone, lest it loses the monopoly over its spoils.

was willing to practice Western liberal democracy. Even so, the Nationalists were by no means a flock of doves sheltered in the parliamentary building, having committed numerous mutinies and assassinations before they succeeded in the Wuchang Uprising,[47] not to mention that the institutions they set up after the 1911 Revolution were entirely alien to the Chinese political tradition in which both they and their rival, Yuan Shikai, were brought up. Both revolutionaries and anti-revolutionaries are prepared to do whatever necessary for the exclusive attainment of absolute power as their ultimate objective, and neither side is willing to negotiate with the other according to the procedures and distribution of powers as dictated in a constitution. More often than not, the constitution is but a façade under which unlimited power struggles are carried out, and it is easily dispensed with if it is deemed useless for its assigned purpose. Far from bringing constitutional order to the country, revolutions aggravate despotism, since a successful revolution requires an efficient party machine built on organisational discipline and unconditional obedience to party leaders. A successful revolutionary party, then, is necessarily accustomed to centralisation rather than separation of powers and will; and once it has succeeded in gaining the state, the successful party will continue to operate in a mode suitable to itself but diametrically opposed to the spirit of modern constitutionalism.

Finally, authoritarian states not only breed revolutions but also expose themselves to the grave danger that fake revolutionary promises will be blindly accepted by a naïve population. Unlike a democracy in which the desirability and practicability of political proposals, together with the capacity and credibility of their advocates, are repeatedly subjected to public debate and scrutiny, an authoritarian state prohibits genuine debate and deliberation and thus will lack the very means to examine the veracity of those splendid promises that revolutionaries use to garner social support. The Nationalists fulfilled their promise to yield the presidency to Yuan Shikai, but only out of fear of the heavy armed forces under Yuan's control; such fear was absent when it came to dealing with the Communists in 1927, and the promise to establish a liberal republic was not honoured. Even though the promise was made in good faith before the Nationalists gained power, there was nothing to compel its fulfilment or to prevent the Nationalists from changing their minds

---

[47] Before the Wuchang uprising, for example, the Nationalists had attempted more than one mutiny in Guangzhou, all brutally suppressed by the Qing army.

once circumstances had changed. The Communists for their part persuaded the peasants to stand on their side by promising them the right to own the land on which they had previously toiled under the landlords, and such policy was indeed implemented in their revolutionary bases. Soon after the Communists came to power in 1949, however, the peasants not only lost all right to land by successive rounds of collectivisation but became the most tragic victims of institutional discrimination, even forbidden to form associations for their own protection. And once a revolutionary party has gained control of the state, it is obviously too late for society to find out its real agenda and withdraw the support that enabled it to rise to the summit of the power pyramid that it can now use to subjugate the entire population.

China is, then, trapped in an authoritarian dilemma that stoutly defies constitutionalism. If constitutional reform fails in face of the powerful status quo, which inevitably opposes any change that will diminish its power, a revolution can but make things worse by creating an even more powerful group under a new status quo, whose ground for legitimacy will take many decades to dissolve and whose appetite will take even longer to satisfy. Certainly, the rule of a party that is forged by modern revolution is more effective than the traditional rule of 'one man' (寡人, *guaren*, ie, the Emperor), who could only rely on the bureaucratic machinery working for him personally. In contrast, a modern revolutionary party has organisational strength, buttressed by self-legitimising ideology, which will enable the party to reach every corner of society. If the effectiveness of the Nationalist rule was weakened by foreign invasions and domestic turmoil, Communist rule was all the more strengthened by relative peace – though it was frequently disturbed by political campaigns instigated on its own initiative and is nowadays troubled by large-scale social conflict as a result of institutional corruption and abuse of power. In the end, Mao Zedong was not far from truth when he bragged that 'we exceed Qin Shihuang (the First Emperor) by a hundred times'. The tragedy at Tiananmen in 1989 was but the most recent testimony to the invincibility of the authoritarian dilemma, which China today has yet to transcend. The key to overcoming such a formidable dilemma is to be found in the new developments taking place almost a century after the founding of the First Republic, within a very different constitutional framework and social context.[48]

---

[48] See below chs 3 and 7.

FURTHER READING

Chen, H, *An Introduction to the Legal System of the People's Republic of China*, 4th edn (Hong Kong, LexisNexis Butterworths, 2011) ch 1.

Chow, T, *The May Fourth Movement: Intellectual Revolution in China* (Cambridge, MA, Harvard University Press, 1960).

Hahm, C, 'Ritual and Constitutionalism: Disputing the Ruler's Legitimacy in a Confucian Polity' (2009) 57 *American Journal of Comparative Law* 135–204.

Kim, HI, *Fundamental Legal Concepts of China and the West: A Comparative Study* (London, Kennikat Press, 1981).

Spence, JD, *The Search for Modern China* (New York, WW Norton, 1990) 230–43.

Thompson, RR, *China's Local Councils in the Age of Constitutional Reform* (Cambridge, MA, Harvard University Press, 1995).

2

The New Constitutional Order of the People's Republic

THE SECOND REPUBLIC: THE COMMUNIST REVOLU-
TION OF 1949 – The May Fourth Movement and the Communist
Ascendance – The Founding of the People's Republic –
Revolutionary Legacies – THE 1982 CONSTITUTION – The
1978 Reform – An Overview of the 1982 Constitution – Basic State
Structure in the 1982 Constitution – CONSTITUTIONAL
AMENDMENTS – Previous Amendments: Towards a Market
Economy and the Rule of Law – The 2004 Amendments:
Recognising Human Rights and Private Property – CONSTITU-
TIONAL TRANSFORMATIONS – Reform and the Constitution:
The Benign Violation Paradox – From Popular Sovereignty to
Human Rights: A Paradigm Shift for Constitutional Jurisprudence
– The Rise of 'Rights Consciousness' and 'Populist Constitu-
tionalism' in an Inchoate Civil Society

T HE SECOND CHAPTER will begin with the political and ideological development of the current socialist regime in China,
which saw a turning point in 1978. The chapter will sketch out
the new constitutional order that was promulgated in 1982 and is still
effective today. I will explain the socio-political background as well as
the guiding principles for the drafting of the constitution before describing the main features of the new constitution, and then successively
trace four constitutional amendments. The chapter will end with a summary of significant constitutional transformations during the last three
decades of reform, which have witnessed not only fundamental shifts in
the methodological approach to constitutional jurisprudence, which laid

the theoretical foundation for constitutional reform, but also the rapid rise of a popular consciousness of human rights, perhaps for the very first time in Chinese history. These events and developments occurred despite the arrest of the reform momentum by the June Fourth Incident (六四事件, *liusi shijian*, also referred to in English as the Tiananmen Protests).

I. THE SECOND REPUBLIC: THE COMMUNIST REVOLUTION OF 1949

A. The May Fourth Movement and the Communist Ascendance

The Chinese Communist Party (CCP) and the Nationalists once were deadly rivals, but they shared a common nature as revolutionary parties. And they became enemies precisely because they shared the revolutionary conviction that each was pursuing the absolutely 'correct' cause for the good of the Chinese people. This not only made their own political cause sacred and solely legitimate against all rivalries but also lent moral supremacy to each party, as well as justification for using any means, including physical violence, to eliminate all impediments in the way of achieving unconditionally salutary objectives. In that sense, both parties were revolutionaries against the old Confucian imperial order, but both inherited from Confucianism the same dogmatic tradition that has run through Chinese history. Sun Yat-sen was a genuine republican, committed to Western liberal constitutionalism, but when he resorted to violent revolution against the last dynasty, he had already embarked on a one-way journey along which his party regularly used violence whenever it met any challenge or competition, whether from warlords or Communists. Following the Nationalist footprints and under the guidance of their common Soviet mentors, the Communists from the very beginning aimed at nothing less than 'the forcible overthrow of all existing social conditions'.[1] Founded in 1921, precisely a decade after the 1911 Revolution, the CCP was in many ways the younger brother who learned from and surpassed its elder sibling in manipulating ideological propaganda and organisational violence, succeeding where the latter failed.

---

[1] K Marx and F Engels, *The Communist Manifesto* (New York, International Publishers, 1948) 44.

The CCP was brought to the fore of China's political arena on 4 May 1919, when an angry assembly of Beijing students allegedly set fire to the Zhao Mansion (赵家楼, *zhaojia lou*) during mass demonstrations against the peace Treaty of Versailles,[2] which transferred the rule of Shandong province from the defeated Germany to the victorious Japan. US President Woodrow Wilson, who otherwise sympathised with the Chinese demand for sovereignty over its own land, yielded first to the white Australian policy and rejected Japan's perfectly legitimate claim for ethnic equality in the Asia Pacific region, then succumbed to Japanese pressure to grant it illegitimate control over the Chinese territory, as if it were 'compensation' for the earlier wrong and in exchange for Japanese support for the League of Nations.[3] This apparently innocent realist strategy proved detrimental to China's pursuit of constitutionalism by arousing Chinese nationalism and antipathy against liberal democracy, which ultimately paved the way toward communism.

Unlike the signing of the Shimonoseki Treaty with Japan, which led to civilised scholarly petitions by Kang Youwei and other elites, the Versailles Treaty resulted in radical student reaction. It is to be remembered that after Japan defeated China in 1894, the Chinese viewed this 'tiny island' with awe and inspiration rather than hatred. During the quarter century following 1894 – notwithstanding continual skirmishes over what should be preserved as China's 'core' values – Westernisation and institutional modernisation seemed to be the theme of the era. For a time the Chinese seemed to have forgotten the humiliations of defeats and unequal treaties from which they had suffered since the Opium War of 1840. By 1919, despite its tenuous involvement in the First World War, China was treated as being victorious and viewed itself as such, expecting to regain full control of its own territory. The Treaty of Versailles served a disheartening blow to such optimistic expectations,

---

[2] The mansion's resident was Cao Rulin (曹汝霖), then the Minister of Transportation and a graduate from Japan. The students broke into the mansion and destroyed some furniture, though doubts remain as to whether they were responsible for the ensuing fire. Anyway, the 'burning of Zhao's Mansion' became the symbolic event of student radicalism after the May Fourth Movement. For an incisive narrative account of the May Fourth Movement, see T Chow, *The May Fourth Movement: Intellectual Revolution in Modern China* (Cambridge, Harvard University Press, 1980) 84–115.

[3] See PG Lauren, *Power and Prejudice: The Politics and Diplomacy of Racial Discrimination* (Boulder, Westview Press, 1988) 80–99; and TA Bailey, *Woodrow Wilson and the Great Betrayal* (New York, Times Books, 1963) 75, 161–64 and 407.

however, and sorely reminded China of its disgraceful past and the opposition between peremptory Western powers, now including Japan, on the one side, and a weak and humiliated China on the other. That did not stop China from experimenting with Western democratic constitutionalism right away, but it did inculcate a mood of the opposite kind. Even Liang Qichao, an eloquent defender of Western constitutionalism, began to express doubts about the future of Western civilisation following the mass destructions of WWI and reservations concerning China's Westernisation efforts.[4]

No wonder, then, that when the new Soviet regime established by the 'October Revolution' of 1917 actively peddled Marxist Leninism to its disgruntled neighbour in order to convert it into a political ally, the new doctrine was welcomed with enthusiasm, especially among radical intellectuals and young students. True, Marxism was also a Western product, but it shared no part with the Western ideological mainstream; on the contrary, it was fiercely critical of the bloody capitalist order that would inevitably turn into global imperialism, and of which China was a victim. Better yet, it prophesied that the death knell of such an oppressive order would sound sooner or later in the human evolution toward communism. Communism instead of constitutionalism, then, seemed to be the 'right' theory for China because it offered bright hope for the weak to ultimately defeat the powerful and avenge itself for past humiliations. When the Soviet Union extended its embrace to a country just abandoned by the Western powers at the Paris Peace Conference, the offer turned out to be more than China could resist. The once shelved nationalism now fought its way back under the name of 'patriotism', putting an end to the liberal enlightenment of the New Culture Movement (新文化运动, *xinwenhua yundong*).[5] Chen Duxiu (陈独秀), who had been a liberal faculty member at Peking University and had co-initiated the 'vernacular literature movement' (白话文运动, *baihuawen yundong*) with Hu Shih, now turned himself into a founding theorist of Chinese communism, which quickly spread out like a wildfire throughout the

---

[4] See Liang Qichao, *Reflections on the European Trip: Travel Memoir of a New Continent* (Beijing, East Press, 2006).

[5] It has been a common practice for mainland scholars to extend the 'May Fourth Movement' back to 1915 so as to embrace the New Culture Movement, even though the youth movement initiated on 4 May 1919 proved to be the end of China's cultural enlightenment.

country. A mere three decades after the start of the May Fourth Movement, the Communists succeeded, through unexpected twists and turns of historical contingencies, in replacing their Nationalist predecessors as the absolute ruler of China, and despite great calamities caused by major policy failures and political upheaval, they have managed thus far to maintain the institutions established by their revolution.

B. The Founding of the People's Republic

Having renounced traditional Confucianism as anachronistic 'feudalism' on the one hand and Western constitutionalism as capitalistic 'imperialism' on the other, the new People's Republic of China (PRC, 中华人民共和国, *zhonghua renmin gonghe guo*) started to build its own legal infrastructure from the ground level. Even before it took over power in 1949, the CCP had already undone every Nationalist accomplishment in rule of law by repealing all 'six basic laws' (六法, *liufa*), including the Nationalist constitution. In contrast to the Nationalists, the CCP has never been keen on constitutionalism and has never devised, as Sun Yatsen did, any practical procedure for transition from 'tutelage' to constitutionalism, whereby political power could be returned to the people.[6] In a sense, there was nothing to be 'returned', since the people supposedly already possessed all the powers under 'democratic dictatorship' and the Communist leadership, so much so that the former Party Secretary of Hunan province, Zhang Chunxian (张春贤), created quite a shock wave in China's media by speaking of 'returning power to the people' in 2009,[7] six decades after the Communist takeover. Indeed, the ruling party was not quite prepared to adopt a formal constitution but for Stalin's prodding that a constitution might add to consolidation of the regime's legitimacy. Since then, China has had one provisional and four formal constitutions, none of which were seriously implemented – hence a seemingly unique phenomenon of constitutions without constitutionalism.[8]

---

[6] See above ch 1, ss III and IV.

[7] 'Zhang Chunxian on Ideological Emancipation: Not Only Benefits, but also Powers are to be Returned to the People', *Changsha Evening News* (1 September 2008).

[8] In contrast, the Vietnamese Communist Party seems to be rather serious in debating its constitutional drafts and amendments. See M Sidel, *The Constitution of Vietnam: A Contextual Analysis* (Oxford, Hart Publishing, 2009) ch 1.

The first constitutional document of the People's Republic was the provisional Common Programme (共同纲领, *gongtong gangling*), passed in 1949 by the new Political Consultative Committee (PCC), which differed from the old in that it was now composed of political parties and associations dominated by and friendly to a new ruling party. In seven chapters and 60 articles, the Common Programme laid down completely new principles for all the later constitutions. Its Preamble proclaimed a 'people's democratic dictatorship' (人民民主专政, *renmin minzhu zhuanzheng*), that is, a power based on a 'united front' (统一战线, *tongyi zhanxian*) made up of classes of workers, peasants, petty and national bourgeois and other 'patriotic democratic elements', based on the alliance between workers and peasants, led by the working class. The first chapter on General Principles (总纲, *zonggang*) provided for civil and political rights and promised to protect not only state public property but also the 'economic interests and private properties of workers, peasants, petty bourgeois and national bourgeois' (Article 3), reflecting the CCP's willingness to accommodate a wide variety of interests while it was consolidating its political power. The second chapter on the Organs of Political Power defined the People's Congresses (人民代表大会, *renmin daibiao dahui*) at various levels as the basic form of political institutions.

The first formal constitution was drafted in 1953 and passed the following year with an unanimous vote among the 1197 representatives of the first National People's Congress (NPC). As the first socialist constitution in China, the 1954 Constitution served as the prototype for the current constitution, with textual and institutional designs that are familiar today. It contained 106 articles in four chapters. The first chapter on General Principles proclaimed that all powers belonged to the people, who were to exercise their powers through the NPC and local People's Congresses (LPC) at various levels (Article 2) and reaffirmed the flexibility in the Common Programme that recognised the legitimate coexistence of various types of ownership during the 'transitional period' of China's socialism, even though the state-operated economy (国营经济, *guoying jingji*) was to enjoy a dominant position and preferential development by the state (Article 6). Chapter II on State Institutions defined the basic structure of the government, which is still in effect today, consisting of the NPC and its Standing Committee (NPCSC), the State President (国家主席, *guojia zhuxi*), the State Council (国务院, *guowu yuan*), LPC at various levels and their People's Committees (local governments), governments for the ethnic autonomous areas, the courts and procuratorate. Like the American president, the State President wielded substantial power, not only as the symbol of the state but also as commander-in-chief and chairman of the Supreme State Conference, a decision-making body of the central government (Articles 40–43). Chapter III provided for 19 articles of 'Fundamental Rights and Obligations of Citizens', among which 15 were about the protections of rights and liberties.

C. Revolutionary Legacies

Although the 1954 Constitution was generally well received in China, it was not implemented with any serious effort and failed to curb calamities of massive scale caused by abuse of state power. Partly out of a need to maintain power against competing rivals within the party, Mao Zedong initiated a series of radical political campaigns, from the suppression of 'counter-revolutionaries' (1950–51) and the 'anti-rightists movement' (1957) to the Great Leap Forward (1958), which eventually led to the greatest famine in the world,[9] and the Great Proletarian Cultural Revolution (1966–76), the Chinese version of the Holocaust, which diminished human dignity and rule of law to the point of annihilation.

These campaigns decimated the basic rights of ordinary citizens, be they 'enemies' of the state like the 'bureaucratic bourgeois', landlords and kulaks, and 'counter-revolutionaries' (反革命分子, *fangeming fenzi*) of different kinds, or marginal groups like the petty bourgeois, middle-class peasants and intellectuals, later classified as the 'stinky ninth category' (臭老九, *chou laojiu*), or for that matter, the poor peasants who constituted the vast majority of the population and the very foundation of the state. Indeed, when Mao Zedong, the State President in charge of drafting the constitution, was approached about the constitutionality of some of these measures, he frankly responded that he could not

[9] Although the death toll remains disputable, it is commonly estimated that roughly 30 million peasants died of starvation, see Yang Jisheng, *The Tombstone: A Documentary History of China's Great Famine in the 1960s* (Hong Kong, Tiandi Books, 2008). According to the most recent estimate based on the declassified documents, the death toll rose to 45 million: F Dikötter, *Mao's Great Famine: The History of China's Most Devastating Catastrophe, 1958–1962* (New York, Walker, 2010).

quite recall what the Constitution was about.[10] When he launched the Cultural Revolution in order to save his own authority from declining within the party in 1966, he committed plainly unconstitutional acts by putting Liu Shaoqi (刘少奇), who succeeded him as State President, and other high-ranking leaders under house arrest, and by later removing Liu from his post without the approval of the NPC, which was essentially suspended during the tumultuous era. When Liu, referred to as 'China's largest capitalist roader', protested in vain to the Red Guards (红卫兵, *hongweibing*) in a 'mass denunciation meeting' held in August 1967 that his freedom of speech and personal right were violated, he merely illustrated a simple point that an unenforced constitution was as useless to the State President as it was to a plain citizen.

In 1975, the NPC reconvened after a long hiatus and managed to pass a revolutionary constitution right before the end of the Cultural Revolution. The 1975 Constitution was structurally similar to its more conservative predecessor but was severely politicised and abridged by the removal of most human rights and institutional provisions, leaving only 30 articles. It reduced the 15 provisions of human rights in the 1954 Constitution to merely three and eliminated the latter's requirements for open and independent trials. It did add the right to strike (Article 28) and the 'Four Big Freedoms' (四大自由, *sida ziyou*) of expression, airing (views), debating and writing 'big character posters' (大字报, *dazibao*), which were introduced as new means to carry out the socialist revolution (Article 13).[11] This constitution conflated the party and state functionaries and dramatically enhanced the role of the CCP by authorising the chairman of the Central Committee 'to command the national armed forces' (Article 15); replacing the LPC and local governments with the 'revolutionary committees' (Articles 22 and 23); and substituting the township governments in rural areas with the People's Communes (人民公社, *renmin gongshe*). In a sense the 1975 Constitution was merely a political declaration, at most an outline for a politicised constitution; a constitution was in any case quite meaningless in an era when rights and laws were trampled on with distain as 'bourgeois influences' (资产阶级流毒, *zichanjieji liudu*).

---

[10]   See Liu Zheng, 'Why the 1954 Constitution Gradually Fell into Disuse after Three Years of its Promulgation' (2002) 14 *China People's Congress* 42, 43.

[11]   These wall posters were particularly popular during the Cultural Revolution for expressing mass political views.

This is not to say that the Cultural Revolution, which has been widely and justly condemned for wreaking massive destruction, had produced nothing positive. At the very least, the tumultuous decade helped to inculcate a critical and reflective generation that, despite its deficiency in concrete knowledge, was courageous enough to challenge the legitimacy of the ruling party and undertake a painstaking search for the institutional causes of the revolutionary upheavals.[12] In retrospect, the Cultural Revolution marked both the high tide and low ebb of the leftist ideology initiated by the May Fourth Movement and paved the way for the return of the liberal democratic spirit in the April Fifth Movement (四五运动, *siwu yundong*) in 1976, which began as a protest against the leftist perversions and culminated in the June Fourth Incident of 1989.

Following Mao's death in 1976 and the subsequent purge of the Gang of Four (四人帮, *sirenbang*) as the chief culprits of the Cultural Revolution, the NPC enacted a third constitution in 1978. Extended to 60 articles, the 1978 Constitution deleted some of the leftist provisions in the 1975 Constitution, supplemented human rights and institutional provisions and set the 'Four Modernisations' (四个现代化, *sige xiandaihua*) in industry, agriculture, defence, and science and technology as the new primary objective. These moves were unmistakably reminiscent of the Modernisation Movement of the 1860s. Still under the influence of the Cultural Revolution, however, the 1978 Constitution retained such leftist phrases and concepts as 'continuing revolution under the proletarian dictatorship', 'class struggles', the revolutionary committees and the People's Communes (Articles 7 and 34). Not until the end of 1978 when the CCP convened its Third Plenum of the 11th Congress (十一届三中全会, *shiyijie sanzhong quanhui*) was the Cultural Revolution formally denounced as turmoil and the direction of the state realigned from the 'class struggles' to economic construction. The Constitution was accordingly revised in 1979 and 1980, before it was completely replaced by the current constitution in 1982.

---

[12] In this respect it might not be mere coincidence that quite a few liberal dissidents now active overseas were activists during the Cultural Revolution, eg, Wei Jingsheng (魏京生) and Wang Xizhe (王希哲).

II. THE 1982 CONSTITUTION

A. The 1978 Reform

The CCP's Third Plenum of the 11th Congress in 1978 proved to be a landmark for China's open-door reform (改革开放, *gaige kaifang*). By 1982, the moderates in the mainstream of the CCP who had been ousted by the revolutionary radicals managed to come back and consolidate their powers around Deng Xiaoping, then the Chairman of the Central Military Commission (中央军委, *zhongyang junwen*). It was not surprising, then, that the 1982 Constitution borrowed heavily from the first constitution enacted in 1954, when the CCP mainstream under Liu Shaoqi and Deng Xiaoping shared power with Mao Zedong. In fact, the main programme of the opening and reform by and large reverted back to the industrialisation and limited liberalisation of the rural economy that had begun in the 1950s and early 1960s. Although the 1982 Constitution got rid of most of the revolutionary rhetoric in the previous two constitutions, it was overall a rather conservative – indeed, out-dated – constitution, given its resemblance to its remote predecessor, which had been enacted three decades earlier in a very different social context.

The post-1978 reforms did carry a novel strain of their own, however, with far-reaching significance for China's constitutional development. The economic reform, though legitimised and sometimes positively promoted by the central government, was far from a top-down process; to the contrary, its participants – and even initiators – included the rank and file from the very beginning. In December 1978, 18 peasants in Xiaogang Village (小岗村, *xiaogang cun*) of Fengyang county (Anhui province) signed a private agreement among themselves to divide the public land, each household to be responsible for the farming and yield of its own land.[13] That move, later officially sanctioned and promoted nationwide, appears commonplace today. Indeed, it had by and large been the situation in rural China since the early 1950s, until the collectivisation movement agglomerated the land under individual ownership into the collective land owned by the People's Commune; and it was the situation to which rural China reverted following the colossal failure of the Great Leap Forward in the early 1960s.

[13] See Chen Guidi and Chun Tao, *The Story of Xiaogang Village* (Beijing, Huawen Publisher, 2009).

Keep in mind, however, that such 'revisionist' (修正主义, *xiuzheng zhuyi*) policy had become the chief crime of the deposed State President Liu Shaoqi by the time of the Cultural Revolution, when harsh criticisms would fall on even 'a flash of the "private" word in the mind'.[14] Moreover, China in 1978 was supposedly governed by a constitution under which the People's Commune was the sole legitimate owner of rural land. At that time it took these peasants great courage to break away from the collectivist yoke and pioneer the 'household responsibility system' (家庭联产承包责任制, *jiating lianchan chengbao zerenzhi*), which triggered wholesale economic reform throughout the country. Like the scholars' gatherings in 1895, the signing of the peasant agreement in 1978 marked the rise of spontaneous civil participation in reform, only this time the peasants did not petition any emperor but took actions for themselves. Even more significant, they were peasants, not elites; and they took actions for their own good rather than begging any elite intermediary to represent their cause. This fundamental difference set the Xiaogang experiment apart from the Hundred Days Reform that had failed 80 years before, and provided fresh hope for the latest reform.

It was against this background that the current Constitution was enacted in 1982. As a product of reform, the new constitutional order carried with it both the momentum and the constraints of a century's worth of alternating episodes of reform and revolution. The new episode played out in a different constitutional framework and sociopolitical context.

B. An Overview of the 1982 Constitution

The 1982 Constitution symbolised a new, reformist order that has lasted to this day. It was enacted in order to purge the revolutionary rhetoric that remained in its 1978 predecessor and confirm the shift of national focus to economic construction, as proposed in the CCP's Third Plenum of its 11th Congress. In February 1982, the Committee for Constitutional Revision, composed of legal scholars, proposed a draft, and a revised draft was published by the NPCSC in April. Based upon the

---

[14] 狠批私字一闪念 (*henpi sizi yishannian*), meaning that one was forbidden to even momentarily flirt with the idea of private interest.

opinions and comments solicited from society at large, the draft constitution was further revised and approved on 4 December, which has since been annually celebrated as 'Constitution Day' (法制宣传日, *fazhi xuanchuan ri*).

Though a mark of the new order, the 1982 Constitution was in nature by and large a reversion to the pre-Cultural Revolution era, which had been dominated by the CCP's moderate mainstream, only this time without the fatal destructions from its own demigod, Mao Zedong, who permanently shelved the constitution he himself had drafted by initiating the Great Leap Forward and the Cultural Revolution. As such, it inherited the basic socialist spirit from the 1954 Constitution and indeed from even the 1949 Common Programme. To highlight the new order under the party leadership, the 1982 Preamble explicitly expressed Deng Xiaoping's insistence on the Four Cardinal Principles (四项基本原则, *sixiang jiben yuanze*), which included the political leadership of the CCP, the state foundation on the 'people's democratic dictatorship', the economic system of the 'socialist road' and the ideological guidance of Marxism, Leninism and Mao Zedong Thought. Added to this list are 'Deng Xiaoping theory' and the 'important thoughts of three represents' (三个代表, *sange daibiao*), which demands that the ruling CCP should 'represent the most fundamental interest of the overwhelming majority of the people', by the constitutional amendments of 1999 and 2004, respectively. In practice, the most important and perhaps the only relevant principle today is regarding the CCP leadership, which ironically runs counter to the spirit of constitutionalism. The Preamble did highlight the legal nature of the constitution by defining it as 'the fundamental law of the state with supreme legal effect'. The legal force of the Constitution is reaffirmed by Article 5, which explicitly provides that 'no laws or administrative and local rules or regulations may contravene the Constitution'.

The Constitution contains 138 articles in four chapters. Paraphrasing the Marxist ideology expressed in the 1949 Common Programme, the first chapter on General Principles defines the nature of the state as 'a socialist country of people's democratic dictatorship led by the working class and founded on the worker–peasant alliance' , where socialism is the 'fundamental system' of the state, the disruption of which is strictly 'prohibited' (Article 1). All state powers belong to the people, who exercise their powers through the NPC and LPC at various levels of government (Article 2). The state institutions follow the principle of 'democratic centralism' (民主集中制, *minzhu jizhong zhi*), which means that the NPC and LPC at various levels are made 'responsible to the people' by periodic elections, and the deputies thus constituted in turn supervise all administrative, judicial and procuratorial departments by electing the leadership of these departments at their levels. As a compound of two opposite orders, one bottom-up and the other top-down, the principle of democratic centralism also implies that a People's Congress at a higher level is to be created either by one at a lower level or directly elected by their constituencies (the democratic element[15]), but the government at the higher level is to direct and supervise the one(s) below (the centrist element[16]). In practice, given the ineffectiveness of elections and electoral checks on power, the centrist inclination has always overwhelmed the democratic counterpart, thus reducing the apparently balanced principle to a lopsided structure in which the top-down supervision alone exerts force. The Constitution makes no effort to delimit central and local powers but adopts a vague principle of 'giving full scope to the initiative and enthusiasm of the local authorities under the unified leadership of the central authorities' in attempt to guide their functional divisions (Article 3).

A major structural difference between the 1982 Constitution and its predecessors lies in the order of chapters: 'Fundamental Rights and Duties of Citizens' used to be provided in Chapter III but now precedes the 'State Structure' as the second chapter, partly to reflect the enhanced status of individual rights. The scope of protection is also expanded, as the number of rights provisions has increased to 24. The most important rights include the rights to equality (Article 33), elections (Article 34), freedom of speech, press, assembly and association (Article 35), religious freedom (Article 36), personal freedom (Article 37), personal dignity (Article 38), privilege of residence (Article 39), freedom and privacy of correspondence (Article 40), to criticise, make suggestions and receive compensation for losses caused by state infringements of civil rights (Article 40). The last four provisions were absent in the previous constitutions and were added in view of the great atrocities committed against human rights and dignity during the Cultural Revolution.

Perhaps as a result of duty-oriented Confucian influence, some of the rights are also accompanied by corresponding duties on citizens. For

[15] See below ch 5.
[16] See below ch 3.

example, not only is the obligation of the state to protect religious freedom limited to 'normal religious activities', but private citizens are prohibited from 'making use of religion to engage in activities that disrupt
public order, impair the health of citizens or interfere with the educational system of the state' (Article 36.3); a citizen is free to press charges
against any state functionary for violation of the law or dereliction of
duty but is explicitly prohibited from 'fabrication or distortion of facts
for purposes of libel or false incrimination' (Article 41.1).[17] Like other
constitutional provisions, however, these provisions have not been seriously implemented, partly owing to the lack of judicial review and the
ineffectiveness of the legislative review that is supposed to be exercised
by the NPCSC (Article 67.1).

C. Basic State Structure in the 1982 Constitution

A brief sketch of the state structure is in order before detailed
discussion of China's government institutions. It is necessary particularly because, unlike the Nationalists and even warlords, contemporary
Chinese leaders have repeatedly rejected the Western models of federalism and separation of powers and thus have purported to create a novel
constitutional structure with unique 'Chinese characteristics'.[18] In reality,
however, any institutional design is to be evaluated by its efficacy in fulfilling certain social needs common to every human society and, indeed,
described by a common set of functional vocabularies. China's 1982
Constitution is no exception, and its basic features can be summarised
as a unicameral legislature, a dualist judiciary and a tripartite administrative system at the national level.

The 1982 Constitution, resembling in this respect the British parliamentary model but explicitly rejecting the American model of separation of powers, in which the executive and judicial branches share power
with the Congress, vests China's primary legislatures, the NPC and LPC

---

[17] For a criticism of including private duties in the Constitution, see Zhang
Qianfan, 'What the Constitution Should Not Provide' (2005) 3 *Journal of East China
University of Politics & Law* 25–33.

[18] Deng Xiaoping, for example, repeatedly rejected the separation of powers idea
as 'bourgeois' during the 1980s, though curiously, he also criticised excessive con-
centration of powers. See *Selected Works of Deng Xiaoping*, vol 1 (Beijing, Renmin
Press, 2002) 328.

at various levels, solely with the constituent and thus nominally supreme power. Consistent with socialist ideology, which usually presupposes the presence of a simple majority will,[19] all People's Congresses are unicameral legislatures, and any law or local regulation needs only to pass one particular Congress to take effect. The Standing Committee of the NPC or LPC above the county level is sometimes seen as the 'second chamber'; it *is* a 'second chamber' in view of its independent authority to pass laws or local regulations alone. But this does not make China's legislature 'bicameral', since both a whole Congress and its Standing Committee are capable of passing legislations of almost equal legal force,[20] and since the work of a Standing Committee is also supposedly subject to review of the entire Congress (Article 62 of the Constitution). In this sense a Standing Committee is an inferior though independent and alternative legislature. Above all, the Standing Committees were created not for the purpose of an alternative representative scheme (for example, regions rather than population) or legislative check and balances, but rather to facilitate law-making and, indeed, to lead the whole Congress.

It is perhaps somewhat justified to characterise China's representative system as 'quasi-bicameral' since, in addition to the People's Congresses and their Standing Committees, the Political Consultative Committees at various levels also play some legislative role, convening at the same time with their congressional counterparts every year. The PCCs are not, however, a formal institution defined in the Constitution, and their resolutions, however influential on state policymaking, lack formal binding force. To be precise, the NPC and LPC are the sole legislative bodies from which other state institutions are created.

Beneath the People's Congresses are 'one government and two (judicial) chambers' (一府两院, *yifu liangyuan*). The government and the judiciary are supposed to be elected and supervised by the People's Congresses at their respective levels, while maintaining independence among themselves, though it is common for the government to dominate over the judiciary. While in most countries legal prosecution is

---

[19] Chinese constitutional scholars are well aware of the dilemma raised by French scholar Sieyes a century ago: if the House and the Senate in a bicameral system disagree, which should be seen as representing the 'general will' expressed by the majority of the people? See Miao Lianying, 'The Legislature' in Zhang Qianfan (ed), *Studies of Constitutional Law*, 2nd edn (Beijing, Law Press, 2008) ch 7.

[20] See below ch 4.

normally part of the administration, the procuratorate in China was made a separate and supposedly independent institution within the judicial branch (Article 129 of the Constitution) – an echo of its central role in imperial China – and it constitutes with the courts a 'dualist' judiciary. While the judges are in charge of trials and appeals, the procurators are primarily responsible for prosecutions and investigations for official corruption. The two judicial branches with separate functions check against each other in some respects but often act in concert on major policy initiatives.[21]

Finally, while many modern 'mixed' constitutions incorporate a presidency within a parliamentary framework, resulting in a 'dual heads' scenario (usually a directly elected president and a cabinet created by and accountable to the parliamentary majority), the powers of China's central government are divided among three institutions. If the State President serves mostly as a honorary symbol of the state, the State Council holds most substantive powers of administration in its capacity as the Central People's Government (CPG, 中央人民政府, *zhongyang renmin zhengfu*), and military power is vested in a separate Central Military Commission, which ordinarily overlaps with its counterpart in the CCP, which has exactly the same name.[22] Deviating significantly from the 1954 Constitution, whereby military power was vested in the State President, this arrangement is often criticised for politicising the military and facilitating the CCP's ultimate control over the state.[23]

Without the military and symbolic components, the structure of a Local People's Government (LPG) is a good deal simpler. The only complication comes from the fact that government at each level is matched with a Party organisation, which is in charge of overseeing government decision-making. In fact, the Party is an omnipotent and omnipresent shadow over every branch of public power; the two judicial branches and even the LPC are likewise under the supervision of their own party organisations.[24] The structure of the ruling party is not

---

[21]   See below ch 6.

[22]   See below ch 5 for exceptional cases where the two CMCs do not exactly coincide.

[23]   Thus, liberals often call for the 'nationalisation of armies' (军队国家化, *jundui guojia hua*). See Charter 08 signed by over three hundred intellectuals in China and published on 10 December 1998, http://www.vckbase.com/bbs/viewtopic2.asp?rid=3537795&sf=96.

[24]   See further below ch 3.

stipulated in the 1982 Constitution other than the general leadership dictated by the first 'Cardinal Principle' in the Preamble, but it is the decisive factor for allocating powers to each formal institution defined in the Constitution.

III. CONSTITUTIONAL AMENDMENTS

The 1982 Constitution was drafted and promulgated in the initial stage of China's opening and reform, when Chinese society had barely begun to reopen itself to new ideas after decades of revolutionary bigotry, self-enclosure and self-destruction. It inherited from the 1949 Common Programme and the 1954 Constitution a political and ideological framework that badly needed adjustment, to say the least, in order to comply with the fast-changing demands arising both from economic developments and from a legal and constitutional consciousness that gradually taken root in the minds of ordinary people since the 1978 reforms. Fortunately, the Constitution allowed for timely revisions through a simple procedure, entailing approval by a two-thirds majority of the NPC. As a result, the Constitution was amended in 1988, 1993, 1999 and 2004. So far, most of the amendments have been revisions of the economic system defined in the Preamble and the General Principles, but a few amendments have supplemented fundamental constitutional principles on the rule of law and human rights.

A. Previous Amendments: Towards a Market Economy and the Rule of Law

On 12 April 1988, two constitutional amendments were approved in the first session of the Seventh NPC, both on the economic system. The first supplemented Article 10.4 by allowing 'the rights to the use of land be transferred according to law', thus giving limited space to market transactions within the straitjacket of public land ownership – the hallmark of socialism purporting to have under public ownership every major 'means of production' (生产资料, *shengchan ziliao*). The second amendment supplemented Article 11 of the Constitution by allowing 'the private sector of the economy to exist and develop within the limits prescribed by law'. The private economy, which used to be the target for 'transformation' (改造, *gaizao*), was now 'a complement to the socialist public economy', which is to be 'guided, supervised and controlled' by the state but whose lawful rights and interests will also be protected by the same state.

On 29 March 1993, the Eighth NPC approved a total of nine amendments in its first session. It changed the Preamble to highlight that China is in 'the primary stage of socialism', during which the basic task of the state is 'socialist modernisation along the socialist road with Chinese characteristics'. In order to reflect the new idea of separating management from ownership, whatever enterprises used to be 'state-run' were all changed to 'state-owned', implying that the state was no longer in charge of daily management of public enterprises. The planned economy provisions in Articles 15, 16 and 17 were deleted and replaced by the notions of 'socialist market economy' and 'macro regulation', to be implemented by the state through economic legislation. The 1993 amendment also deleted, belatedly, the term 'People's Commune' and transformed the system of collective ownership in rural areas by implementing the household responsibility system, whereby a commune's lands are distributed to individual peasant households. Last but not least, the term of LPCs at the county level was extended from three to five years (Article 98). LPCs at the township level were not extended to the same term until 2004, when a constitutional amendment made the term of People's Congresses at all levels a uniform five years.

On 15 March 1999, the Ninth NPC approved six amendments in the second session. First, it reassured the validity of the previous amendments by emphasising that 'China will be in the primary stage of socialism for a long time to come', during which the public economy, as the principal component in the socialist economic system, is to develop together with 'multiple forms of economies' (Article 6). The status of the private sector was elevated from 'a complement' in the 1988 Amendment to 'the important constituent component' of the socialist market economy (Article 11). And the political notion of 'counter-revolutionary activities' punishable by the state was changed to the more legalistic term 'unlawful activities that harm state security' (Article 28), followed by corresponding changes in the Criminal Law. More significantly, the 1999 Amendment inserted in the beginning of Article 5 a declaration that China is committed to 'administration of the state according to law' and construction of a 'socialist rule of law state'.

B. The 2004 Amendments: Recognising Human Rights and Private Property

In comparison to the previous amendments, the most recent set of amendments in 2004 was the most extensive in scope, revising 14 provisions. It was the product of the new regime headed by Secretary General Hu Jingtao (胡锦涛), who succeeded President Jiang Zemin (江泽民) in 2003, shortly before the outbreak of the severe acute respiratory syndrome (SARS) epidemic and the landmark Sun Zhigang incident (孙志刚事件, discussed in detail in chapter three). The latter prompted the ruling party to give constitutional recognition to 'human rights' for the first time since the founding of the People's Republic, a notion that had once been ridiculed as a 'bourgeois sentiment'. Now Article 33 provides: 'The state respects and protects human rights.' Notably, what are to be respected and protected are not only rights for workers, peasants and any other 'good class' but rather 'human' rights in general – that is, rights of all human beings, which, literally understood, include even such 'enemies' as those who used to be called 'counter-revolutionaries'.

The 2004 Amendment, then, signifies a partial repudiation of the Marxist class-based cosmology underlying all previous constitutions – 'partial' because the class language in the Preamble and General Principles remains intact in the 1982 Constitution, creating tensions between the original text and recent amendments, which are products of quite a different spirit. The new cosmology is confirmed in corresponding amendments to the Preamble, expanding the 'patriotic united front' to embrace 'all socialist working people, builders of the socialist cause' and inserting the 'Three Represents' theory, according to which the CCP is supposed to 'represent the most fundamental interests of the broadest range of the people'.

Consistent with the ideological shift and continuing with the momentum of the previous amendments, the 2004 amendments further strengthen the equal protection of the private economy. The notion of 'individual and private' sectors is generalised to that of 'non-public' economies, whose 'lawful rights and interests' are protected by the state (Article 12.2). The new Article 13 goes so far as to declare that the 'lawful private property of citizens is inviolable' – almost a paraphrase of Article 12, which dictates that 'socialist public property is inviolable'.

Not only is the status of private property thus elevated to a position almost parallel with that of public property, but for the first time, the taking of private property for the public interest now explicitly gives rise to a requirement to provide 'compensation' (Article 13).[25] Although mere 'compensation', if literally taken, is meaningless without a require- ment to be 'just', these revisions nonetheless reflect significant changes in the constitutional consciousness of China's legislators, officials, scholars and ordinary people since the promulgation of the 1982 Constitution.

Much like the Nationalists had done with earlier constitutions, all post-1949 constitutional amendments in China had been proposed and drafted by the CCP. In fact, it was normal practice to incorporate the amendments first in the CCP Charter (党章, *dangzhang*) in a Party Congress held a few months before the NPC convenes, and then move the amendments from the Party charter to the Constitution verbatim. In comparison, the 2004 Amendments were more 'democratic' in origin for a few reasons.[26] First, while the previous amendments were decided by the Central Committee of the CCP before they were open to public comments and suggestions, the 2004 Amendments were based on sur- veys that solicited the opinions of the central and local governments, corporate entities and scholars before they were summarised and digested in July 2003 in the form of a draft for recommended amend- ments. The recommendations were then discussed and approved by the Politburo (政治局, *zhengzhi ju*) of the Central Committee and its Standing Committee before they were distributed to the Party commit- tees of provincial governments and ministries of the central govern- ment, as well as to the central committees of satellite parties, economists, legal scholars and political theorists. After the second round of solicit- ing opinions, the central committee in charge of constitutional amend- ments revised its recommendations and submitted them to the Politburo

[25]   The original 1982 Constitution did provide for the 'public interest' condition for state appropriation, though without requiring 'compensation'. The other major revisions include the authorisation of the State President to conduct 'state visits' (Art 81) and a change of vocabulary from 'martial law' to 'state of emergency' (Art 67.20) in wake of the SARS epidemic in 2003, when the central and local govern- ments were compelled to take non-military action for protecting the public interest.
[26]   See Wang Leiming and Shen Lutao, 'An Important Measure for Implementing the Basic Strategy of Governing the State According to Law: Recording the Birth of the Constitutional Amendment', *Guangming Daily* (22 March 2004).

and its Standing Committee for further deliberation. While the previous amendments were decided by the Politburo, the final version of the 2004 Amendments was submitted to and approved by 342 members of the Third Plenum of the 16th Party Congress in October 2003, when the formal amendment proposal, consisting of 14 recommended revisions, was submitted to the NPC. After the NPCSC unanimously approved the proposal in December, it was introduced to the plenary session of the NPC when it convened in March 2004, during which the 14 amendments were passed by 2903 members of the NPC with overwhelming approval, against only 10 objections and 17 abstentions.[27]

IV. CONSTITUTIONAL TRANSFORMATIONS

China's constitutional progress neither began nor ended with textual changes. Ever since the opening and reform initiated in the late 1970s, Chinese society has been exposed to a myriad of new ideas and practices. From classical liberalism to the New Left, various schools of economic, political and legal thought have been translated and introduced to Chinese readers of different generations. If a version of democracy was already enshrined in the original text of the 1982 Constitution, the Western concepts of human rights, private property, rule of law, judicial review and constitutionalism, to name a few, gradually found their way into the Chinese literature, some even into laws and the Constitution, though with Chinese modifications. Perhaps more importantly, the spread of legal and constitutional knowledge has led to institutional practices that, however limited and defective, have helped to inculcate popular consciousness for defending the individual rights provided for in the Constitution and in laws, which in turn has raised new expectations for institutional performance and reform. Nor have all salutary transformations taken place within the existing constitutional and legal framework. In a unitary state like China, some local reforms of constitutional nature can take place only in spite of the uniform constitutional provisions to the contrary, giving rise to the unique paradox of 'benign constitutional violations'.

---

[27] Ibid.

A. Reform and the Constitution: The Benign Violation Paradox

It cannot be taken for granted that the Constitution is necessarily on the people's side. Quite to the contrary, for an authoritarian state like China, the constitution is often authoritarian and contains provisions that deprive or restrict rather than protect individual rights. This gives rise to a dilemma whereby the constitution itself need be broken in order to make constitutional progress. In fact, the progressive reforms in the PRC since 1978 were carried out in the shackles of a conservative constitutional framework that badly needed be reformed, if only to get itself out of the way of social progress. Unlike the Constitution of the United States, in which clauses regarding due process and equal protection have served as legal grounds incubating innovative social change,[28] China's constitution offered no such possibility; on the contrary, it had acted as a straitjacket, such that no social or political innovation was possible.

As a case in point, the Xiaogang experiment was plainly inconsistent with the 1978 Constitution, which dictated:

> The rural economy based on the People's Commune is an economy of collective ownership belonging to socialist labour masses. . . Only on the condition that the absolute dominance of the collective economy based on the People's Commune is guaranteed, is a member of the People's Commune allowed to manage a small quantity of private plot and household sideline (Article 7).

The household responsibility system, which allotted parcels of land supposedly owned by the People's Commune to the individual peasant household, obviously exceeded the 'small quantity' provision; in fact, it not only failed to satisfy the 'absolute dominance' condition but effectively dissolved the entire system of the People's Commune itself, when the State Council decided to duplicate the Xiaogang experiment throughout the country in 1983.[29] It is perhaps a 'Chinese characteristic' of the constitutional system that the out-dated provisions stayed on the books despite their glaring inconsistency with social reality. Indeed, surprisingly, the People's Commune provision was preserved in the 1982

---

[28] See, for example, *Brown v Board of Education of Topeka* 347 US 483 (1954); and *Roe v Wade* 410 US 113 (1973).

[29] Central Government, 'Notice on Printing and Distributing the Basic Problems of Agricultural Economic Policy' (1983).

Constitution, even when the household responsibility system was widely implemented, well received and soon formally adopted by the central government, and now covers as much as 97 per cent of farmland nationwide. The provision was replaced only by one of the constitutional amendments of 1993. For a decade between 1983 and 1993, then, the household responsibility system was an officially sanctioned but unconstitutional institution.

Today only a few leftist diehards maintain that such constitutional violations, if violations at all, are anything but 'benign' to China, a country that suffered from a great famine in the aftermath of the hysterical Great Leap Forward and was in constant danger of food shortages under the yoke of the People's Commune. The household responsibility system undoubtedly stimulated great incentive in ordinary peasants to produce the basic means of sustenance for this populous country and enabled it to bid farewell to an on-going food crisis by providing the peasants with limited freedom to manage the land under their possession. Such a salutary reform was made 'unconstitutional' only by an anachronistic and excessively restrictive constitutional framework that deprived the basic personal and property rights of the peasants and thus should not have been part of the constitution to begin with. The real culprit for the unconstitutionality, then, was the Constitution itself, and reform should be carried out despite its 'benign violation' of the Constitution or of laws still in effect at the time.

At its crux, the 'benign violation' (良性违宪, *liangxing weixian*) thesis argues that, since the constitution and laws often lag behind rapid social changes in a transitional society like China, some violations should be allowed and legitimised in view of their salutary society effects, which could not be achieved otherwise.[30] Hence a state measure can produce benign social effects paradoxically by violating the state's own constitution or basic law. Even though most constitutional violations invariably involve serious vices, China's example of the household responsibility

---

[30] Hao Tiechuan, 'On Benign Violation of the Constitution' (1996) 4 *Chinese Journal of Law* 90; and Hao Tiechuan, 'Social Transformation and Limitations of Written Constitutions' (1996) 6 *Chinese Journal of Law* 23. For a critique arguing that apparently 'benign' constitutional violations in terms of immediate effects might bring permanent damages to establishing constitutionalism and rule of law, see Tong Zhiwei, ' "Benign Violation" Should Not Be Approved' (1996) 6 *Chinese Journal of Law* 19; and Tong Zhiwei, 'The Bottom Line of Flexible Implementation of Constitution' (1997) 5 *Legal Science Monthly* 15.

system illustrates that occasionally the yoke imposed by the Constitution itself can be shaken off only by 'benign violation'.

Such a paradox may hardly be felt in an advanced democratic state, where the constitution and laws are usually updated in time for necessary social changes to take place, it but does present a genuine problem to a transitional state in which not only does society changes at a rapid pace, but its lack of democratic apprenticeship under the authoritarian tradition may well prevent its legislature from functioning effectively to allow timely constitutional and legislative adjustments. China's NPC, for example, is supposed to be the supreme legislature responsible for enacting and amending the Constitution and basic laws, but it convenes only once a year for a mere dozen days, during which hardly anything of moderate complexity can be accomplished; above all, of course, it is handicapped by its 'rubber stamp' status and is empowered to act only to the extent it is permitted by the ruling party as the *de facto* supreme power. In fact, the 'benign violation' paradox would have disappeared had the Constitution been enacted by an assembly truly accountable to the people – not only because such a constitution could be amended in time by a competent institution but more fundamentally, because a constitutional provision that so seriously deprives the basic freedom of several hundred million peasants could not have been enacted in the first place. It is conventional wisdom in liberal democracies that a constitution is supposed to protect rather than deprive rights, unless such deprivation is necessitated by the preservation of a public interest of sufficient weight. The benign violation paradox is but another strange dilemma created by an authoritarian regime with neither popular participation in fundamental decision-making nor a genuine commitment to liberal constitutionalism; the unique role of a modern constitution, as opposed to ordinary laws, lies in protecting individual rights rather than imposing obligations on citizens.[31]

The paradox takes a different twist, however, when the liberal understanding of rights protection is extended to cover local self-determination of policies, procedures and institutions. This problem is not removed simply by reorienting the constitution to protect substantive rights and amending it in time for it to catch up with the pace of social reforms; in a

---

[31]   See Zhang Qianfan, 'What the Constitution Should Not Provide' (above n 17), arguing that it is inadequate for a constitution to include duty provisions, among other things.

unitary framework such as the PRC, the problem may in fact become acute (see below chapter three) if the national constitution expands its scope and lays down local institutional structures, thus producing once again a straitjacket, this time to suffocate local innovation.[32]

An example is provided by China's 1982 Constitution, which not only defines the form of the central government and provides basic democratic principles for local governance but also proceeds to define the form of local governments in detail: like the central government, every local government is to be elected by the LPC at the same level (Article 101). It is unconstitutional, then, for a township government to be elected directly by the local electorate, even though China's local experience has definitively proved that direct election, as opposed to indirect election by the LPC, is more competitive and effective in obliging elected officials to respond to their constituencies.[33] Once again, such local institutional innovations are benign in effect and consistent with the democratic principle of the 1982 Constitution but plainly contravene its specific provisions. It would have been better to leave them as 'benign violations' than to take these provisions seriously and prohibit salutary local initiatives, since the fault lies instead in the excessive uniformity imposed by the unitary constitution. When the Secretary-General of the NPC declared in 2006 that direct elections in counties and townships were 'unconstitutional',[34] he merely put a pre-emptory stop on another 'benign violation' that could have provided some hope and vitality for the dismal character of local elections in China today.

The most recent example of the benign violation paradox is the new regulation on associations and organisations issued by the Guangzhou civil affairs bureau,[35] which dramatically simplified the application

---

[32] Zhang Qianfan, 'Constitutional Flexibility and Local Experiments' (2007) 1 *Chinese Journal of Law* 63.

[33] For a synopsis of local experiments with direct township elections, see Zhang Qianfan, *Introduction to Constitutional Law: Principles and Applications*, 2nd edn (Beijing, Law Press, 2008) 435–40.

[34] Sheng Huaren, 'Work Out the Turnover Elections of the Township and County People's Congresses According to Law', *Party Construction of Yongjia County* (23 August 2006).

[35] Notice Regarding the Further Deepening of the Registration Reform of Social Organisations and the Boosting of Social Organisation Development, see Li Qiang and Wen Yanmei, 'Guangzhou Social Organisation May Apply Direct Registration, Many Associations may be Established in Same Sector', *Southern Daily* (23 November 2011).

process, reduced the time period for review and approval, did away with requirement for the sector approval and, most importantly, removed the restriction that only one association was allowed in any specific area, a restriction explicitly laid down in the Regulation on the Registration and Administration of Social Organizations enacted by the State Council.[36] Although some procedural simplifications and the reduction of the review period are not necessarily inconsistent with the central regulation if it is interpreted, for example, as defining the maximum review period allowed for the administration, the removal of the requirement on sector approval and restriction on the number of associations seems to plainly contradict the Regulation as a higher norm. But promoting freedom of association is not only good for local public interest but also consistent with the specific requirement of the 1982 Constitution laid down in Article 35.[37] The Guangzhou regulation may violate a higher, central norm, but that norm itself has arguably violated the supreme law of the land, the Constitution, the plain words of which do seem to prohibit unnecessary and excessive restrictions of freedom to association.

As a matter of rule, of course, China's constitutional progress has taken place within the existing constitutional framework, however defective it is. And reforms since 1978 have been pushed forward as much by open-minded officials and the intellectual community as by 'public interest' lawyers and a people ever more conscious of their constitutional rights. It is their combined efforts that have made the Constitution and laws both better and more effective in terms of protecting individual rights.

B. From Popular Sovereignty to Human Rights: A Paradigm Shift for Constitutional Jurisprudence

Just as institutional change is often preceded by intellectual groundwork, China's constitutional and legal reform has been guided by legal scholarship that has experienced rapid changes of its own. As the early case of Kang Youwei illustrates vividly, Chinese intellectuals have long played a pivotal role in social transformation, serving as 'antennae', as it were, for receiving and disseminating new ideas. Three decades ago, hardly any-

---

[36] For more detail, see below ch 8.
[37] See below ch 8.

one had heard of 'administrative litigation' (行政诉讼, *xingzheng susong*) or thought of the possibility of suing an official for a violation of the law, just as a child brought up in the Confucian tradition could not imagine the possibility of suing her parents. Nowadays, however, the Chinese courts entertain hundreds of thousands of such litigations every year, thanks to the enactment of the Administrative Litigation Law in 1989. But that law could not have been enacted without a major change of mentality, whether traditional or revolutionary, brought about by massively introducing Western jurisprudence and legal practices that help to fill the void left by the relentless destructions of the Cultural Revolution. And the same applies to China's constitutional jurisprudence, which used to be just another manual for political education but has undergone slow but fundamental change since the initiation of the reforms.

The 1982 Constitution shares several basic features with the 1949 Common Programme and the 1954 Constitution; it is largely political (as opposed to legal) in content, collectivist (as opposed to individualistic) in ideological orientation, and lacks a feasible enforcement mechanism. To begin with, a constitution is necessarily more 'political' than ordinary laws in the sense that it embodies the fundamental political beliefs of a nation and defines the nature and structure of a political system. And particularly so is China's 1982 Constitution, which opens with a lengthy, glorifying account of the ruling party gaining historical victories that are supposed to provide legitimacy for its permanent leadership over the nation. Even the main text is filled with legally unenforceable yet politically high-pitched notions such as 'people's democratic dictatorship' (Article 1), 'democratic centralism' (Article 3), 'sacrosanctity' (referring to 'socialist public property', Article 12) and numerous references to the undefined and probably indefinable notion of 'socialist system' throughout the text. Even though the term for China's constitution literally means 'constitutional law' (宪法, *xianfa*), the pervasive use of political vocabulary has greatly inhibited the legal enforcement of the 1982 Constitution.[38] After all, a constitution filled with political slogans not only is difficult to enforce but may well have never been meant to be seriously enforced at all.

The political nature of the Constitution helped to politicise the legal and constitutional scholarship built around it. Far from being a value-neutral comparison and examination of world constitutions, free from

---

[38] See further below ch 6.

the political values expressed in its own national constitution, China's constitutional study used to be but an extension of the Party's mouthpiece for affirming, glorifying and disseminating its political views. The primary task of a Chinese constitutional scholar was not to freely interpret or evaluate, much less criticise, the Constitution, but simply to pass the Party's orthodox doctrines to students and society at large. As a result, China's constitutional community developed a highly self-centred inclination for self-affirmation and, together with it, xenophobia. Western constitutions were studied only to be criticised for their pernicious 'bourgeois' influences, which ultimately had to be warned against, even if one was presenting a positive introduction to Western institutions. Such a xenophobic attitude could be maintained, of course, only by indulging oneself completely in theoretical self-construction and resolutely turning one's head away from reality. Since the 1982 Constitution is not equipped with a meaningful enforcement mechanism and has so far afforded only one disputed constitutional 'case' to speak of,[39] Chinese constitutional scholars are used to being preoccupied with lofty concepts and general theories, without paying attention to enforcement mechanisms and the legal application of the Constitution to concrete cases.

The situation emerged from the Chinese context of a holistic mentality that traditionally immersed an individual in the collective – whether the family, the community or the state – and was exacerbated by the post-1949 collectivist movements. A convenient illustration is found in the holistic notion of 'popular sovereignty', which, to be sure, seems to express a democratic principle that finds its primary locus in Article 2 of the Constitution: 'All power in the People's Republic of China belongs to the people.' Both the notions of 'people' and 'power' were, however, taken as holistic fictions in their singular form, incapable of being broken down into individual components and thus finding concrete applications in real life. Under the pervasive influence of the simplistic collectivist thinking that had dominated China from 1949 to 1978, during which all private lands of individual peasants were taken away and placed under the supposedly collective control of 'People's Commune', China's constitutional community in 1982 could not meaningfully answer questions such as 'Who are the "people"? 'What powers can be divided or shared among different institutions bearing different rela-

---

[39] *Qi Yuling v Chen Xiaoqi et al.* See below ch 6.

tionships to their constituencies?' In an article entitled 'Theory and Practice of People's Democratic Dictatorship', for instance, the author cited a standard definition of the 'people': 'The agency of people's democratic dictatorship is, of course, the people. At the time when the new China was founded, the people included the working class, the peasant class, the petit bourgeoisie in the cities and the national bourgeoisie.'[40] Such a definition reduced the notion of 'people' into several 'classes', but 'class' in itself is a collective concept, which is not only opposed to the notion of equality among all individuals but also fundamentally alien to the liberal premise that everyone is to be respected irrespective of the class to which he or she may belong.

The holistic mentality proved to be disastrous for China: the rights of individual persons were completely overwhelmed by the higher interests of such grandiose yet fictitious entities as the 'people' (人民, *renmin*), the 'state' (国家, *guojia*), the 'nation' (民族, *minzu*) and the 'collective' (集体, *jiti*); and pervasive 'class struggles' during the Cultural Revolution and other political movements brought calamities of unprecedented scale to the entire nation.

Although the holistic legacy has lingered to this day – the collectivist notions in the original Constitution remaining untouched by amendments – both the conscious and subconscious minds of China's legal community and society at large have undergone a painful but decisive shift toward individualism since the time of opening and reform. The main theme of this shift has been learning from the useful experiences of advanced countries. Deng Xiaoping's 'cat theory',[41] for example, implies that 'the sole touchstone for truth is practice' (实践, *shijian*) rather than any *a priori* edicts.[42] In 1979, a major ideological dispute broke out between the remains of the Maoist camp on the one hand and pragmatists on the other hand, with the latter buttressed by a

---

[40] Translated from Zhang Youyu et al, *Collection of Essays on Constitutional Law* (Beijing, Social Science Literature Press, 2003) 48–66.

[41] Paraphrasing a Sichuan proverb, 'It does not matter whether the cat is white or black, as long as it is good at catching mice.' The implication is that what matters to social well-being is not so much ideological left or right, and a 'bourgeois' experience can be worth studying – even copying – if it proves to be useful to China's development.

[42] This is in reference to the doctrine of 'two whatevers' (两个凡是, *liangge fanshi*): 'Whatever Chairman Mao has decided, we will firmly uphold; whatever Chairman Mao has directed, we will always follow.' See Editorial Commentary, 'Study Well the Files and Capture the Crux', *People's Daily* (7 February 1977).

neo-conservative mainstream that came to dominate the party.[43] With the Maoist ideological obstinacy gradually giving way to the pragmatic CCP mainstream, Chinese jurisprudence in general and constitutional scholarship in particular transformed accordingly. Reading law books and articles published three decades ago,[44] one cannot fail to be amazed by the scale of transformation in China's legal and constitutional paradigms, which are in many ways more fundamental than the textual changes that aim to make the Constitution into more of a legal document than a political declaration.

In a span of three decades, despite major political setbacks since June 1989, Chinese constitutional jurisprudence has completely transformed not only its outlook but also its spirit. If it used to be self-centred, xenophobic, purely text-oriented and woefully negligent of practical applications and enforcement mechanisms, it has now adopted quite an opposite attitude. Chinese constitutional scholars today are not only anxious to learn about foreign constitutional theories and practices but also willing to borrow from the salutary experiences of developed constitutional systems, particularly mechanisms of judicial review and the vast body of case law that applies constitutions to specific, real issues of social life. While books on foreign legal and constitutional systems used to be treated as 'bourgeois' taboo, hundreds of foreign law textbooks and treatises have been translated and introduced to China during the past 20 years. The translations of legal classics and popular textbooks have been a thriving enterprise since the 1980s for the Chinese presses, who have managed to maintain that momentum, adding a bewildering amount of foreign legal literature to China's market every year. During the early 1980s, Chinese students would be vexed at the extreme shortage of foreign legal scholarship and would gleefully grab any such book found in a bookstore; such student may still be vexed today, but only because they would be at a loss as to which one to pick among a dozen bearing similar titles. And constitutional law is no exception. Since the late 1990s, several influential works on Western (especially American)

---

[43] See Special Commentary, 'Practice is the Sole Test for Truth', *Guangming Daily* (11 May 1978).
[44] For representative works around 1980, see Zhang Youyu et al, *Collection of Essays on Constitutional Law* (above n 40); and Zhang Youyu et al, *Collection of Essays on Jurisprudence* (Beijing, Social Science Literature Press, 2003).

constitutional law have been introduced to China.[45] The translations are unsurprisingly uneven in quality, but they nonetheless provide Chinese readers with a knowledge base for approaching foreign (mostly Western) constitutional law.

Stimulated by the massive influx of foreign legal scholarship, its indigenous counterpart has grown rapidly. Even by the middle of the 1980s, the representative work in public law was limited to *Comparative Constitutional and Administrative Law*, a comprehensive but rather thin volume on two vast areas by Professor Gong Xiangrui (龚祥瑞), a liberal Peking University scholar who studied with Harold Laski during the 1920s; by the end of the 1990s, comparative constitutional studies were producing multiple volumes.[46] Comparative law scholarship has helped improve domestic constitutional research; few serious contributions nowadays are content with quoting provisions or citing general principles of the national Constitution without making reference to relevant foreign experiences.[47] In fact, the lack of judicial review and direct application of the Constitution in China make comparative studies all the more essential to delineating solutions for its own problems.

More profoundly, China's constitutional study used to be nothing but political ideology, but it is now evolving towards a value-neutral, positive science, shifting focus from empty, generalist jargon such as 'people', 'class', 'state' and 'sovereignty' to tangible individual rights, which are increasingly demarcated in concrete cases and controversies. In proportion to the consistent diminution of ideological content in constitutional law scholarship, Chinese constitutional scholars are increasingly paying attention to the application of constitutional theories to practical social problems. As a result, the Constitution is no longer a political

---

[45] See, eg, the American constitutional law casebook, P Brest et al (eds), *Processes of Constitutional Decision-Making: Cases and Materials*, 4th edn, which was fully translated by Qianfan Zhang et al and published by the China Politics and Law University Press in 2002. The last edition of Professor Konrad Hesse's classic *Outline of the Basic Law* was translated into Chinese from the original German version and published by the Commerce Press (Beijing) in 2007.

[46] See, eg, Li Buyun (ed), *Comparative Studies of Constitutional Law* (Beijing, Law Press, 1998); Shen Zongling, *Comparative Constitutional Law: A Comparative Study of Constitutions of Eight States* (Beijing, Peking University Press, 2002); and Zhang Qianfan, *The Western Constitutional Systems*, vol 1, 'The American Constitution' and vol 2, 'The European Constitutions' (Beijing, China University of Politics and Law Press, 2000/2001).

[47] For a representative collection of articles, see Jiang Min'an et al (eds), *China's Road to Constitutionalism* (Beijing, Law Press, 2005).

declaration of lofty ideals but becoming a fundamental legal document for protecting concrete individual rights. The 'human rights' provision in the 2004 Amendment is but a reflection of this basic change of mind-set, which is now almost exclusively interested in individuals. It is true that 'human rights' can also be collectivised, as it were, into a holistic 'right of mankind', but unlike the singular, monolithic, conglomerate 'popular sovereignty' – a term hardly ever used anymore – the notion of 'human rights' ultimately rests on the rights of individual human beings, with immediate implications in real life. The human rights amendment signals a decisive shift of priority from the collective to the individual in China's constitutional jurisprudence.

C. The Rise of 'Rights Consciousness' and 'Populist Constitutionalism' in an Inchoate Civil Society

Unlike the constitutional reform movements in the late Qing period, China's constitutional transformation in the last three decades is no longer limited to the efforts of a few elite jurists or enlightened officials but rather is positively supported and promoted by a vast population of workers, peasants and the younger 'internet generation'. A small number of liberal scholars and students have certainly made valuable, even indispensable contributions to the enlightenment of the Chinese masses, not only by initiating policy changes and propagating legal and constitutional knowledge in classrooms but also by turning constitutionally significant events into constitutional cases through litigation.[48] As the numerous failures of previous reforms have repeatedly illustrated, however, without popular support, these individual efforts would have been suffocated in their cradles by the formidable status quo. In the landmark Sun Zhigang incident, which sparked national reactions in 2003, for example, several legal scholars petitioned the NPCSC and requested its review of the State Council's Custody and Repatriation Measures.[49] The petition itself failed to establish a precedent for constitutional review in China but did receive overwhelming public support and helped to channel public anger into expressions for institutional reform within the existing·constitutional

---

[48] For a representative work, see Zhou Wei, *A Study on the Judicial Remedies of Constitutional Basic Rights (Xianfa Jiben Quanli Sifa Jiuji Yanjiu)* (Beijing, China People's Public Security University Press, 2003).

[49] See further below ch 3.

framework, which eventually succeeded in pressuring the State Council to rescind its odious Measures, which severely deprived personal freedom and discriminated against peasants. In fact, the reform has origins in 1978 with a group of 18 common peasants in Xiaogang village – not with academic or government elites, and this key difference sets the contemporary reform apart from all previous elite-initiated reforms, both in the scope and the depth it has been able to reach. In this sense, the 1978 reform was far more than a top-down adjustment of national economic policy; it was in essence a self-emancipation movement initiated from below, through which the people educated themselves about the constitutional rights they ought to enjoy in strenuously fighting for their own subsistence and basic well-being.

Since the initiation of the reform that shook off the yoke of the People's Commune from the peasants and that of the state-owned enterprises over city workers, the state has been gradually loosening its grip on society, and Chinese people have enjoyed an increasing degree of freedom. Through continuous communication with the rest of the world through multilateral exchanges in persons, goods, services and ideas – facilitated most recently by the Internet – orthodox ideology has quickly lost its appeal for the young generations, giving rise to unprecedented varieties of competing theories, doctrines and opinions; leftist (or neo-leftist) and rightist ideologies have exchanged fire both in the academic community and in wider public debates, but in neither case at the behest of the government mainstream.[50] Added to the diversity of views is the proliferation of civic associations (NGOs) that exist outside government-sponsored 'people's organisations' (人民团体, *renmin tuanti*), despite tight legal and political control over these burgeoning associations.[51] As a result, an inchoate civil society is taking shape. While the central government is still capable of cracking down on any targeted idea or association, it has afforded enough space for the brewing of a civic spirit that thinks and occasionally acts for itself. Concurrent with the transformation of China's constitutional law and legal community, the Chinese public in general has experienced a rapid growth of consciousness for vindicating its own rights and applying the Constitution to ordinary life. It is not exaggerating to characterise China's last three decades as 'an era toward rights'.[52]

[50] See the Maoist website 'Utopia' (*wuyouzhixiang*), http://www.wyzxsx.com/.
[51] See below ch 8.
[52] Xia Yong et al, *An Era toward Rights: A Study of the Development of the Rights of Chinese Citizens* (Beijing, China University of Politics and Law Press, 1995).

The rise of the public's rights consciousness is facilitated both by institutional innovations brought about by legal reform and by growing social dislocation in a less regulated society. Ever since 1979, Chinese legislation has experienced radical expansion, in part to sustain the transition toward a market economy. Yet many of the rights promised in legislation and in the Constitution remain unimplemented, leaving a good number of government regulations inconsistent with higher laws and many more official practices that plainly deprive ordinary people of their fundamental rights. Article 37 of the 1982 Constitution states, for example, that 'personal freedom . . . is inviolable', and Article 8 of the Law on Legislation explicitly requires legislative support in laws enacted by the NPC for any 'compulsory measures and penalties that restrict personal freedom'. But the deportation and repatriation system that clearly restrict personal freedom without prior legislative authorisation was enacted by the State Council and had been implemented by all local governments for nearly half a century before it was repealed in 2003 following the Sun Zhigang incident. Likewise, both the Constitution (Article 13) and the Property Law (Article 66) provide that 'lawful private property' will be protected by law, but in both city planning decisions and the urbanisation of rural areas, the people's land and houses continue to be taken without just compensation, creating a massive amount of social conflict and tragedy.[53] Left unprotected by state institutions, the people are obliged to study the Constitution and laws themselves, and to push the governments at all levels to perform their constitutional and legal obligations. In urban renovation projects, for example, more than a few residents have taken the Constitution as the basis for defending their property rights.[54] While constitutionalism through official channels is blocked indefinitely for lack of both an effective enforcement mechanism and a genuine incentive for implementing the Constitution, there is nonetheless a genuine alternative in 'populist constitutionalism', whereby the general populace can play a more active role in making the Constitution into what its plain words are meant to be.

In retrospect, it is not altogether impossible to transcend the dilemma of reform and revolution that confronts an authoritarian state, which

---

[53]   See below ch 7.

[54]   See, eg, Duan Hongqing, 'Awaiting the Supreme Court's Judicial Interpretation for Demolition', *Finance (Caijing)* (5 June 2004) 104.

was sketched out above in chapter one. In fact, the apparently insurmountable dilemma was created by the very nature of authoritarianism and illustrates a plain truth: so long as ordinary people remain bystanders to rather than actors in the political arena, the end of the political game will never turn out in favour of their interest because the more conscientious, altruistic or enlightened faction within a ruling regime is always weaker than the dominant, self-regarding status quo that controls the state machinery. And a revolution led by a small, elite group of self-appointed 'vanguards' can only re-establish a despotic regime that will be equally if not more resistant to popular participation. Somehow, the people, in order to protect their own interests, will have to stand up and make their voices count in the political games.

From mid-April to early June 1989, in wake of the untimely death of the reformist and widely loved former General Secretary Hu Yaobang (胡耀邦), young students and Beijing residents came out in large numbers to make clear demands of the ruling regime, but the demonstrators were too weak to make a difference in the outcome of the political struggle at hand. Like the Hundred Days Reform almost a century earlier, the popular movement and the reformist faction within the Party were simply crushed. Yet the popular momentum for reform remained alive, and the Communist regime is under as much pressure to reform as the imperial regime was when it was forced to promulgate the first constitutional Outline in 1908. Hence Deng Xiaoping's Southern Tour in 1992. If anything, the current government is under even more pressure to exhibit the 'maintenance of stability' (维稳, *weiwen*) and 'social harmony' (社会和谐, *shehui hexie*),[55] because continuing economic 'reform' without political checks and balances has so far meant the further accumulation of wealth by the rapacious status quo at the expense of the ordinary people's interest and livelihood – even their lives. Such a predatory process cannot help but create a plethora of social conflict and

---

[55] 'Social harmony' was the major banner of Hu Jintao, who succeeded Jiang Zemin as the General Secretary on the 16th Congress of the CCP in 2002. According to an informal report, the government expense spent on 'maintenance of stability' (including activities, for example, on resolving petitions for grievances and, in most cases, forcibly returning the petitioners to their homes from Beijing or provincial capitals, where they usually gather) has been continuously escalating over the years, now to the point of exceeding the military expense, which is roughly 15 per cent of total revenue.

tragedy, and tarnish the image of a regime purported to be founded on and work for the people (Article 2 of the Constitution).

One of these many tragedies, fallen on the young man named Sun Zhigang, sparked a new round of civil activism in a new, internet environment and opened a new chapter in China's constitutional history.

FURTHER READING

Cai, D, 'The Development of Constitutionalism in the Transition of Chinese Society' (2005) 19 *Columbia Journal of Asian Law* 1.

Chen, H, *An Introduction to the Legal System of the People's Republic of China*, 4th edn (Hong Kong, LexisNexis Butterworths, 2011) ch 2.

Deva, S, 'The Constitution of China: What Purpose Does it (Not) Serve?' (2011) 2 *Jindal Global Law Review* 55.

Dikötter, F, *Mao's Great Famine: The History of China's Most Devastating Catastrophe, 1958–1962* (New York, Walker, 2010).

Feng, L, *Constitutional Law in China* (Hong Kong, Sweet and Maxwell Asia, 2000).

Lieberthal, K, *Governing China: From Revolution through Reform*, 2nd edn (New York, WW Norton & Co, 2003).

Lubman, S, 'Bird in a Cage: Chinese Law Reform after Twenty Years' (2000) 20 *Northwestern Journal of International Law & Business* 383.

Pu, Z, 'A Comparative Perspective on the United States and Chinese Constitutions' (1989) 30 *William & Mary Law Review* 867.

3

Governing the Goliath: China's Central and Local Relations

———◆◆◆———

INTRODUCTION: THE SUN ZHIGANG TRAGEDY – THE CONSTITUTIONAL LANDSCAPE – KEEPING LAWS IN ORDER – The Hierarchy of Legal Norms – Leaving Room for Local Autonomy – Curbing 'Legislation Fights' in a Unitary State – Limitations of the Law on Legislation – BOTTOM-UP OR TOP-DOWN? RULE OF THE PARTY REINFORCED – Between the Text and the Reality of Laws: The Latent Rules – Top-Down Control and the Role of the Ruling Party – The Dual Responsibility Paradox – Limitations Inherent in Top-Down Control – PLURALISM WITHIN A UNITARY SYSTEM – The Regional Autonomy of 'Nationalities' – 'One Country, Two Systems': Special Administrative Regions (SARs) – Divided Sovereignty across the Taiwan Strait

I. INTRODUCTION: THE SUN ZHIGANG TRAGEDY

IN MARCH 2003, when China and the rest of the world were grappling with an epidemic of severe acute respiratory syndrome (SARS), a personal tragedy struck Guangzhou and eventually triggered a public outcry against the age-old system for treating migrant populations in Chinese cities. Sun Zhigang (孙志刚), a 27-year-old graduate from the Wuhan Science and Technology College in Hubei province, came to work as a fashion designer in the economically booming city of Guangzhou, once known in the West as Canton. On the fateful night of 17 March, he went to visit an internet cafe as usual, without bringing his temporary residence permit as an identification document.

He was mistakenly detained by police as an illegal immigrant to the city and was brought to the Guangzhou internment and deportation transfer center. Apparently, having quarreled with the management personnel about his treatment, he was battered by fellow inmates and died a few days later.[1] The medical record of the official report asserts that Sun died of 'heart-attack' and 'cerebrovascular accident', a claim belied by the autopsy report, which displayed massive bruises on his back. For over a month afterwards, despite studious efforts by Sun's relatives and friends, the Guangzhou city police refused to explain the true cause of Sun's death.

The silence was broken first by a news report of the *South Metropolitan Daily* (南方都市报, *nanfang dushi bao*), one of most outspoken newspapers in China today, entitled 'Who Should Be Responsible for a Citizen's Abnormal Death?'[2] The report triggered mounting public outcries, fuelled by exchanges on the relatively unregulated Internet. Although similar events occurred quite routinely – if not always as dramatically – the Sun Zhigang incident shocked the conscience of the entire nation. After the event was first publicly reported, storms of curses and condemnations directed at the Guangzhou police broke over the Internet, which was as yet a rapidly developing medium for expressing a variety of ideas in China. For a short time, the local government remained adamant that Sun had died of natural causes and that the local police were impeccable throughout the process.[3] Such responses fuelled further public dissatisfaction. Eventually, the accident and the public criticisms attracted the attention of high-level leaders in the central government and the Guangdong provincial government, and demands were made for a thorough investigation, the culprits to be severely punished.[4] Under political pressure from above, the Minister of Public Security was reported to have instructed as many as seven times that the responsible persons be apprehended. And when the central government intervened, justice was quickly served.

---

[1]   There were disputes as to where the battery actually took place, and some have proposed that it occurred in the police bureau instead, but this book adopts the official report, due to a lack of other reliable sources.

[2]   *South Metropolitan Daily* (25 April 2003).

[3]   *Beijing Youth Daily* (1 May 2003).

[4]   'The Sun Zhigang Case has Achieved a Breakthrough', *Xinhua Daily* (14 May 2003).

Although the Sun Zhigang tragedy triggered mounting moral condemnation, the Chinese public did not stop at simply condemning the official misconduct but rather took a further step by questioning both the legality and the legitimacy of the Guangzhou police's authorisation to seize and detain Sun in the first place. The legislative culprit was the Measures for Custody and Repatriation (收容遣送, *shourong qiansong*) of Urban Vagrants and Beggars (hereafter 'Custody and Repatriation Measures'), a regulation enacted by the State Council in 1982, ironically the same year as the current Constitution, which states that 'personal freedom . . . is inviolable. Unlawful detention or deprivation or restriction of citizen's freedom of the person by other means is prohibited' (Article 37). Custody and 'repatriation' as an institutional practice was, however, almost as old as the People's Republic itself, designed initially to clean up the remaining Nationalist bandits, prostitutes and wandering beggars in the early 1950s, then to contain and settle the starved peasants pouring into the cities as a result of the radical Great Leap Forward movement in the early 1960s, and to curb the so-called 'blind migrations' (盲流, *mangliu*) of 'peasant workers' seeking employment in the cities during the 1980s. Over the years, custody and repatriation deteriorated into a practice that provided local polices with unchecked opportunities for profiteering and abuse of power, and it had caused several tragedies even before the Sun Zhigang incident.[5] In addition to its moral dubiousness, the Measures also ran into legal trouble with the promulgation of the Law on Legislation (hereinafter LL) in 2000, which reserves certain areas of powers to the National People's Congress (NPC) and its Standing Committee (NPCSC). Among the reserved areas is the 'deprivation of the political rights of citizens, or compulsory measures and penalties that restrict personal freedom'.[6] While custody and repatriation obviously involves 'compulsory measures . . . that restrict personal freedom', the Custody and Repatriation Measures had never been legally authorised by the NPC or NPCSC in the form of law,[7] thus obviously running counter to the LL requirement.

---

[5] Zhang Qianfan, Chinese Legal Reforms in the Aftermath of the Sun Zhigang Incident (2007) 4 *Asia Law Review* 1–39.

[6] Law on Legislations, Art 8.5.

[7] Art 9 of the Legislation Law does allow the State Council to develop certain regulations in the prohibited areas if it is authorised by the NPC/NPCSC, but such authorisation may not be given to enactments involving compulsory measures and penalties that restrict personal freedom, the deprivation of the political rights of citizens, or crimes and criminal penalties.

It was against this background that three young legal scholars initiated a constitutional review process, which is provided for in Article 90 of the LL,[8] and sent to the Legal Works Committee (法工委, *fagongwei*) of the NPCSC a recommendation for reviewing the constitutionality and legality of the Custody and Repatriation Measures. Their petition received overwhelming public support. The NPCSC failed to take any action as usual, but the State Council, now under severe national pressure and under the leadership of a new Premier, Wen Jiabao, moved promptly to repeal the Custody and Repatriation Measures, which authorised the compulsory relocation of 'vagrants and beggars'. On 1 August 2003, less than five months after the Sun Zhigang tragedy occurred and within three months after it became publicly known, the State Council promulgated a new regulation of an entirely different nature, as revealed even by its title: Measures for the Administration of Relief for Vagrants and Beggars without Assured Living Sources in Cities. Based on the principles of 'receiving aid of one's own free will' and 'giving help gratis', relief for vagrants and beggars was now to be administered with compassion and according to individual circumstances, so that recipients could have access to food, lodging, medical care, means of communication and transportation to their hometowns. In a surprisingly short period, a system that had been enforced for half a century and fraught with local interests was levelled to ground, upon which an entirely new relief system was built up.

The incident that triggered this transformation was obviously a personal tragedy for Sun Zhigang and his family, but it was a seminal moment for China's constitutional development. It not only led to the repeal of an age-old, iniquitous institution that discriminated against the massive population of peasants but, more profoundly, consummated a model initiated by the Xiaogang experiment that can be properly labelled as 'populist constitutionalism'. Unlike the elite scholarly gathering called by Kang Youwei in 1895, Sun Zhigang and millions of his sympathisers were but ordinary folks expressing their reactions against a discriminative and restrictive institution – reactions that were conspicuously absent when the Hundred Days Reform was suppressed by the conservative clique of the Manchu rulers; when the warlord Yuan Shikai persecuted

[8] Art 90 of the Law on Legislation confers a sort of 'citizen standing' that allows ordinary persons to request the NPCSC to review the constitutionality or legality of an administrative or local regulation even if that person is not directly related to a particular dispute.

the Nationalists and won his 'presidency' by kidnapping Parliamentary voters; when the Nationalists actively eliminated the Communists through multiple military campaigns under its strict one-party rule; when members of the two parties killed each other in a bloody civil war as soon as the victory of the Sino-Japanese War was achieved; and when the government-mandated Great Leap Forward left over 30 million peasants in graveyards. Even when the Xiaogang villagers decided to set themselves free from the yoke of the People's Commune and initiated rural reform in 1978, the nationwide expansion of the family responsibility system was unilaterally deployed by the central government; the vast majority of peasants were but passive followers in the process. In contrast, after the Sun Zhigang incident, the people stood up, openly expressed their opinions and pressured the government to take action; institutional reform was helped by intellectuals, but it was initiated and decisively promoted by the people.

The significance of the Sun Zhigang tragedy, a subject to which this book will constantly return, can be appreciated from many different perspectives. It was obviously a criminal case of personal assault and an administrative case of official dereliction and incitement; it was equally a constitutional case involving a variety of human rights – the right to freedom of the person; the right to due process; the right to equal treatment of peasants and city residents; and last but far from least, the right to free speech and press, which should enable the public to air their opinions about events such as the Sun Zhigang incident. The Sun Zhigang case also illustrates how an institution, in spite of the will of the vast majority of people, can be enacted, maintained and rigorously enforced for decades in a 'people's republic'; how the constitutional guarantee of 'popular sovereignty' is rendered nugatory once the rule of the people over the government has been effectively replaced by rule of the party; and how even positive laws such as the Law on Legislation can fail to produce any effect on such secondary norms as the State Council's Custody and Repatriation Measures. Yet it is above all a vivid illustration of the working of China's inter-governmental relationships.

Keep in mind that the Custody and Repatriation Measures was central legislation uniformly implemented by local governments throughout the vast country, and it was uniformly repealed by a single command from the same central government. The local governments at various levels may to some extent adapt a regulation to local circumstances, but only within the regulatory framework and without contravening the basic spirit of the central regulation; with regard to the Custody and Repatriation Measures, they were as powerless to resist the uniform implementation of the national regulation prior to 2003 as they were to save it after the State Council pronounced its demise. Just as the central government was positively promoting official misconduct when it uniformly enforced the Measures, it was efficiently promoting the national good when it uniformly repealed such regulation – but even here, the national regulation may have inevitably placed the local governments on a Procrustean bed, creating the pervasive problem of 'cutting uniformly with one knife' (一刀切, *yidao qie*). In other words, some local governments may well find themselves obliged to detain beggars and vagabonds or adopt other compulsory measures restraining personal freedom under special circumstances, without legislative authorisation of the NPC or its Standing Committee, since necessities for these measures are found only in special local circumstances rather than felt nationwide; it would have been both inadequate and inefficient for a national legislature to adopt regulation of local interests, and indeed, it is practically impossible for the massive NPC (with nearly 3000 representatives) in its short annual session (roughly ten days) or for its overwhelmingly busy Standing Committee to adopt any such measure. As a result, local governments are left with two unappealing options: either be handicapped and do nothing in the absence of central approval, or step outside their legal competency in order to do good for the local community. Yet Article 8 of the LL, the very legal basis used to challenge the validity of the infamous Custody and Repatriation Measures, requires precisely such result and illustrates how good purpose is achieved in a unitary regime like China: powers are taken away from the local legislatures and relegated to the central authority in order to prevent abuses and to protect certain fundamental rights. In this sense, the way by which the institutional cause of the Sun Zhigang tragedy was removed only revealed a deeper institutional pattern that left many more problems unresolved.

This chapter introduces the basic framework of central and local relationships in China. It first provides an overview of the institutional landscape and hierarchies, in particular, some basic statistics for government and civil service at various levels, which are important for appreciating the difficulties of governing a giant country like China. It then explains the hierarchy of ordinary legislation in mainland China, as well as the institutional causes of the pervasive legislative conflicts. But laws do not always mean what they say, and account must be given to the role of the ruling party, which vitally affects the distribution of central and local powers as well as the entire mode of governance. The chapter will end with an introduction to several exceptions from the unitary model – namely, the nationalities' autonomous regions, the special economic zones and the Special Administrative Regions (Hong Kong and Macao) – as well as the unresolved conundrum that is the outstanding territories of Taiwan and other islands ruled under the Nationalist Constitution.

II. THE CONSTITUTIONAL LANDSCAPE

As a state with the longest unitary history in the world, China has maintained its centralised framework since it was united in the Qin dynasty some 2500 years ago, during which period the central government has always enjoyed supreme authority over the people and local governments, limited only by its own capacity. Due to its enormous size, the absence of effective means of transport and communication, and the limits of centralised control itself, China's unitary framework is destined to be fractured by numerous local factors. Not only had impediments to economic and cultural exchange produced a diverse set of stable local enclaves and settlements, but limited central power has long necessitated a degree of local self-governance. In the past, this system of self-governance relied primarily on Confucian scholars. The Communist takeover in 1949 dramatically accelerated centralisation in many aspects, but even they could not eliminate the local diversities inherent to Chinese society; in fact, the developmental policies that discriminated between urban areas and rural ones only served to reinforce local differences. To encourage local initiative, the open-door reform further devolved significant amounts of power to local governments, resulting in a system that was still unitary but with unique pluralistic characteristics.

With the world's largest population (nearly 1.4 billion) and third largest territory (9.6 million square kilometres), mainland China is extremely uneven in the distribution of population, resources, wealth and degree of economic development. Divided among four municipalities (直辖市, *zhixiashi*), five nationality autonomous regions (少数民族自治区, *shaoshu minzu zizhiqu*, hereinafter 'NARs') and 23 provinces (省, *sheng*), most of the population is concentrated in the interior provinces, which are rich in farmland, and the coastal provinces, which have received preferential development since the opening and reform, leaving the vast mountainous areas in the northwest sparsely populated. While talent and commerce are concentrated in municipalities like Beijing, Shanghai and Tianjin, as well as in affluent provinces like Jiangsu, Zhejiang and Guangdong, natural resources are disproportionally found in the north-west peripheries. More generally, although economic and social inequalities have been exacerbated everywhere, particularly in the cities ever since the market reform of the mid-1990s, the institutionally enforced urban–rural divide continues to dominate the systematically maintained social injustice, despite the on-going reforms initiated by the Sun Zhigang incident.[9] The determining factor for any province's prosperity is still the proportion of its land in comparison to the proportion of its rural population.

The 1982 Constitution provides for a four-level governance structure (Article 95). From top to bottom, these are the central government; the provinces (including municipalities and NARs); the cities (市, *shi*) and counties (县, *xian*); and townships (乡, *xiang*) within counties, and districts (区, *qu*) within the cities, with 'towns' (镇, *zhen*) usually standing for urbanised townships. The reality is more complex, however, as an extra level was created between the provinces and the counties in order to facilitate domination of the cities over the counties. Thus large 'prefecture-level cities' (地级市, *dijishi*), to be distinguished from smaller cities at the 'county level', contain counties that are further divided into townships and districts. Although a few provinces have begun to experiment with 'direct provincial control over counties' (省管县, *sheng guan xian*), which promotes county governments to the same level as that of the cities, the control by large cities over counties remains the norm so far.[10] In addition, below the townships and city districts are villagers' committees (村民委员会, *cunmin weiyuanhui*) and city residents' committees (居民委员会, *junmin weiyuanhui*), respectively; both are 'grassroots mass self-organisations' (基层群众自治组织, *jiceng qunzhong zizhi zuzhi*) in name, but in effect they are quasi-official entities with varying degrees of executive power devolved from the local governments. Taking into account these additional government bodies, China is actually, in spite of Article 95, characterised by a complex governing structure with six levels of governments.

---

[9] See further below ch 7.

[10] Xu Lifan, 'China Is About to Initiate Administrative Zoning Reform, Planning to Establish a Government System of Two Levels Containing Provinces and Counties', *Huaxia Times*, 1 September 2005.

According to the census performed in 2004, China has 283 large cities, 374 small cities, 852 districts, 2862 counties, 17781 townships, 19171 towns, and over 652718 villages. The average population of a town or township is about 25000, and that of a village roughly 1500. But the distribution is extremely uneven. While the average township population may well reach 50000 in dense provinces such as Guangdong, Shandong, Jiangsu, Hubei, and Henan, that in the sparsely populated NARs is fewer than 10000; the average township population in Tibet, for example, is only 3300, a fifteenth of Guangdong province.

Critique has frequently been offered about the high number of officials and civil servants in China. It is undeniable that the proportion of civil servants in the population has increased rather dramatically. By 1996 what amounted to publically salaried personnel (including public school teachers) reached 36.7 million, among whom roughly eleven million were cadres in the Party or government offices. This was an 82.3 per cent increase from 1978, while the population increased by only 27 per cent during the same period. Although the proportion between public employees and the population increased from two per cent to over three per cent (1:28), and since then roughly a million were added to China's civil service cohort every year, China's governmental scale as a whole is still not particularly 'big', even if measured by Western standards since the advent of 'administrative states'.[11] By 2003, the total number of civil servants in mainland China was roughly 6.54 million, and there was one state employee for every 198 citizens.

In fact, contrary to the conventional wisdom, the official body of civil servants is often too 'small' to seriously undertake major public programmes involving, eg, social welfare and environmental protection. The central government, the apex of national powers, for example, has undergone several rounds of 'institutional streamlining' (机构精简, *jigou jingjian*) since 1980s, but even before dramatic cuts in 2001 reduced the civil servants directly affiliated with the central bureau by nearly a half, they numbered only slightly over 340,000.[12] A small central government

---

[11] See Ma Haoliang, 'Official-civilian ratio reached 1:18, experts called for strict control of official inflation', *Legal Daily* (13 June 2005).

[12] The initial guiding document for the institutional reform at the beginning of the economic reform was Deng Xiaoping's speech made at the Enlarged Conference of the Central Politburo, Reforming the Party and State Leadership Institution. See Duan Hongqing, 'Two Decades of the Chinese Administrative Institutional Reform', *Finance* (20 March 2004) 46–47.

is made possible in China through the delegation of most of the regulatory implementation to local governments at various levels and even to villages, which, as 'mass self-organisations', are not formally part of the state institutions.

The image of 'small' Chinese government is dramatically changed, however, once massive quasi-public bodies of various sorts are taken into account. Other than civil servants in the government, there are several million cadres and workers in the Party organisations, whose ranks and remuneration parallel those of the civil servants. In addition, by 2004 there were roughly 20 million county, township and village managerial personnel who were not officially employed by the government and lived on fees and fines, including 7.3 village cadres. Finally, official retirees, who constitute another 10 million, enjoy the same privileges they did before retirement. Taken together, the overall public burden is rather onerous.[13]

III. KEEPING LAWS IN ORDER

At least since the Qin dynasty was established by the 'First Emperor' in 221 BC, China has maintained a unitary framework in which the central laws are unlimited in competence and unconditionally superior to all local regulations. Indeed, the very term 'law' (法律, *falü*) is monopolised by the national legislature; local assemblies at whatever level and scale are entitled to pass only 'regulations' (法规, *fagui*), 'ordinances' (法令, *faling*) and 'rules' (规章, *guizhang*). 'Laws', much less separate constitutions, which exist in some federal systems, are beyond their purview. Except for a brief period of provincial constitutional experimentation during the 1920s,[14] there has always been only one Constitution in China, despite the fact that the Basic Laws of Hong Kong and Macao are sometimes dubbed 'mini-constitutions'; but in reality, even they are passed by the NPC. The unlimited competence of the central government notwithstanding, a degree of conflict often remains between local legislation on the one hand and the rules enacted by departments of the central government on the other hand. The result is a complex structure of legal norms.

---

[13] Ma Haoliang, 'Official-Civilian Ratio Reached 1:18, Experts Called for Strict Control of Official Inflation', *Legal Daily* (13 June 2005).

[14] See above ch 1.

A. The Hierarchy of Legal Norms

In January 2011, the Chairman of the NPC Standing Committee confidently announced that a 'socialist legal system with Chinese characteristics' had been established, leaving China with 236 effective national laws; over 690 sets of administrative regulations; 8600 sets of local regulations; and many more rules and norms of lower rank.[15] In the current hierarchy of legal norms, the 1982 Constitution theoretically occupies the highest place, though it is not a 'law' in its complete sense, due to the lack of an effective enforcement mechanism, even though the last paragraph of its Preface states that the Constitution is 'the fundamental law of the state and has supreme legal authority'. Article 5 emphatically declares:

> No laws or administrative or local rules and regulations may contravene the Constitution. All state organs, the armed forces, all political parties and public organisations and all enterprises and institutions must abide by the Constitution and the law. All acts in violation of the Constitution or the law must be investigated. No organisation or individual is privileged to be beyond the Constitution or the law.

The Constitution is ineffectively enforced partly because courts and other judicial tribunals are not authorised to apply constitutional provisions in their decisions;[16] rather, constitutional review of legal norms is entrusted to the NPCSC, which is given the function 'to interpret the Constitution and supervise its enforcement' (Article 67.1). However, this power has not been exercised by the NPCSC a single time since the Constitution came into force in 1982, even in in the face of cases that involve egregious violation.[17]

Second in the hierarchy of legal norms are the 'laws' (法律, *falü*) in their narrow sense – statutes enacted by the NPC or its Standing Committee.[18] Unlike a federal framework, in which central legislation is

---

[15] Chen Baocheng, 'Wu Bangguo Declares that the Chinese Legal System Has Been Established', *Southern Metropolitan Daily* (10 January 2011).

[16] See further below ch 6.

[17] See below chs 7 and 8.

[18] China is one of the few countries in which the Standing Committee of the national legislature is constitutionally authorised to make laws that become effective without the need for further approval of the latter. The Legislation Law provides that the NPC shall 'enact and amend criminal, civil, state-institutional and other basic laws', while the Standing Committee can make 'other laws'. See also below ch 4.

required to lie within the scope of powers authorised by the federal constitution, China's unitary structure imposes no limits on the scope of national legislation. Though the word 'unitary' (单一制, *danyi zhi*) is not explicitly spelled out in the 1982 Constitution, it does provide a list of general areas on which the NPC or its Standing Committee may legislate, but they are not limited to legislation in these areas. Instead, any law will be deemed constitutional as long as it does not contradict specific constitutional provisions. Indeed, Article 8 of the LL specifically reserves several areas of competence to national laws, such as matters with respect to state sovereignty; the structure and powers of governments at all levels; the autonomic governance of NARs and Special Administrative Regions (SARs); the civil and criminal systems; 'deprivation of the political rights of citizens or compulsory measures and penalties that restrict personal freedom'; 'expropriation of non-state assets'; basics of taxation and the economic system; and the litigation and arbitration systems.

Below the Constitution and the laws are administrative regulations (行政法规, *xingzheng fagui*) enacted by the State Council. Just as the function of China's Constitution is not to 'grant' (though it does 'limit') legislative powers, the function of these regulations is not to 'grant' (though, again, they do 'limit') administrative powers; an administrative regulation is not required to be pre-authorised by the laws but is deemed lawful as long as it does not contravene any specific legal provisions. Even for areas reserved to the national legislatures, the NPC or its Standing Committee may pre-authorise the State Council to enact administrative regulations 'as needed', except in matters relating to criminal law; the judicial system; and deprivation of citizens' political rights or compulsory measures and penalties restricting citizens' personal freedom (Article 9). In these exceptional areas, a law must be enacted before the State Council may impose its regulations. The national laws and administrative regulations are binding nationwide and are superior to local legislation and departmental rules of the central government. The structure of legal norms in China becomes less clear when one looks at the next level – local regulations (地方性法规, *difangxing fagui*) enacted by the provincial LPCs (including those of municipalities and nationality autonomous districts) and 'departmental rules' (部门规章, *bumen guizhang*) made by ministries and commissions (部委, *buwei*) under the State Council. Although an administrative regulation made by the State Council always supersedes local regulations, this does not apply to a nationally applicable rule made by its department. In other words, the normative hierarchy as between central and local legislation becomes unclear for any rules or norms below the national laws and administrative regulation. In fact, not only is the hierarchy as between a provincial regulation and a departmental rule unable to be decided *a priori*, but even local regulations enacted by the local People's Congress (LPC) of a 'relatively large city' (较大市, *jiaoda shi*) and local rules (地方规章, *difang guizhang*) enacted by its government are not necessarily pre-empted by a national rule in case of conflict,[19] though a local rule is supposed to conform to the local regulations of the same jurisdiction in addition to national laws and regulations (Article 73). The Law on Legislation explicitly provides that local rules have the 'same legal force' as that of departmental rules (Article 82).

Last, but by no means the least, below regulations and rules is a massive body of 'normative documents' (规范性文件, *guifanxing wenjian*), such as orders, decisions, notices and instructions of general applicability made by a variety of government units at all levels. However, without even an assigned term, these Chinese versions of 'red tape' (红头文件, *hongtou wenjian*) are marked not only by their sheer number but also by the effectiveness of their implementation in practical life, especially in comparison with the Constitution and laws. For example, a local zoning plan aiming to take a piece of village land or demolish residential buildings in a city, or a local standard that minimises the compensation for such takings of property, would be executed forcibly and swiftly because such a decision literally means revenue to the local government.[20] Many of these red tape orders are not published, even though the Regulation on Disclosure of Government Information (政府信息公开条例, *zhengfu xinxi gongkai tiaoli*), promulgated by the State Council in 2007, explicitly requires such publication by governments at all levels (Article 6).

---

[19] According to the Law on Legislation, the category of 'relatively large cities' includes provincial capitals, special economic zones (SEZs) and 'any other city so approved by the State Council' (Article 63). The State Council has so far approved 36 such cities, including Qingdao, Dalian, Xuzhou, Ningbo, Suzhou, Wuxi, Changzhou and other relatively developed cities.

[20] See below ch 7.

B. Leaving Room for Local Autonomy

Although within its unitary constitutional framework, China's central legislature enjoys plenary legislative powers, local legislation is not constrained in a straitjacket but is left with plenty of room to adapt to local needs and circumstances. Article 63 of the LL provides that a provincial People's Congress and its standing committee may 'enact local regulations according to the specific circumstances and actual needs of the jurisdiction, provided that such enactment does not contravene any provision of the Constitution, laws or administrative regulations'. The LPC and its standing committee of a relatively large city may do the same, provided that the implementation is approved by the provincial Local People's Congress Standing Committee (LPCSC), which is required to review the legality of the lower regulation and grant approval within four months if such regulation does not contravene any provision of the Constitution, laws, administrative regulations or provincial regulations (Article 63).

The Law on Legislation further provides that local regulations may be enacted for two types of matters. First, they can be made for the purpose of implementing a national law or regulation if more specific provisions are required in light of local circumstances (Article 64.1). Virtually all provinces have enacted, for example, local regulations for implementing the Measures for the Administration of Relief for Vagrants and Beggars, which was adopted by the State Council in the aftermath of the Sun Zhigang incident. Second, an independent local regulation can also be enacted with respect to 'local concerns', presumably referring to matters not covered by the central legislations (Article 64.2). In addition, the LPCs and their standing committees of provinces and relatively large cities may, 'according to the specific situation and actual demands of the locality, make local regulations for those matters for which no laws or regulations have been enacted' (Article 64.3). Parts of such regulations inconsistent with national laws or regulations enacted later shall be repealed or amended by the enacting body. A local rule is authorised to do by and large the same: to implement laws, administrative regulations or local regulations, and to enact independent rules 'within the regulatory scope of the local jurisdiction' (Article 73).

China's local autonomy is fatally limited, for good reason, by the lack of trust in local governments, which leads to the abrogation of local competences and reservation to the national legislatures of certain key areas specified in Article 8 of the LL. Although some of these areas – such as matters relating to 'state sovereignty', the organisation of the central government, the division of competences between the central and local governments, and basic economic and legal institutions – may properly be said to belong to the tasks of national legislation, some of these reservations plainly contradict the democratic principle of local autonomy. A typical example is the reservation of 'compulsory measures and penalties that restrict personal freedom' in Article 8.5 of the Law on Legislation. In other words, a local legislature may pass a regulation on these compulsory measures or penalties only as an implementation of a pre-existing national law that involves these measures, and lacks independent authority to legislate these measures for local needs without the authorisation of a national law. Personal freedom is undeniably an important individual right, but in mature democracies, local governments are generally entrusted with maintaining local order and promoting legitimate public interest by whatever means they judge necessary. A central government usually intervenes only when a local legislation positively contravenes a provision in the national constitution or legislation. This is usually achieved through judicial intervention – which is uniquely effective for protecting fundamental rights of 'discrete and insular' minorities and checking against the 'tyranny of the majority'[21] – rather than through direct legislative or executive intervention, much less through an outright deprivation of local competence in legislating on these matters. Trust in local governments is well deserved, however, only when they are held sufficiently accountable to the local people by effective electoral or judicial mechanisms. In China, where such mechanisms are simply absent and local officials are held responsible, if at all, to their superiors rather than to the electorates or the judiciary, the distrust of local government is well grounded, since such legislative powers, once delegated to the local governments, may well be abused.[22]

---

[21] These terms were coined respectively by Chief Justice Stone in the famous Footnote 4 of *United States v Carolene Products Co* (1938) 304 US 144 and by Alexis de Tocqueville, *Democracy in America*, G Lawrence (trans), JP Mayer (ed) (New York, Harper & Row, 1969) 250–54.

[22] In November 2009, for example, the Court, the Procuratorate, the Public Security Bureau and the Bureau of Justice of Shenzhen city, Guangdong province, jointly issued a Notice Regarding Handling of Abnormal Petition Acts According to Law, which authorised the local police to place those who repeatedly engage in 'abnormal petitions' in the 'education through labour' (*laodong jiaoyang*) programme

Even so, reserving legislative competence according to the importance of a subject matter rather than the scope of its influence invariably handicaps governance under the rule of law and aggravates legislative lawlessness by providing legitimacy to local disregard of national laws.

Finally, a word should be spent here on the 'revenue-sharing scheme' (分税制, *fenshui zhi*) established in 1994, which provides for 'local taxes' (地方税, *difang shui*) for the first time in the history of mainland China; previously, the central government had monopolised the power to collect tax and disperse revenue.[23] Paradoxically, however, the revenue-sharing scheme, superficially a form of 'fiscal federalism', has increased the central share of the total tax revenue at the expense of local shares. The reform was initiated essentially to halt the double decline of central revenue's share of total state revenue and of state revenue's share of GDP, which had continued for 15 years since the economic reform was initiated. And it successfully achieved the goal of enhancing state power in general and central power in particular.[24] In fact, the central government maintains a monopoly over tax legislation – again, apparently for good reason – and local governments are authorised to collect revenue only via minor taxes and at rates fixed by central legislation. Of course, the central government disperses a large amount of its revenue to provincial governments and, occasionally, lower levels through transfer payments, but these payments are usually calculated according to projects and programmes, which exacerbates local dependence and intensifies local lobbying for central funds. In retrospect, despite the former Premier Zhu Rongji's own defence of the matter,[25] tax reform has made local revenue at the county level and below insufficient to meet basic local needs, whether legitimate (eg, public expenses for school teachers, medical care, social security, law and order, and enforcement of national or local public policies) or illegitimate (eg, corruption, lavish government buildings, luxury official vehicles and leisure tours at public

(of which see below ch 7). This Notice was viewed by many as flagrantly infringing the basic freedom of the petitioners and inconsistent with Article 8 of the Law on Legislation. See 'Shenzhen Provides that Repeated "Abnormal Petitions" Will Be Treated with Education Through Labour', *Guangzhou Daily* (12 November 2009).

[23] He Fan, *Making a Constitution for Market Economy: The Fiscal Problems in Contemporary China* (Beijing, China Today Press, 1998) 174–84.

[24] The theoretical basis of the reform was expounded in Wang Shaoguang and Hu Angang, *A Report on China's State Capacity* (Shenyang, Liaoning People's Press, 1993) 120–21, which deplored the 'decline in the state capacity' of China.

[25] Zhu Rongji, *Record of Zhu Rongji's Speeches* (Beijing, Renmin Press, 2011).

expense). In one way or another, it has prompted local governments to exact funds on their own, primarily through land-taking in the country-side and house renovation in the cities; in other words, it has authorised local governments to profiteer in the name of 'development', at the expense of the common people's livelihoods. The tragedy of Tang Fuzhen,[26] which will be discussed below in chapter seven, in many ways replicated the events surrounding the Sun Zhigang incident – but in the context of land-taking context. It was but a natural consequence of the new developmental policy taking shape after Deng Xiaoping's Southern Tour, of which the revenue-sharing reform was an essential part.

C. Curbing 'Legislation Fights' in a Unitary State

Once local authorities gain freedom to provide for local interests, con-flicts between local and central legislation become inevitable. The prob-lem is especially acute for a giant country like China, where central and local legislative competences are not constitutionally delimited. Article 3 of the 1982 Constitution merely states a vague principle of 'giving full scope to the initiative and enthusiasm of the local authorities under the unified leadership of the central authorities', which provides little guid-ance for dividing the central and local functions. As a result, China's central–local relationship has been trapped in a rather lawless state, in which conflict between legislation at different levels, commonly known as 'legislation fighting', has been both pervasive and perennial. In 2000, the Law on Legislation was enacted precisely to curb legislation fighting by specifying the order of legal norms and their law-making procedures, as well as the ways to resolve legislative conflict. In this sense it is the 'law of laws', with a prominent status next to the Constitution.[27]

Unlike the Constitution of the United States, the Law on Legislation does not provide an absolute principle of national supremacy but employs a complex ex post facto review procedure to resolve the con-flicts between local regulations and national legislation that is below the

---

[26] 'A Relocatee in Chengdu Died of Self-immolation after Resisting the Urban Demolition Team for 3 Hours', news.163.com/09/1202/10/5PH8QC3K00011229. html (2 December 2009).

[27] For a concise explanation of the Chinese legal structure, see Albert (Hongyi) Chen, *An Introduction to Legal System of the People's Republic of China,* 4th edn (Hong Kong, LexisNexis Butterworths, 2011) chs 1 and 2.

level of administrative regulations. If discrepancy occurs between a local rule and an administrative rule, or between administrative rules concerning a similar matter, a ruling shall be made by the State Council (Article 86.3). If a discrepancy occurs between a local regulation and an administrative rule concerning the same matter, then the process becomes more cumbersome:

> The State Council shall give its opinion; where the State Council deems that the local regulation should apply, in the local jurisdiction the local regulation shall be applied; where the State Council deems that the administrative rule should apply, it shall request the Standing Committee of the National People's Congress to make a ruling.[28]

Since China lacks a centralised mechanism for reviewing the legality of legislation, the Law on Legislation is at pains to define a complex hierarchy of reviewing authorities. Generally, a state institution has the authority to review legislation enacted by another that is situated at one level below in the constitutional hierarchy, and an enabling agency has the authority to directly invalidate delegated legislation beyond the scope of authorisation or inconsistent with the objective of the enabling decision (Article 88.7). For example, while the NPC has the power to 'amend or withdraw any inappropriate law enacted by its Standing Committee' (Article 88.1) and to 'amend or withdraw any inappropriate administrative rule or local rule' (Article 88.3), the NPCSC has the power to invalidate, among other things, any administrative regulation that contravenes the Constitution or any law, and any local regulation that contravenes the Constitution or any law or administrative regulation (Article 88.2). Likewise, while the State Council has the authority to amend or invalidate an inappropriate departmental or provincial rule (Article 88.2), a provincial Local People's Government (LPG) has the power to amend or withdraw any inappropriate local rule enacted by the LPG at the next lower level (Article 88.6). To facilitate legislative review, an inferior agency is obliged to report its legislation within 30 days of its promulgation to its superior (Articles 88 and 89). This complex setup of cascading review aims to ensure the legality of legislation at all levels.

Finally, the Law on Legislation grants to state institutions, social organisations and individual citizens the right to request review of legislative conflict. Unlike judicial review, which usually requires personal standing to initiate review procedures, China's legislative review process

---

[28] LL Art 86.2.

may be initiated by almost anyone. First, Article 90 provides that certain state institutions can request and initiate the review process by right, even though such request has never been put forward since the promulgation of the LL in 2000. The State Council, the CMC, the Supreme People's Court (最高人民法院, *zuigao renmin fayuan*, hereinafter 'SPC'), the Supreme People's Procuratorate (最高人民检察院, *zuigao renmin jianchayuan*, hereinafter 'SPP'), a special committee of the NPCSC or a standing committee of a provincial LPC may all make written requests to the NPCSC for review if they deem that an administrative regulation or local regulation contravenes the Constitution or any law. The 'working office' of the NPCSC, the Legal Affairs Commission (LAC) (法工委, *fagong wei*), distributes such requests to the relevant special committees of the NPC for review and comment, a process that may eventually lead to the NPCSC deliberating on and deciding the matter.

Second, a private citizen or social group may also make written proposals to the NPCSC for review if any of the above kinds of legislation is deemed to contravene the Constitution or any law, but their proposals will be 'studied' by the LAC and distributed to relevant special committee for review and comments only 'where necessary' (LL, Article 90, paragraph 2). So far, although hundreds and perhaps even thousands of such private requests have been made, none of them has been deemed 'necessary' enough to initiate the review process; even the request made by legal scholars to invalidate the egregious Custody and Repatriation Measures, which was repealed shortly afterwards by the State Council itself, failed to initiate the review process in the aftermath of the Sun Zhigang incident. In fact, although a special office has been created for 'regulatory review and record' (法规审查备案室, *fagui shencha bei'an shi*) in 2005 under the LAC, it has never even published the list of requests received, making it impossible to assess the number or nature of such requests. In any case, despite the minimal standing requirement, private individuals have never been able to trigger the seemingly well-designed albeit convoluted review process provided for by the Law of Legislation, while no public institution has ever even bothered to try.

D. Limitations of the Law on Legislation

As the 'law of laws', yet seldom if ever used since its promulgation in China, the Law on Legislation suffers from several limitations. First, although its original purpose was to curb legislation fighting, it has done little to strengthen the uniformity of national legislation and to clarify the order of different norms below administrative regulations. In contrast to a federal system such as that of the United States, where federal powers are limited to those granted in the Constitution but have supremacy vis-à-vis state and local legislation,[29] China's central legislation needs no constitutional grant; however, neither are they supreme over local legislation in the complete sense – a departmental rule is not necessarily superior to a local regulation or rule, even if it is entirely consistent with national laws and regulations that in turn comply with the Constitution. Far from curbing legislation fighting, then, the Law on Legislation runs the serious risk of encouraging conflict between legislative acts that sit below the level of administration regulations. While it may accommodate local diversity and prevent 'cutting across the board with one knife' by departmental rules or decisions, it undermines legal uniformity as a basic requirement of the rule of law.

Second, it is not only impossible to decide a priori the rank of a departmental rule vis-à-vis a local regulation or rule, but also extremely difficult to apply the review mechanism in practice. If a conflict between a departmental rule and provincial regulation or rule occurs, a request for review will have to be submitted to the State Council, an extremely busy bureaucratic centre that has only one Legal Affairs Office (LAO) (法制办, *fazhiban*) to handle issues of legislative conflict, and this results in long delays in conflict resolution. Added to that agony, if the State Council decides for its department against a provincial regulation, the matter will have to be appealed further to the NPCSC, which is preoccupied with its own legislative agenda.[30] This process is meant to both temper the natural inclination of the State Council toward its own departments, which would disqualify it as a neutral arbitrator in dispute resolution, and make up for any democratic deficiency inherent in a process where the national administration imposes its decisions on locally elected People's Congresses. In reality, however, it simply prolongs an already lengthy process and creates further delays.

On the whole, both the State Council and the NPCSC are preoccupied with their own administrative and legislative work and thus can hardly devote significant time to resolving pervasive legislation fighting in such a

---

[29] Art 6, Constitution of the United States.
[30] See below ch 4.

massive state as China or to processing the massive number of individual complaints that are made possible by the lack of a standing requirement. Timely resolution of legal conflicts requires a far more decentralised process, whereby impartial judicial institutions across the country are able to take up and speedily dispense with the local complaints.

This leads to the third and most important point: the conspicuous absence of courts in the entire review process. Indeed, the Law on Legislation completely leaves out the courts. This is consistent with the Administration Litigation Law, which limits the scope of judicial review to 'concrete administrative acts' and does not extend to 'abstract administrative acts' such as laws, regulations, rules or any normative documents of general nature.[31] In fact, the courts are obliged to take laws and regulations as 'legal grounds' (法律依据, *falü yiju*) in adjudications (Article 51). That the courts play no role whatsoever in resolving legislation conflicts merely reinforces the impression that the review provided for in the Law on Legislation is purely legislative – or more accurately, political rather than judicial in nature. Not only is the review of legislation directed to purely abstract norms with no requirements about personal standing – and thus able to avoid the concrete cases and controversies normally associated with judicial review – but when review is conducted by a non-judicial institution without the guidance of any higher legal principles such as the supremacy of national legislation, legal criteria are completely absent. When the State Council or the NPCSC confronts a conflict between a departmental rule and a provincial regulation deemed to be of the same rank, what can possibly be the legal ground that predictably governs its ruling except ad hoc policy considerations? As a result, the legislative review contemplated in Article 90 of the LL is nothing but ex post facto law-making by the reviewing agency, which does so at best with a vague idea of the relevant situation at the time of review. For other review systems in which the hierarchy of legal norms is well defined, such clear violations of higher norms as found in the Custody and Repatriation Measures can be meaningfully reviewed even without a concrete case, but they are best conducted by an impartial institution of a judicial nature since, as Chief Justice Marshall pointed out in *Marbury v Madison*: 'It is emphatically the province and duty of the judicial department to say what the law is.'[32]

---

[31] See further below ch 5.
[32] *Marbury v Madison* 5 US 137 (1803).

Unfortunately, the courts in China are excluded from this task, leaving the basic objective of curbing legislation fights unfulfilled.

In fact, precisely two centuries after the *Marbury* decision, a similar case appeared in Luoyang, Henan province, but the very opposite result was reached. The case itself was simple enough: a seed company agreed with the plaintiff to provide an amount of corn seed but defaulted by selling the seed to other parties at market price. The dispute came to the Luoyang City Court in 2003, focusing on the amount of damages liable to the plaintiff. While the plaintiff insisted on payment of the market price according to the Seed Law enacted by the NPCSC, which would amount to damages of CNY¥700,000, the defendant, citing Article 36 of the Henan Provincial Regulation on Crop Seeds enacted by the provincial LPCSC, claimed that the 'government guidance price' should be the standard for calculating the damage, which would amount to CNY¥20,000. The assistant judge presiding over the case, Li Huijuan, found for the plaintiff, interpreting the Seed Law as having established the principle of applying a market price standard. Since the Henan Regulation was local legislation, which is below the level of national law in the legal hierarchy, its provision that conflicted with the Seed Law was null and void.[33]

The case did not even implicate any constitutional provisions as *Marbury* did, although the nature of the question was similar: does the court have *any* power in reviewing abstract norms, if only to safeguard the supremacy of the Constitution and national laws?[34] And the answer provided by the Luoyang court was commonsensical enough in any jurisdiction committed to rule of law: of course, the court, through the pivotal role of judicial review, is obliged to maintain a rational legal order, and reason dictates that a higher law be given effect, notwithstanding lower laws to the contrary. But the Henan provincial LPCSC reacted strongly against the decision and forced the City Court to renounce the judgment.[35] When the courts are unable to defend the law, local protectionism necessarily runs amuck, fatally damaging the uniformity of the entire legal system.

---

[33] See Guo Guosong, 'The Judge Stroke Struck? Down a Local Regulation: Is She Violating the Law or Vindicating the Law', *Southern Weekend*, 20 November 2003.

[34] See below ch 6.

[35] See further below ch 6.

IV. BOTTOM-UP OR TOP-DOWN?
RULE OF THE PARTY REINFORCED

A. Between the Text and the Reality of Laws: The Latent Rules

That the Law on Legislation fails to work in the way it was designed does not mean, of course, that the relationship between China's central government and its many local governments is out of order; on the contrary, it is quite well under control in many aspects, though not in ways spelled out in the Constitution or in laws like the LL. What the law demands is ignored in reality; but the practice is *not* lawless chaos but instead follows another set of rules and conventions, which are mostly found nowhere in any law book. The stark contrast between the text and the reality of law in China has already been illustrated above in the discussion of the Sun Zhigang incident. Another startling disparity between text and reality in China's constitutional law is the role of local democracy in the relationship between central and local government. The 1982 Constitution envisages a democratic state governed by the people from the bottom up through the election of congressional representatives close to them at the township and county levels; these representatives are supposed to elect the provincial LPC, and the latter ultimately elect the NPC, which is to be made responsible to the electorate through this cascade of elections. In other words, the entire government regime is supposedly made responsible to the people because the various People's Congresses elect the major government officials at the same levels. In reality, however, power flows in precisely the opposite direction, with the representatives of the LPCs at lower levels appointed by the superior governments.[36] If China desperately needed law-making when recovering from the lawlessness of the Cultural Revolution during the early 1980s, it now confronts the greater task of applying these laws; otherwise, the great legislative achievements in the recent three decades are but a facade for a dark reality. The disparity between text and reality is even greater with regard to China's Constitution since, in contrast to ordinary laws, the Constitution is not implemented by any credible mechanism.

In fact, such disparity is anything but a contemporary novelty; it has been with China throughout its recorded history. It was reported that

---

[36] See further below chs 4 and 8.

Emperor Jing of Han (who reigned 156–140 bc) once repealed cruel corporal punishments, replacing them with flogging; had this measure been faithfully implemented, China would have been the first nation in the world that succeeded in abolishing state-sanctioned cruel and unusual punishment. Yet the apparently benevolent edict resulted in even more deaths than before because the officers enforcing the edict abused their power in carrying out the floggings, and the situation was resolved only after the Emperor subsequently reduced the number of floggings for each individual crime, defined the size and shape of bamboo whips and prohibited the practice of changing executioners midway through a sentence in order to increase suffering.[37] Not every type of law enforcement task can be narrowed down to bamboo sizes, however, and the ambiguities and vagueness inherent in any law had lent the enforcement officers ample opportunity for misusing their discretion, producing effects contrary to that which the letter of the law dictated. The duality between law and reality is aptly captured by the term 'latent rules' (潜规则, *qian guize*), rules operating in reality as opposed to rules laid out on the law books.[38] The omnipresence of these latent rules has perplexed China not only throughout the long dynasties but also during the legal reform of the last three decades.

Laws and constitutions, of course, do not always mean what they say; it is often joked that the Americans and the Canadians might do better by trading constitutions because the Constitution of the United States was meant by its framers to establish a circumscribed federal power, but it has ended up with an almost unlimited one, while the Canadian counterpart has experienced quite the opposite. In any country, a gap between the text and reality of law is inevitable to a certain extent because the implementation of law is affected by a variety of social, historical, customary and personal factors. In China, however, this gap has been of a different order of magnitude. Not only is what is expressed in the Constitution or laws not enforced faithfully in practice, but the governments often systemically practice a set of 'latent rules', rules not found in open texts but formed and carried out beneath what appears on the surface, often without public knowledge. This explains the apparently

---

[37] See Annals on Emperor Jing and Criminal Law Report in *Book of Han* (*Hanshu*). For an introduction to the penal reform during this time, see Yan Xiaojun, 'The Penal System of Early Han Dynasty' (2004) 4 *Legal Science Monthly* 160-180.

[38] The term was coined in Wu Si, *Latent Rules: Real Games in the Chinese History* (Kunming, Yunnan People's Press, 2001).

irrational phenomenon that sees rules of the lowest order, particularly unpublished 'red-tape' rules made in closed meetings without public consultation and usually against public interest, zealously enforced, while laws in the higher echelon of the normative order get paid lip service, and the Constitution as 'the fundamental law of the state' with 'supreme legal authority' turns out to be the least useful for the purpose of safeguarding the rights of ordinary people. One must keep this in mind when studying China's constitutional law.

A major source of the 'latent rules' is the fact that China's Constitution and government are overshadowed by a ruling party whose power is hardly defined in the Constitution and the law. The 1982 Constitution does highlight the leading role of the Chinese Communist Party (CCP) as the first 'cardinal principle', and the party's 'obligation to uphold the dignity of the Constitution and ensure its implementation' is stated in the Preamble, but it is never mentioned in the main text, the part commonly viewed as having binding force; nor is it referred to by name in most laws or regulations of the state. In fact, the CCP and its satellite parties are not registered as legal entities in China, thus leaving no ground for estimating their legal status and capacities. In reality, however, the CCP as the sole ruling party has completely permeated China's social structure and has extended its control over every corner of government. Governments and organisations at all levels are paired with and led by Party committees at the same levels, which decide the key personnel of the leadership circles; even private law firms are equipped with Party organisations today. Unlike the Nationalist 'tutelage politics' during the late 1920s and 1930s,[39] when it was explicitly stated that there was to be 'no single party outside this (Nationalist) party', in the PRC today there *are* eight satellite 'democratic parties' (民主党派, *minzhu dangpai*) recognised as legitimate by the CCP. However, these parties are totally overshadowed and are supposed to play only a supplementary role to the CCP's leadership. And like its Nationalist predecessor, the CCP also leaves virtually 'no politics outside the party', having taken charge of all major policy initiatives, an example of which was vividly illustrated in the constitutional amendment process described above in chapter two. Ultimately, it is the political control of the ruling party that provides the order in China's central–local relationship.

---

[39] See above ch 1.

B. Top-Down Control and the Role of the Ruling Party

The political party system of a state is particularly important to the relationship between central and local government, since the organisation and power of parties matter a great deal to the division of central and local powers in practice. The Mexican federal constitution is, for example, virtually a copy of the United States Constitution, but the reality of federalism has been dramatically changed by the practice of the National Party, which dominated Mexican national politics for decades.[40] The former Soviet Union contained a dozen 'republics' together with their 'presidents', a constitutional context that would suggest an extremely loose confederation made up of over a hundred ethnic minorities, but the reality was precisely the opposite, owing to the orchestrating role of the Soviet Communist Party. Likewise, its Chinese progeny, the CCP, has maintained a tight grip on Chinese society and government at all levels since 1949. In each case, a highly centralised governance structure emerged in an extremely diverse country through a rigorously organised party machine.

The strict hierarchy within the CCP commands rigorous obedience from Party members and cadres in deference to their superiors so as to ensure the will expressed from the top of the power pyramid, now the Standing Committee of the Politburo, will be carried out unimpeded through all levels, until it reaches the very bottom. The parallel control the CCP exercises over state institutions at various levels then enables the mere nine members of the Standing Committee to carry out their supreme political commands over the whole of China and replaces the essentially bottom-up democratic design expressed in the People's Congress provisions of the 1982 Constitution with a top-down control mechanism in daily political practice.

One rule that does operate effectively to govern the party–state relationship in China is the Working Regulation on Selections and Appointments of the Party and Government Leading Cadres (党政领导干部选拔任用工作条例, *dangzheng lingdao ganbu xuanba renyong gongzuo tiaoli*), published by the CCP Central Committee in 2002 to replace the previous Interim Regulation of 1995. Note that the Working Regulation applies not only to the selection of the ruling party's own cadres but also

---

[40] KS Rosenn, 'Federalism in the Americas in Comparative Perspective' (1994) 26 *University of Miami Inter-American Law Review* 1.

to appointments to government offices in general, such as those in branches and departments in the People's Congresses, the Political Consultative Committee (PCC), governments, courts, and procuratorates – in fact, even to cadre selections in government-affiliated enterprises, public universities and the People's Organisations such as the Communist Youth League (共青团, *gongqing tuan*), the All-China Federation of Trade Unions and the Women's Alliance Association (妇联, *fulian*).

Divided into 13 chapters, the Working Regulation specifies the conditions for party and government appointments in detail, according to which the candidates for posts above county level are to be rigorously measured. The first chapter on 'General Principles' defines six principles governing cadre selections, the most important of which confirms the 'party control of cadres' (党管干部, *dang guan ganbu*). Besides ideological loyalty and career qualifications (Articles 6 and 7), a successful candidate is to pass a series of procedures, including 'democratic recommendations' (Chapter 3), 'investigations' (考察, *kaocha*) and 'deliberations' (酝酿, *yunniang*), 'discussions and decisions' (Chapters 4–7), all orchestrated by the Organisation Department (组织部, *zuzhi bu*) in the Party committee above the department in which the selection process is carried out. For example, in selecting a mayor, the Organisation Department at the provincial level will conduct the 'democratic recommendation' to solicit opinions from the provincial Party committee members, the leading Party groups of the LPCSC, the provincial government, the PCC, the Discipline Inspection Commission (DIC) (纪检, *jijian*), the local court and the procuratorate, as well as the leading members of the city government and its Party committee. It shall then report without publishing the results to the provincial Party committee. Based upon these results, the city Party committee shall come up with a list of candidates after consulting with the provincial Party committee and begin to 'inspect' and 'deliberate' upon the candidates through interviews and solicitation of opinions in a wider circle. Based on these results, the provincial Party committee shall nominate the final candidate and cast an anonymous vote; if successful in acquiring majority support, the candidate will be voted into office by the city LPC in the next convention to make the Party decision legally effective.

For the leading posts in government departments that are appointed by the government itself, the procedure is even simpler; they are just appointed after the matter is discussed and decided by the Party committee (Article 45). Given the heavy-handed manipulation of the Party committees throughout the whole appointment process, the ruling party can virtually put anyone it desires in a leading post. Even so, the Working Regulation provides several loopholes to guarantee that the Party's will be implemented. For example, in deciding a list of candidates, a Party committee shall primarily rely on the results of 'democratic recommendations' but shall at the same time 'avoid simply deciding a person on his votes' (Article 17). If, at the final legitimising stage, a candidate recommended by the Party committee or nominated by the LPCSC fails to acquire the majority vote of the LPC, he or she is to be 'further deliberated upon according to the needs of work and his or her personal condition' and be recommended in another LPC session, although a candidate who fails twice consecutively cannot be recommended for the same post at the same location (Article 48). Such loopholes give rise to enormous personal discretion for the Party committee, which not only creates tremendous opportunity for corruption but also produces far-reaching consequences for China's central–local relationship.

C. The Dual Responsibility Paradox

The cascading control of the ruling party over cadre appointments has created a top-down authoritarian accountability system in which a cadre is practically made responsible to his superior, who controls his opportunity for promotion, rather than to the LPC as stipulated in the Constitution and in the Local Organic Law on the People's Congresses and the People's Governments at Various Levels (hereinafter 'Local Organic Law'). These laws require, instead, not only that a leading local cadre be elected by the LPC at that level but also that an LPC at or above county level is empowered to elect and supervise the People's Congress at a higher level (Article 97 of the Constitution),[41] which is supposed in turn to elect and supervise the major cadres at that level. Such bottom-up democratic accountability contemplated in the Constitution and the law is dramatically subverted by the rigid organisational control of the ruling party. Not only is the direction for the flow

---

[41] The LPC at or below the county level is to be elected directly by the electorates. Constitution, Art 97. See also below ch 4.

of control reversed when an official is in practice made accountable to his superiors instead of to the constituencies he is supposed to serve, but the constitutional framework of the People's Congresses itself is fatally undermined by the pervasive infiltration and manipulation of the ruling party and is reduced to little more than a sanctuary for 'rubber stamps' (橡皮图章, *xiangpi tuzhang*).

Thus democratic accountability is compromised both politically and legally. Although the Constitution and the Local Organic Law define a bottom-up framework through a cascade of elections to the People's Congresses, they also contain distinctively centralising characteristics that imply a legal order operating in the opposite direction. First, a local government is obliged to implement legal norms enacted by superior governments. Thus, an LPC shall 'ensure the observance and implementation of the Constitution, the laws and the administrative regulations in their respective administrative areas' (Article 99 of the Constitution); in addition, LPCs above the county level shall ensure the observance and implementation of the resolutions made by superior People's Congresses and their standing committees (LL, Article 44), and LPGs above the county level are obliged to implement not only the resolutions of the LPC and its standing committee at the same level but also the 'decisions and commands of superior state administrative organs' (Local Organic Law, Article 59).

Second, the superior governments are empowered to direct the work of inferior governments and revoke their inadequate decisions, treating them as subordinate departments within the government. One of the functions of LPCSCs above the county level, for example, is to 'revoke inappropriate resolutions of the LPC at the next lower level' (Constitution, Article 104). An LPG above the county level has the power to direct the work of its subordinate departments and the LPGs at lower levels, and to alter or revoke their inappropriate decisions (Constitution, Article 108; LL, Article 59). Thus, the administrative functions of local governments are legally subject to both horizontal and vertical supervision. While an LPG is nominally accountable to the LPC and its standing committee at the same level, it is effectively responsible and obliged to report its work to the 'state administrative organs at the next higher level'; all LPGs are 'state administrative organs under the unified leadership of the State Council, to which they are all subordinate' (Constitution, Article 110).

Third, the dual responsibility scheme is applied not only to the legislative and administrative relationships between different levels of governments but also to their judicial relationship. In any country, of course, the lowers courts are invariably obliged to follow the decisions of the upper courts to ensure uniform application of laws; even in federal countries, such as the United States, with dualist judicial frameworks whereby federal and state courts parallel each other in dealing with separate bodies of laws and jurisprudence, the federal supremacy principle implies that state judges must follow federal precedents established by the federal supreme court.[42] Following the Continental tradition after the French Revolution,[43] China does not recognise the *stare decisis* doctrine and the prospective binding effect of judicial decisions as 'case law'; nonetheless, upper courts not only enjoy the regular prerogative of reversing and revoking lower judgments through formal appeals but also exercise the function of supervision (监督, *jiandu*) over the lower courts not found in jurisdictions with an established rule of law. While higher courts generally supervise judicial works of lower courts in their jurisdictions, the SPC 'supervises the administration of justice' in courts of all levels (Constitution, Article 127). The other judicial branch, the procuratorate, is governed by a similar vertical relationship, except that procuratorates at higher levels 'lead' (领导, *lingdao*) as opposed to merely 'supervise' the work of those at lower levels (Constitution, Article 132), implying a heightened degree of superior control. In addition, the election or recall of a chief procurator is not solely decided by the LPC at the same level but 'shall be reported to the chief procurator at the next higher level' and submitted to the LPCSC at that level 'for approval' (Constitution, Article 101), indicating direct vertical control of local procuratorates.

Finally, traces of vertical control can be found even in 'grassroots mass self-organisations', the villagers committees, which are outside the formal state structure. Article 4 of the Organic Law on the Villagers Committees provides that township governments 'may not interfere with the matters that lawfully fall within the scope of the villagers self-

---

[42]   See *Martin v Hunter's Lessee* (1816) 14 US 304.

[43]   All French judges, for example, are supposed to be 'equal before law' in spite of their ranks, and appellate reversals are not directly binding on the lower courts in reassessing the facts and interpretations of laws. In practice, however, the Court of Cessation as the supreme common law court has managed to impose its decisions on the lower courts out of the obvious interest for uniformity of laws in a unitary state. See A Túnc, '*Loi Badinter* or Traffic Accident and Beyond' (1991–92) 6/7 *Tulane Law Forum* 27.

government' but at the same time 'shall guide, support and help the villagers committees in their work'; and the villagers committees shall, on their part, 'assist' the local governments in their work. In practice, the villagers committees are used by township governments as an executive instrument for implementing such state mandates as tax collection, birth control and maintenance of local order, even though the original purpose of creating such 'grassroots mass self-organisations', which were supposed to be elected by and accountable to the villagers, was obviously to serve local village interests.

D. Limitations Inherent in Top-Down Control

The top-down control scheme, powerful as it seems, suffers from several inherent limitations that fatally undermine its effectiveness. First and foremost, a scheme that runs diametrically opposed to the democratic principle laid out in the constitution of a state cannot possibly serve the genuine interest of the people, since the national government at the very top of the power pyramid simply lacks such incentive. It is to be kept in mind that some of the most sinister policies and regulations in China were enacted precisely by the central government. The discriminatory policies of urban industrial development at the expense of agricultural areas, together with the household registration system and the Custody and Repatriation Measures that led to the Sun Zhigang tragedy, are but the most conspicuous examples that have positively harmed the vast majority of the nation for over half a century.

In such a political system, peasants, who used to constitute over two thirds of the total population, cannot meaningfully participate in elections; moreover, until 2010 their voting rights had been expressly reduced by national election law to a quarter or less of those of city residents.[44] The interests of this large and 'vulnerable group' (弱势群体, *ruoshi qunti*) can therefore hardly be said to be meaningfully represented and protected. Nor are the interests of city residents, a relatively privileged group compared to the peasants, securely protected against the official encroachments authorised by such national legislations as the Regulation on Urban House Demolition (城市房屋拆迁管理条例, *chengshi fangwu chaiqian guanli tiaoli*, hereafter 'Urban Demolition

---

[44] See further below ch 8.

Regulation'), which, in the name of 'urban development', has caused even more tragedy than the Custody and Repatriation Measures.[45] Indeed, in the type of unitary system described here, the national government may not only fail to legislate for the majority interests by itself but even positively prevent progressive local governments from conducting salutary experiments to benefit their own people.[46]

Even if national legislation is itself benign, it is doubtful that a national government that is not responsible to the national electorate will have sufficient incentive to seriously implement its own laws and protect its people against local governments. More likely, every national law with a nice appearance will be crippled by its lack of an enforcement mechanism, and it will remains little more than a pretty facade for maintaining the legitimacy and dignity of the state; in practice, governments at all levels will follow 'latent rules', which bear no resemblance to the laws in the books, and the people will be institutionally incapable of making any use of the latter for protecting themselves.

The Constitution itself serves a good example. After debates for at least a decade since the Qi Yuling case was decided in 2001,[47] it has now become clear that China needs to establish some sort of judicial review to make the words of its Constitution mean anything, yet not only has there been no single positive action along this direction, but the Qi Yuling decision itself was repealed by the SPC after several years, and the whole subject matter of 'constitutional judicialisation' (宪法司法化, *xianfa sifa hua*) has been banned from public discourse. Nor is the central government well equipped to implement its own laws even if it is willing to do so. Unlike the 'dual sovereign' arrangement in the United States, whereby the federal government is equipped with the full panoply of executive functions and replies primarily on its own resources in enforcing federal laws, China's unitary framework necessitates that the central government limits itself largely to legislation pertaining to national interests, while delegating most of its implementation to local governments. The central government *is* in charge of overseeing local implementation through inspections and disciplinary investigations, but it is in serious shortage of personnel and resources for effectively ensuring that centrally issued statutes are faithfully implemented in such a vast and diverse country.

---

[45] See further below ch 7.
[46] See the 'benign violation paradox' discussed above ch 2.
[47] See further below ch 6.

This leads to the third and most fundamental limitation on the capacity of the central government: it simply lacks adequate knowledge to keep track of the massive amount of daily official activity in 32 provincial units, over 600 large and small cities, nearly 3000 counties and 40000 towns and townships, not to mention over half a million villagers' committees that exercise some legislative and executive powers. No single central government, omnipotent as it is, can afford to keep its eyes on any particular local power out of myriads in a country this vast, unless that particular issue is somehow brought to its attention. The cascading control scheme enables vertical separation of functions and to a degree ameliorates but cannot cure the root problem or prevent collusion among different levels of governments. In fact, the Party Secretary-General and the Premier would never have heard of Sun Zhigang's name, much less take major policy action, had his tragedy failed to shock the conscience of the entire nation and aroused public indignation about the egregious misconduct of a local government. No wonder, then, that 'the central laws and policies can hardly get out of the Forbidden City' (政令不出中南海, *zhengling buchu zhongnanhai*), since 'for every national policy made above, there are thousands of local countermeasures from below' that effectively boycot its implementation (上有政策、下有对策, *shangyou zhengce, xiayou duice*), and the central government is helpless to prevent its own policy from being twisted out of shape by local implementing agencies.

Thus, if the central government prohibited the levying of taxes on peasants without approval of national laws or regulations, then what used to be a 'tax' could easily turn into a 'fee' outside the scope of central prohibitions, resulting in rampant 'arbitrary charges' (乱收费, *luan shoufei*). For example, Article 46 of the 1982 Constitution provides that a citizen has a right (and indeed, an obligation) to 'receive education', and the Education Law provides that compulsory education shall be freely provided; but it has been common practice for elementary and middle schools (particularly those with good reputations) to impose fees on certain classes of students, despite frequent prohibitions of such fees being issued by the Ministry of Education.[48] If the central government were to require review and approval for the taking of land above a certain acreage, the requirement could easily be sidestepped by dividing

---

[48] See Xie Yong, 'The Tuition Is Fiercer Than a Tiger', *China News Weekly* (26 July 2004).

the land into several pieces, each ostensibly under a project of a different name.[49] If the central government were to lay out a specific quota of local governments in proportion to the size of their jurisdictions, then the overall structure could be streamlined to satisfy the central plan, but a number of leading posts could be retained for relatives and friends in lucrative departments,[50] creating the perplexing contrast between a government structure too small to satisfy public need and the pervasive popular image of 'big government'.[51] If the national Labour Contract Law specifies that workers who have served for ten consecutive years cannot be fired at will, it can be easily be common practice for them to be fired on the last day of their ninth year of employment.[52] And so on.

Having witnessed good laws and negligible (and occasionally worse) effects, one cannot fail to appreciate both the omnipotence and futility of China's central authority. That the project of implementing national law has not been fundamentally improved since the time of Emperor Jing of Han's humanist criminal reform is an ample illustration of the fact that, if the people cannot protect themselves by holding their local governments accountable, then any attempt by the central government to protect them will be in vain.

V. PLURALISM WITHIN A UNITARY SYSTEM

Thus far we have seen the complexity of China's unitary framework. Centralisation has a long tradition in China, where it is characterised by an absence of constitutional limitations on the legislative competence of the national government. But the centralised tradition is qualified by

[49] For a notorious such case, see He Yuxin and Chen Fang, 'The Tieben Fiasco', *Finance* (20 May 2004) 77–86.

[50] Some small counties are staffed with many 'vice mayors' and dozens of 'assistant mayors'. See Wang Wenzhi and Xiao Bo, 'A Poor County in Shandong Is Equipped with 6 Vice Mayors and 15 Assistant Mayors', *Economic Reference News* (10 August 2007); and Chen Jianfen, 'A State Level Poor County Is Equipped with 11 Vice Mayors', *Wellbing (Xiaokang)* (18 August 2006).

[51] According to the field investigation of Professor Xiang Jiquan of the Rural Area Research Centre of Central China Normal University, the population of a small county in Hubei province increased by 63% from 1949 to 1990, yet the number of cadres multiplied 43 times during the same period. Unpublished papers filed with the author.

[52] Chen Xiaojing and Chen Lei, 'China will Pay for the Labour Contract Law', *Southern People Weekly* (21 November 2007).

several factors arising from local diversities, such as limitations in the efficacy of curbing 'legislation fighting' due to the lack of a feasible mechanism and in the central capacity to fully carrying out its imperatives against local resistance; the absence of a strict hierarchy of legal norms below the level of administrative regulation; and deliberate compromises made to accommodate local experiments that exceed the boundary marked by the current Constitution and laws.[53] The four Special Economic Zones (SEZs) (经济特区, *jingji tequ*) – Shenzhen and Zhuhai in Guangdong province; Xiamen and Shantou in Fujian province – are good examples of the latter category. They were established in 1982 as 'windows' for the reform and open-door experiment.[54] Although the SEZs are no longer so 'special' today, given the widespread delegation of legislative power to the local governments as the reform proceeds, they nevertheless illustrate how certain yokes of the unitary framework may be shaken off to allow trials of far-reaching institutional breakthroughs.

More significant, however, is the fact that China accommodates even greater disparity than ordinary institutional compromises within its unitary framework. Indeed, some of its special arrangements afford structural diversity and autonomy even greater than that in a federal state. A Hong Kong resident, for example, is obliged neither to obey most national laws nor to pay taxes to the central government; arguably, even the Constitution itself does not apply to this Special Administrative Region (SAR) (特别行政区, *tebie xingzheng qu*), except the provision authorising the NPC to enact its Basic Law (Article 31). Briefly examined below are the special arrangements made for the SARs and nationality autonomous regions, as well the unresolved issues of divided sovereignty across the Taiwan Strait.

A. The Regional Autonomy of 'Nationalities'

The northwest frontier of China has always been troubled by ethnic problems, to which the CCP leadership have attended seriously ever since the founding of the People's Republic. In fact, the CCP had

---

[53] See the 'benign violation paradox' discussed above ch 2, s IV.

[54] See C Carter, 'A Tale of Two Chinese SEZs: From Exogenous to Sustainable Endogenous Growth?' in C Carter and A Harding (eds), *Special Economic Zones in Asian Market Economies* (New York, Routledge, 2010) 54–61.

consistently advocated a version of ethnic federalism to facilitate the unification of Tibet, Mongolia and Xinjiang from as early as its Second Congress, held in the 1920s, until the Declaration of the People's Liberation Army in October 1947, which proclaimed the freedom of minorities to 'freely join the Federation of China'.[55] After it succeeded in expelling the Nationalists to Taiwan and establishing monopolistic one-party control over the mainland in 1949, however, federalism and the right of minorities to self-determination became taboo subjects and were forbidden in public discussion. But the ruling party did come up with a special arrangement for five peripheral regions with major clusters of minority populations by borrowing from the former Soviet model. In contrast to the 'melting pot' strategy practiced in the United States, where racial classifications are reviewed by the court with 'strict scrutiny' and racial segregation is deemed 'per se invalid',[56] the Soviet and Chinese policies positively distinguish ethnic minorities and separate their major clusters from other ethnicities – in the Chinese case, from the dominant Han ethnicity. Indeed, the minority ethnicities were not treated as ordinary ethnic groups (族群, *zuqun*) in one nation but as autonomous 'nationalities' (民族, *minzu*), implying special status in an otherwise unitary state.

The special institution of 'nationality regional autonomy' (民族区域自治, *minzu quyu zizhi*) was established in China in 1952, when the central government promulgated the Outline for Implementing Nationality Regional Autonomy, and was reinforced in both the 1982 Constitution and the Law on Nationality Regional Autonomy, which was enacted in 1984. The Preamble of the Constitution devotes a paragraph specifically to nationalities, defining China as 'a unitary multi-national state created jointly by the people of all its nationalities', whose 'common prosperity' is to be promoted by the state:

> All nationalities in the People's Republic of China are equal. The state protects the lawful rights and interests of the minority nationalities and upholds and develops a relationship of equality, unity and mutual assistance among all of China's nationalities. Discrimination against and oppression of any

[55] 'Declaration of the Second National Congress of the Chinese Communist Party' in Ministry of United Front, the Central Committee of the CCP, *Documentary Compilation on the Ethnic Problem: July 1921–September 1949* (Beijing, Central Committee of Chinese Communist Party School Press, 1991) 18.

[56] See *Brown v Board of Education* (1954) 347 US 483.

nationality are prohibited; any act which undermines the unity of the nation-alities or instigates division is prohibited (Constitution, Article 4).

The regional autonomy principle applies not only to the five nationality autonomous regions (NARs) at the provincial level but more generally to 'areas where people of minority nationalities live in concentrated communities' in ordinary jurisdictions (Article 4). Chapter 3 of the Constitution has a section that specifically deals with the 'organs of self-government of nationality autonomous areas', which provides for LPCs and LPGs in autonomous regions, autonomous prefectures and autono-mous counties (Art. 112). China has established so far a total of over 140 autonomous areas, which include five autonomous regions, 31 autonomous prefectures and 104 autonomous counties. Within these areas are 44 different ethnic minorities (among a total of 56 in China as a whole), 85 per cent of the total minority population and 60 per cent of PRC territory.

Although these nationality autonomous areas are supposed to exer-cise 'the power of regional autonomy' (Article 4), not much autonomy is allowed in practice, primarily in order to maintain national unity in the face of separatist efforts. Indeed, the institutional structure of regional autonomy, together with its practical defects, is remarkably similar to those of ordinary government in China; if anything, an autonomous area is more likely to experience tighter control and supervision from the central government to ensure ethnic peace and loyalty.

However, there *are* a few privileges attached to ethnic minorities. First, all minority nationalities have the cultural freedom 'to use and develop their own spoken and written languages and to preserve or reform their own folkways and customs' (Constitution, Article 4), implying a government obligation to provide services in order to help ethnic minorities to read official documents and to represent themselves in legal proceedings in their own languages. Second, certain leading posts are reserved for the minority group that constitutes the dominant population in an autonomous area, primarily the head of the govern-ment and the chair or vice-chair of the LPCSC (Constitution, Articles 113 and 114).

Third, similar to an SEZ, an autonomous area is authorised to imple-ment its own policies and legislation and to manage local finance and development, among other things (Constitution, Article 117). Although legislation in an autonomous area is generally obliged to be enacted within the framework of the Constitution, national laws and national administrative regulations, certain deviations are permitted as 'flexible provisions of a law or administrative regulation, so long as they do not contravene the basic principles thereof' (LL Article 66.2). The LPCs of autonomous areas are empowered to enact autonomous regulations 'in the light of the political, economic and cultural characteristics of the nationalities in the areas concerned' (Constitution, Article 116), subject to approval by the standing committees of superior People's Congresses. Before taking effect, autonomous regulations of autonomous prefectures and counties must be submitted to the relevant provincial LPCSCs for approval and reported to the NPCSC for record, while those of autonomous regions shall be submitted to the NPCSC for approval (Article 116), subject to the power of the NPC to withdraw any approved regulations in contravention of the Constitution or Article 66.2 of the LL. Furthermore, exceptions are made in implementing generally applicable laws to accommodate ethnic customs. Certain flirtatious conduct between young men and women, for example, would otherwise constitute misdemeanour under national Criminal Law, but it is exempt if it is committed by members of national minorities during ethnic holidays as part of their customs.

B. 'One Country, Two Systems': Special Administrative Regions (SARs)

While the regional autonomy of ethnic minorities is severely limited, genuine autonomy has been conferred on Hong Kong and Macao, former ceded colonies whose sovereignty reverted to China in 1997 and 1999 respectively, under Deng Xiaoping's guiding principle of 'one country, two systems' (一国两制, *yiguo liangzhi*). Unlike the nationality autonomous areas, where deviations from the Constitution and national laws are merely exceptions, the SARs are governed by their own 'mini-constitutions', the two highly similar Basic Laws ('HKBL' for Hong Kong), as the ground for 'the social and economic systems, the system for safeguarding the fundamental rights and freedoms of its residents, the executive, legislative and judicial systems, and the relevant policies' (HKBL, Article 11). Article 2 of both Basic Laws stipulates that the NPC 'authorises' the SAR to exercise 'a high degree of autonomy and enjoy executive, legislative and independent judicial power, including

that of final adjudication'.[57] All laws previously enforced in the SARs
have been maintained except those inconsistent with the Basic Law;
laws enacted by the SAR legislatures must be reported to the NPCSC,
but only for record-keeping purposes and without affecting their legal
force (HKBL, Article 17). Most significantly, national laws simply do
not apply to the SARs except those few explicitly listed in Annex III of
the Basic Laws, such as provisions in the National Flag Law and the Law
on Nationality Regional Autonomy. In many ways the legal autonomy
enjoyed by the SARs far exceeds that of a state or province in federal
jurisdictions, where federal powers granted by a constitution apply uniformly and supersede any local laws in conflict.[58]

Yet the SARs are far from 'independent kingdoms' (独立王国, *duli
wangguo*) that stand alone but rather are subject to potentially far-reaching political control by the PRC central government in a number of
ways. First, the principal officials of the SAR administrations, including
the Chief Executive (CE) as the most powerful official, are 'appointed'
by the State Council, even though the CE himself is elected according
to the Basic Law (Annex I) and other principal officials are appointed
upon his nomination (HKBL, Articles 15 and 47.5). The final appointment procedure may be nominal, but it obviously provides the central
government a powerful instrument for influencing the CE elections
since the result of the election would not be formally effective without
the central approval. Not surprisingly, traces of central guidance have
been quite evident in the running of two CE elections so far in each
SAR. In a nominal sense, the SARs are even less politically autonomous
than ordinary local governments on the mainland, since the chief executives there are supposed to be elected by and directly accountable to the
LPC (Constitution, Article 101) rather than appointed by any superior
government.

Second and more fundamentally, although the members of a SAR's
Legislative Council (Legco) are elected according to the Basic Law
(Annex II), the method of the Legco elections, like the method of the
CE elections, is decided as a part of the Basic Law by the NPC rather
than by a majority of the SAR residents themselves or legislatures
accountable to them. So far only half of the Legco members are elected

---

[57] Similarly, Article 12 of both Basic Laws provides that the SAR shall be 'a local
administrative region of the People's Republic of China, which shall enjoy a high
degree of autonomy and come directly under the Central People's Government.'
[58] See the 'Supremacy Clause' in Art 6 of the US Constitution.

directly by SAR residents; the other half are elected by four 'functional groups' that are composed of disproportionate constituencies that nevertheless enjoy an equivalent amount of voting power. This scheme is clearly at odds with the basic principle of 'one person, one vote'[59] and has been relentlessly criticised by opposition groups in Hong Kong.

In fact, although both Basic Laws emphatically guarantee a 'high degree of autonomy', such autonomy is fatally deficient in making and revising the Basic Laws themselves; after all, the 'Basic Law' is nothing but a national law enacted by the NPC, over which the SAR residents have no control except through a handful of deputies assigned to the SAR, who seem to play little role in NPC law-making. The amendment process is extremely difficult, given that amendment bills originating within an SAR must be agreed upon by the CE, the two thirds of the SAR deputies to the NPC and two thirds of the Legco members – which is more than enough to suffocate any spontaneous initiatives from the majority of SAR residents, not to mention that the amendments are to be ultimately passed by the NPC, which can easily decline to do so for such vague reason as inconsistency with 'the established basic policies' toward the SAR (HKBL, Article 159). If the majority will of the SAR residents is repeatedly frustrated by an unequal voting system and an inability to change such systems by themselves, then there is a serious risk that the SARs will be downgraded into 'local administrative regions' like ordinary mainland governments. Fortunately, under mounting pressure from Hong Kong residents, the central government has announced a timetable for democratic reform and has promised to implement direct elections for the CEs and the full Legcos by 2017–18.[60] The recent compromise reached by the Hong Kong administration and opposition groups on a plan for political reform seems to be a good sign,[61] indicating that the central government is more or less willing to allow Hong Kong residents to take SAR political reform into their own hands.

[59] For Chief Justice Warren's exposition of this principle in a landmark redistricting case, see *Reynolds v Sims* (1964) 377 US 533.

[60] 'Decision of the Standing Committee of the National People's Congress Regarding the Ways by which the Chief Executive and the Legco are Elected and Regarding the Problem of General Elections', issued by the 31st Conference of the Standing Committee of the 10th National Congress (29 December 2007).

[61] 'Elections in Hong Kong: Functionally Democratic', *The Economist* (24 June 2010).

Finally, SAR judiciary is accorded extraordinary autonomy, in particular the power of 'final adjudication' and a judicial selection mechanism free from central control (HKBL, Articles 88–93). But even here, encroachments by the national government are made possible by provisions within the Basic Laws. Fundamentally, the ultimate power to interpret the Basic Laws is, as with every other piece of national legislation enacted by the NPC, vested in the NPCSC rather than in the SAR courts of final appeal (HKBL, Article 158). The NPCSC does 'authorise' SAR courts in adjudication 'to interpret on their own' the provisions in the Basic Law that are 'within the limits of the autonomy of the Region' as well as other provisions, but if interpretation touches on affairs regulated by the central government or 'concerning the relationship between the Central Authorities and the Region, and if such interpretation will affect the judgments on the cases', the Court of Final Appeal (CFA) is obliged to seek from the NPCSC an interpretation of the relevant provisions and follow such interpretation in deciding those cases (HKBL, Article 159). In fact, if the NPCSC considers any law enacted by the SAR legislature inconsistent with the Basic Law regarding affairs 'within the responsibility of the Central Authorities or regarding the relationship between the Central Authorities and the Region', it may invalidate the law after consulting the Committee for the Basic Law of the SAR, which is composed of legal experts from both the SAR and the mainland (HKBL, Article 17).

Although direct invalidation of SAR laws by the national government has not occurred so far, the ultimate interpretive power of the NPCSC over the SAR Basic Laws has led to speculation that SAR judicial independence might be fatally undermined. Indeed, conflicts have occurred between Hong Kong and the mainland over interpretations of the Basic Law, leading one to question more generally the boundary of the NPCSC's interpretive power and the procedure for adequately resolving legal disputes between the central government and the SARs. Detailed discussion of the controversial Ng Ka Ling decision (1999) and the ensuing NPCSC intervention is beyond the scope of this book and can be found in studies of the SAR Basic Laws;[62] it suffices to say here that they illustrate how easily considerations for the principle of 'one country' can run into conflict with considerations of 'two systems'.

---

[62] *Ng Ka Ling and Ors v Director of Immigration* (1999) 1 HKC 291. See T Schneider, 'David v Goliath? The Hong Kong Courts and China's National People's Congress Standing Committee' (2002) 20 *Berkeley Journal of International Law* 575.

C. Divided Sovereignty across the Taiwan Strait

The constitutional experiments entailing 'one country, two systems' were designed and carried out not for the SARs alone but with an even more ambitious prospect of using them as models for the future reunification with Taiwan, the island to which the Nationalists retreated in 1949. While the Nationalists are persistent in claiming sovereignty over the entire mainland under the 1946 Constitution of the Republic of China (ROC), the CCP has never given up on the reunification of Taiwan under the Constitution of the People's Republic, thereby to cleanse the last vestige of 'imperial colonialism' from which China has suffered since 1840.

Taiwan was permanently ceded to Japan by the Treaty of Shimonoseki in 1895, against which patriotic reformists like Kang Youwei vehemently protested.[63] After Japan's defeat in World War II, however, sovereignty over Taiwan reverted to China, despite loopholes in the Cairo Declaration and the Potsdam Declaration that have since served as jurisprudential ground for 'Taiwan Independence',[64] a populist movement that emerged during the political democratisation of Taiwan during the 1970s and 1980s among the island's native peoples (as opposed to the Nationalist mainlanders). The conflicting partisan claims of sovereignty across the Strait, coupled with independence appeals arising from within the island and geopolitical interests of the United States and Japan, have taken Taiwan outside the realm of a conventional treatment of constitutional law, but sheer political complexity does not reduce its significance for China's constitutionalism.

After 1949, Taiwan and the mainland experienced parallel developments of single-party rule. While the Communists under Mao Zedong initiated a series of political movements such as repression of 'counter-revolutionaries' and 'anti-rightists', the Great Leap Forward and the Cultural Revolution, the Nationalists under Chiang Kai-shek imposed the Temporary Regulation During Insurgency Mobilisation immediately after arrival in Taiwan, under which the rights to establish parties and to independent media were suspended for a record-breaking 38 years,

---

[63]   See above ch 1.

[64]   For details, see Peng Ming-min and Huang Shao-tang, *The Status of Taiwan in International Law* (Taipei, Yushan Press, 1995) 126–30; Lee Teng-hui, 'Understanding Taiwan' (1999) 78 *Foreign Affairs* 6.

before the bans on press and political association were lifted by Chiang's heir in 1987. Since then, Taiwan experienced the 'third wave' of democracy, which quickly dissolved the single-party monopoly and developed multi-party politics, culminating in the first presidential election in 1996 and the first regime turnover in 2000, when an 'opposition party', the Democratic Progressive Party (民进党, *minjin dang*, hereinafter 'DPP'), won the presidential election for the first time in the history of China. The DPP administration positively promoted the independence cause and aggravated the relationship with the PRC during its eight-year term, until the Nationalists regained power in the 2008 presidential election. Although the Nationalists and the Communists continue to disagree as to who is the legitimate ruler of China, they do agree on the general prospect for a reunited China, and tension across the Taiwan Strait subsequently seems to have significantly decreased under the Nationalist administration.

Taiwan and the mainland are governed today not only by two different parties and Constitutions but also under two different regimes that operate on fundamentally different logics. While Taiwan successfully put an end to 'tutelage politics'[65] and transitioned into constitutional politics at long last in 1987, mainland China is still deadlocked in its single-party rule and has yet to learn such basic rules of the game as freedom of electoral competition in democratic politics, if only to improve its own image among the Taiwan electorate, who will ultimately decide on the issue of reunion with the mainland. A sovereignty divided between regimes of different natures disrupts peace and stability across the Strait, and further challenges the wisdom, courage and patience of decision-makers on both sides. But it does also present opportunities for creative peace-making and institution-building through mutual adjustments. For an indefinite time to come, Taiwan will serve as a lighthouse, as it were, for the hope of democratic reform in China. And the mainland must live up to that hope in order to fulfil the reunification promise it has been holding so dear.

Montesquieu was accurate when he predicted that a giant empire like China could be maintained only by despotism.[66] As the Sun Zhigang tragedy plainly illustrates, such a despotic empire is far from a felicitous

---

[65] See above ch 1, ss III and IV.
[66] Montesquieu, *The Spirit of the Laws*, AM Cohler, BC Miller and HS Stone (trans and eds) (Cambridge, Cambridge University Press, 1988) Part I, Book 8, ch 16.

paradise. A centralised regime organised from the top to the bottom necessarily relieves government at every level of the obligation to be accountable to the people. In China, the central government itself has been the culprit for initiating such monstrous calamities as the Great Leap Forward and the Cultural Revolution, and for enacting such pernicious national policies as the household registration system, which discriminates against peasants, and the Custody and Repatriation Measures, which caused Sun's death.[67] Even if the central government desires to protect the people from exploitation by their local officials, it is inherently limited in its capacity to obtain the necessary information for enacting wise policies or even merely to discover official misconduct,[68] not to mention its capacity to implement such policies with consistency and efficiency. On its surface the empire may be at peace, even enjoying a degree of 'harmony'; but how meaningful is such order to its potential victims like Sun Zhigang, who is representative of the vast majority of ordinary Chinese people? Without real democracy, which obliges government to 'represent the most fundamental interest of the overwhelming majority of the people',[69] the battle for the people has been lost even before it begins.

FURTHER READING

Committee on International Human Rights, 'One Country, Two Legal Systems? The Rule of Law, Democracy, and the Protection of Fundamental Rights in Post-Handover Hong Kong' (2000) 55 *The Record of the Association of the Bar of the City of New York* 325.

Jia Hao and Lin Zhimin (eds), *Changing Central–Local Relations in China: Reform and State Capacity* (Boulder, CO, Westview, 1993).

Li Yahong, 'The Law-Making Law: A Solution to the Problems in the Chinese Legislative System?' (2000) 30 *Hong Kong Law Journal* 120.

Lieberthal, K, *Governing China: From Revolution through Reform*, 2nd edn (New York, WW Norton & Co, 2003) ch 6.

Landry, PF, *Decentralised Authoritarianism in China: The Communist Party's Control of Local Elites in the Post-Mao Era* (Cambridge, Cambridge University Press, 2008).

[67] See below ch 7.

[68] For discussion of how even a limited degree of free press may help to alleviate these problems, see below ch 8.

[69] This is one of the 'three represents', a theory proposed by Jiang Zemin that was inserted in the Preamble of the Constitution via the 2004 amendments.

Lubman, S, 'Looking for Law in China' (2006) 20 *Columbia Journal of Asian Law* 1.

Potter, PB, 'Governance of China's Periphery: Balancing Local Autonomy and National Unity' (2005) 19 *Columbia Journal of Asian Law* 293.

Schneider, T, 'David v Goliath? The Hong Kong Courts and China's National People's Congress Standing Committee' (2002) 20 *Berkeley Journal of International Law* 575.

4

Democracy with Chinese Characteristics? The Role of the People's Congresses

———◆◆◆———

INTRODUCTION: SUPREMACY ON A RUBBER STAMP? – THE NATIONAL PEOPLE'S CONGRESS (NPC) – The Basic Structure of the NPC – Constitutional Powers of the NPC – Legislative Procedure – THE NPC STANDING COMMITTEE (NPCSC) – A Second Chamber? – Constitutional Functions of the NPCSC – Structure and Legislative Procedure – LOCAL PEOPLE'S CONGRESSES (LPCs) – The Structure and Functions of LPCs – The Structure and Functions of LPCSCs – HOW TO MAKE DEMOCRACY WORK – From Supremacy to Rubber Stamp – Toward a Professional Legislature?

I. INTRODUCTION: SUPREMACY BY RUBBER STAMP?

T̲O FULFIL THE democratic promise that is implied by the very title of its state, the People's Republic laid the groundwork for a representative framework in its constitution. Perhaps the most unique and consistent feature of China's constitutions since 1949, the National and Local People's Congresses (NPC and LPC, respectively) were institutionally designed to have supreme authority so that the 'people' could rule the 'republic' that belongs to them. The design was first contemplated in the 1949 Common Program and then fleshed out and maintained in all the later constitutions. Article 2 of the current 1982 Constitution provides:

> All power in the People's Republic of China belongs to the people. The National People's Congress and the Local People's Congresses at various levels are the organs through which the people exercise state power. The people

administer state affairs and manage economic, cultural and social affairs through various channels and in various ways in accordance with the law.

A primary channel through which the people administer state affairs is the regular elections carried out at various levels. Basically, the people elect the People's Congresses at various levels, which in turn elect and oversee other branches of the governments at the same levels. Article 3 of the 1982 Constitution states:

> The National People's Congress and the Local People's Congresses at various levels are constituted through democratic elections. They are responsible to the people and subject to their supervision. All administrative, judicial and procuratorial organs of the state are created by the People's Congresses, to which they are responsible and by which they are supervised.

The constitutionally grounded power structure is simple enough. Had the national and local governments followed the rules laid down in the Constitution, China would have been the world's largest democracy, with a governance system quite akin to the Westminster model. Unfortunately, practice once again followd 'latent' rules rather than the constitutional text.[1] Although the People's Congresses are given supreme status in the Constitution, they have long been dubbed 'rubber stamps', since their ordinary roles have largely been reduced to endorsing official acts decided by the Chinese Communist Party (CCP), the real holder of supreme power in China. The Party's 'leadership' is in fact explicitly recognised by the Preamble of the 1982 Constitution. In essence, the power structure of the Party, the moving force behind the daily flow of things in the real world, completely subverts the power structure defined in the Constitution, which as far as possible has been interpreted to conform to the dictates of the Party and, when that is not possible, is simply ignored.

For example, it is commonly known that the Chairman of the NPC Standing Committee (NPCSC), the highest position among all deputies, is the second position in the country, next to the Secretary-General of the CCP, who is commonly regarded as the supreme figure in China, despite the fact that the government position he usually holds – the Presidency of the State – renders him but a symbolic figure without substantive constitutional power.[2] In fact, although the NPCSC

---

[1]   See the discussion of 'latent rules' above ch 3, s IV.
[2]   See further below ch 5.

Chairman is officially higher than the Premier (the third in rank), who is supposed to be elected and overseen by the NPC, the Premier is much more powerful in substantive terms – and more popular among the people. The deputies, usually appointed by the Party rather than genuinely elected by the people,[3] are supposed to exercise their constitutional powers over government officials, but in reality they are made docile by Party discipline; and this is no surprise, since well over 70 per cent of the deputies are Party cadres, whose ranks are lower than those holding key posts in the government. No wonder that the People's Congresses and the deputies disappear almost completely from the national scene. No one even expects them to step out and express their voices on such important occasions as the Sun Zhigang event, and they have been duly absent.

This is not to say, however, that the institution of NPC is completely useless. The 'two meetings' (两会, *lianghui*) held in March every year – the annual sessions of the NPC and the National Political Consultative Committee – are still national events, attracting much media exposure, through which policy expectations are expressed by many young people through dialogue with top officials (who are almost without exception NPC deputies). Despite the overall weak position of the People's Congresses and the limited contours within which they may exercise their powers without running into conflict with the Party's prerogatives, there *were* genuine efforts at institution-building at the beginning of the reform period, with the intention of making the NPC a fully functioning legislature. From the time of the first NPCSC Chairman, Peng Zhen, who personally suffered from lawless persecution during the Cultural Revolution, the status of the People's Congresses gradually improved; even the former Premier Li Peng, a hard-line conservative who made himself infamous worldwide by announcing martial law during the Tiananmen Protests in 1989, made positive contributions to strengthen the People's Congresses when he became NPCSC Chairman in 1993. It can be said that the People's Congresses are still 'rubber stamps', but occasionally they do surprise those who take such an image for granted.

Although most deputies are passive, there are a few who fight hard to win elections and dutifully exercise their functions once elected: Yao Lifa (姚立法) from Qianjiang city (Hubei province) and Zeng Jianyu

---

[3] See further below ch 8.

(曾建余) from Luzhou city (Sichuan province) are but two examples.[4] Institutional progress slowed down, or even reversed, during the recent term of Wu Bangguo's leadership of the NPCSC, when independent candidates were targeted for retribution; and deputies' independent activities have been discouraged by the latest revision of the Law on Deputies. However, such retrogression may well be attributed to idiosyncratic leadership rather than to a systemic, irreversible trend. At least one cannot exclude altogether the possibility that, with a new NPCSC Chairman who is more conscious of institution-building and more friendly to deputies' individual initiatives, the People's Congresses will regain vigour and play at least some role in the nation's political life.

This chapter deals with China's legislatures, ie, the National and Local People's Congresses, which are officially regarded as the cornerstone of the current Constitution and the primary symbol of China's democracy. I will begin with a brief discussion on the nature and evolution of People's Congresses in China and then introduce the organisational structure, constitutional powers and legislative procedures of the NPC as the supreme legislator; the NPCSC as the regular national legislator; and the LPCs as local legislators. The chapter will end with both a discussion of the defects in the current legislative system, particularly the lack of representation and the lack of professionalism among the congressional deputies, and with proposals for possible reform measures to make democracy work better for China.

II. THE NATIONAL PEOPLE'S CONGRESS (NPC)

Although the People's Congresses as a whole exercise the constituent power of China, Article 57 of the Constitution explicitly provides that the NPC is the 'highest organ of state power', a status implied in the unitary constitutional structure, where the highest power is singularly lodged in the central (national) government and its laws and regulations enjoy unlimited supremacy.[5] The national deputies are supposed to be elected, however, by deputies of the provincial People's Congresses (Constitution, Article 59), who are in turn elected by deputes at the city or county levels, all for five-year terms (Constitution, Article 60). The

---

[4] See Zhu Ling, *I Object: A Legend of Congressional Deputy's Political Participation* (Haikou, Hainan Press, 2006).

[5] For further discussion, see above ch 3.

elections are held every five years, and all deputies may run for consecutive terms.

A. The Basic Structure of the NPC

Like all the People's Congresses, the NPC convenes once a year. Although the Constitution does not fix the dates and times of legislative sessions, the Rules of Procedure for the NPC provides that the NPC shall convene in the first quarter of every calendar year (Article 2). Since it has now become an established convention that the 'two meetings' take place in early March, an ordinary session lasts no more than three weeks. In practice the NPC meets for about 10 days a year. Although the NPC can hold interim sessions 'at any time the Standing Committee deems it necessary or when more than one fifth of the deputies . . . so propose' (Constitution, Article 61), no such session has ever taken place.[6]

The NPC is a large body, with nearly 3000 deputies. The number is determined by the NPCSC 'in accordance with existing conditions' (Constitution, Article 25), including the number of voters in provinces, municipalities and autonomous regions. But the allocation fell far short of meeting the 'one person, one vote' criterion until March 2010, when the NPC repealed the 'quarter vote clause' in Article 16 of the Election Law on the NPC and LPC (hereinafter 'Election Law').[7] That provision dictated that 'the number of people represented by each rural deputy is four times the number of people represented by each urban deputy', effectively depreciating the value of rural votes to a quarter of that of urban votes. Even though peasants are now in principle equally represented as urban residents, military deputies have remained a glaring exception to the principle of equal representation, taking up as many as 300 seats, roughly 10 per cent of the NPC, while the size of the army is slightly over 0.2 per cent of the entire population. The allocation scheme promotes the participation of women and national minorities to meet

[6] Although there was strong appeal for the NPC to hold an interim session before 4 June 1989, the interim procedure was never initiated. See, eg, Zhang Liang, *June Fourth: The True Story* (Hong Kong, Mingjing Press, 2001) 686–87.
[7] Decision of the National People's Congress on Amending the Election Law of National People's Congress and Local People's Congresses at Various Levels, 14 March 2010.

both the constitutional mandate that 'all the minority ethnic groups are entitled to appropriate representation' (Constitution, Article 59) and the legal requirements, according to which they should be guaranteed 'appropriate numbers' in the NPC and LPC (Election Law, Article 6). The Election Law devotes an entire chapter to minority deputies in order to guarantee a minority presence in the LPCs (Constitution, Articles 18–21).

The NPC plenary session each year is conducted by a cryptically defined group called the Presidium (主席团, *zhuxituan*), which is elected by the NPC in its preparatory meeting, which is in turn chaired by the Standing Committee of the last term before the new session begins (Rules of Procedure for the NPC, Article 8). The Presidium for the First Session of the 10th NPC, formed in 2003, had a total of 181 members, consisting of the major leaders of the ruling Party and the state (including all nine members of the Politburo Standing Committee and the former General Secretary, Jiang Zemin), members of the Central Military Commission (CMC), the chairs of eight satellite 'democratic parties' and the persons in charge of the central state organs, the officially recognised 'people's organisations'[8] and the provincial and People's Liberation Army (PLA) (人民解放军, *renmin jiefangjun*) delegations. With such a composition, the Presidium is commonly viewed as a platform through which the CCP controls the NPC.

The NPC is divided into several special committees. Besides the Standing Committee, which has independent law-making powers, there are nine special standing committees: the Nationalities Committee; the Law Committee; the Finance and Economic Committee; the Education, Science, Culture and Public Health Committee; the Foreign Affairs Committee; the Overseas Chinese Committee; the Judicial Committee of Internal Affairs; the Environmental and Resource Protection Committee; and the Agricultural and Rural Committee.[9] Each committee is composed of deputies who more or less specialise in the particular policy area described by the committee names, and they are responsible for drafting legislation in that area. When the NPC is not in session, all special committees are subject to the leadership of the NPCSC. In fact, each committee is usually headed by a Vice-Chairman of the NPCSC,

---

[8] See below ch 8.

[9] The first six special committees were expressly established by Art 70 of the Constitution.

and most NPCSC members are also special committee members and constitute the majority in the special committees. Like the NPCSC, the special committees convene monthly or bi-monthly, while their directors usually convene once every two weeks. Unlike the NPCSC, however, the special committees lack independent law-making power, their roles being limited to the deliberation and proposition of draft bills in their respective spheres.

B. Constitutional Powers of the NPC

The powers of the NPC are defined in Article 62 of the Constitution and can be categorised into four major types. The first is legislative, including the power to amend and to 'supervise the enforcement of' the Constitution (Article 62, clauses 1 and 2) and the power to enact and amend 'basic laws governing criminal offences, civil affairs, the state organs and other matters' (clause 3). At present, the basic laws governing the state organisations include various organic laws relating to the NPC, the State Council, the LPCs and local governments, the courts and the procuratorates, as well as the Election Law on the NPC and LPCs, the Law on Regional National Autonomy and the Basic Laws for the two Special Administrative Districts (SAR), Hong Kong and Macao. Constitutional amendments can be proposed only by the NPCSC or by more than one fifth of the NPC deputies, and are adopted by the votes of more than two thirds of all the NPC deputies (Constitution, Article 63).

The second type of power involves appointment and removal, including the power to elect the President and Vice-President of the state (Constitution, Article 62, clause 4) and the power to choose the Premier 'upon nomination by the President' (clause 5). The NPC further decides, 'upon nomination by the Premier', the Vice-Premiers, State Councillors, Ministers, the Auditor-General and the Secretary-General of the State Council (clause 5); and elects the Chairman of the Central Military Commission (CMC) and decides, 'upon nomination by the Chairman', all other members of the CMC (clause 6). As a unique 'Chinese characteristic', the NPC not only elects the leading personnel in the government but also appoints the key officials of the judicial branch (clauses 7 and 8), namely the President of the Supreme People's Court (SPC) and the Procurator-General of the Supreme People's Procuratorate (SPP). The NPC, upon majority voting, has the power to remove any of the above

(Constitution, Article 63). One tenth of the NPC deputies may present a motion to remove any of the above persons by presenting a reasoned bill to the Presidium (Article 61). The Presidium will distribute the bill among the deputes, who will discuss the bill within their provincial delegations before it is voted upon by the whole Congress; or the latter may decide to organise a special investigation committee and pass a vote on the bill based on the investigation report later provided by that committee.

The third type of power enjoyed by the NPC is supervisory: the power to inquire into the work of other branches of the central government. Article 16 of the Organic Law of the NPC provides that during an NPC session, a provincial delegation or a group of 30 or more deputies may make a written proposal for addressing inquiries to the State Council and its ministries or commissions, the SPC and the SPP. The proposal shall clearly state the person, the theme and the content to be inquired into, and if the Presidium so decides, it is to be answered by the relevant state agent. If half or more of the deputies who made the inquiries are not satisfied with the reply, they may demand another reply from the agency in question if the Presidium so decides. The NPCSC, the State Council, the SPC and the SPP submit separate annual work reports (工作报告, *gongzuo baogao*) to the general session of the NPC (Constitution, Article 34), though the legal effect of a report that fails to receive approval is unclear.

The fourth type of NPC power is the power to make decisions regarding major national political issues, including the power to examine and approve the State Council's plan for national economic and social development as well as the report on its implementation by governments at various levels; to examine and approve the national budget proposed by the State Council and the report on its implementation; to approve the establishment of provinces, autonomous regions, municipalities and SARs; and to decide on questions of war and peace (Constitution, Article 62, clauses 9–14). For example, the construction of the controversial Three Gorges Dam was discussed and approved by the NPC in 1992, when a record number of the deputies (nearly one third of the total) objected or abstained from voting.[10] Had the NPC been conducting its

---

[10] Resolution regarding the Construction of the Three-Gorges Project on the Yangtze River, passed at the Fifth Conference of the Seventh National People's Congress, 3 April 1992. It was pointed out that the main proponent of the project, Li Peng, was the premier at the time and used the NPC approval process to boost its popularity and to share responsibility for possible future failures.

business in this manner from the start, it would have long rid itself of the 'rubber stamp' title. Unfortunately, its action on the Three Gorges Project has been a lonely exception rather than the rule, and it remains silent and passive with regard to most major national issues. The scale of the 'South-to-North Water Diversion' (南水北调, *nanshui beidiao*) project is many times greater than the Three Gorges Project, yet it was given the green light without even raising an issue in the NPC session.

As commonly is the case in China, the enumeration of powers in Article 62 of the Constitution merely exemplifies the types of the power that the NPC usually exercises rather than confining them to the enumerated powers; otherwise, the 1982 Constitution would have been a federalist constitution rather than a unitary one characterised by the unlimited scope of national legislative power. This is attested by the catch-all clause of Article 62, which provides that the NPC may 'exercise such other functions and powers as the highest organ of state power should exercise' (clause 15). In principle, the NPC as the supreme state power may legislate in any substantive area it deems necessary.

C. Legislative Procedure

Legislation is a lengthy process in the NPC, given its extraordinary size, the paucity of sessions and the procedural complexity involved. The enormous number of bills received every year is divided into three categories. The first of these are urgent bills that require immediate action, which means that they shall be deliberated and possibly enacted in the current legislative term. The second are important bills that need to be enacted in the public interest but may require further investigation into potential problems and into the possible solutions, and they will thus be placed on the legislative agenda for the next legislative term. And third, there are other bills that require further study on their desirability and feasibility. Chapter 2 of the Law on Legislation describes the legislative procedure of the NPC in some detail.

First, many state actors are authorised to initiate the legislative process by proposing bills to the NPC. These include the State Council, the CMC, the SPC, the SPP and all special committees of the NPC; and their bills are placed on the agenda of the current legislative session if the Presidium so decides (Article 12). Since such a bill has usually obtained substantial support among key officials, it stands a good chance of being placed on the current agenda. Although an individual deputy cannot propose a bill in his own capacity, a provincial delegation or 'a group of not less than 30 delegates' may jointly propose a bill to the NPC, and it is up to the Presidium to decide whether to place such bills on the current agenda or to refer them to a special committee for further deliberation (Article 13), during which most proposed bills die out.

It is to be pointed out that although deputies vote independently on bills and decisions, most deliberations and activities are carried out within each provincial delegation at the annual NPC session. In fact, provincial (and PLA) delegations sit in blocs in the NPC plenary session. Only the deputies within a delegation of the same province (or a municipality or national autonomous region) may jointly propose a bill since, as a matter of policy, deputies are prohibited from engaging in cross-delegation activities. Such a prohibition undermines joint activities among deputies across the provincial line and facilitates the control of the Party over the deputies.

Second, once a bill is put on the agenda of a current NPC session, the plenary session shall hear the statements of the bill sponsor and forward the bill to the provincial delegations for further deliberation (Article 15), based on which the NPC Legislative Committee will conduct a general deliberation on the bill and submit to the Presidium a deliberation report containing different opinions and an amended draft law (Article 18). If necessary, the Executive Chairman of the Presidium may convene a meeting of delegation leaders to hear the deliberation opinions of all delegations on key issues of the bill (Article 19), on the basis of which the draft law shall be further amended by the Legislative Committee and be submitted to the Presidium for adoption by the plenary NPC session (Article 22).

Finally, a law passed by simple majority voting in the NPC shall be signed by the President of the State and promulgated by presidential order (Article 23). This last requirement is purely of procedural significance, as the President has no discretion in signing once the law has been enacted by an NPC majority.

III. THE NPC STANDING COMMITTEE (NPCSC)

If the NPC is made somewhat unique by its constitutional status, its size, the paucity of its sessions and its role in China's national politics, the Standing Committee of the NPC is all the more unique because it may well be the only parliamentary committee in the world that possesses independent law-making power.[11] Article 58 of the 1982 Constitution makes it clear that the NPC 'and its Standing Committee exercise the legislative power of the state'. In other words, a bill that acquires a majority of votes among NPCSC members becomes an effective law, as if it had been passed by the plenary session of the NPC. This is extraordinary given the fact that the NPCSC is a much smaller body than the full Congress: it now has just over 160 members, barely more than five per cent of the NPC deputies. Its legislative proficiency can also be gleaned from Article 41 of the Constitution, which prohibits any Standing Committee member from 'holding office in an administrative, judicial or procuratorial organ of the state', while ordinary NPC deputies are not prohibited from taking any of the above offices.

The NPCSC is small precisely in order to solve the problem that the NPC is too large, a problem that implicates issues of legislative efficacy, democratic representativeness and local autonomy. A parliament of almost 3000 deputies is unmanageable and inoperative in any country, but it may well be required in China, which has a population of 1.4 billion, in order to gain sufficient representation of its electorate. Nowadays each NPC deputy represents nearly 500,000 members of the population, which is on par with the representation of American voters by members of the US Congress. Democracy for a large population requires a large representative institution, the very size of which then defeats legislative efficiency and active participation on the part of individual deputies. In other words, the 'rubber stamp' status of the NPC is in a sense predestined by its constitutional design. The simple trade-off between representativeness and efficiency may produce a workable solution for a moderate size democracy[12] but may not for such a large country as China. The NPCSC *is* small and efficient, but its design defeats the democratic purpose that a deliberative body is established to serve. With each member roughly representing a population of 10 million – almost the entire population of a medium-size state – and

---

[11] The only other exception may be Vietnam, where the National Assembly may authorise its Standing Committee to issue 'decree laws' (1992 Constitution, Art 91.4). See M Sidel, *The Constitution of Vietnam: A Contextual Analysis* (London, Hart Publishing, 2009) 96–97.

[12] JM Buchanan and G Tullock, *The Calculus of Consent: Logical Foundation of Constitutional Democracy* (Ann Arbor, University of Michigan Press, 1962) 135–40.

particularly with a membership heavily skewed toward Beijing and other large cities, the NPCSC falls far short of providing adequate representation for the mass of Chinese people.

Of course, that does not mean that China's representative democracy has no way out of the dilemma imposed by its size. If the national legislature is destined to be massive and slow to move, maybe it should not busy itself with ordinary business that is better left to local governments, which are less challenged by the representation–efficiency conundrum. So far, however, China has followed the path of unitary centralism rather than decentralised federalism. The conundrum thus remains, and legislative efficiency is gained by sacrificing democratic representation, as the working of the NPCSC clearly demonstrates.

A. A Second Chamber?

In essence, then, the NPCSC is a 'second chamber' in China, enjoying independent legislative authority. This term is not to be entertained, of course, in the same sense as in bicameralism, which usually requires a bill to acquire majority voting in both chambers in order to be effective law. The Chinese system of allowing either chamber to enact laws on its own is surely peculiar, and the relationship between the two chambers must be carefully defined to avoid legislative conflicts and confusions.

The NPC–NPCSC relationship is indeed an intricate one. On the surface the NPCSC is elected by and subordinate to the full Congress (Constitution, Article 65). One NPCSC responsibility is to submit its annual work report to the NPC during its full session (Article 69), even though the formal effect of the review remains unclear, and the NPC has never failed to approve the report. Among the NPC powers, one is to 'alter or annul inappropriate decisions of the Standing Committee' (Article 62, clause 11), which indicates that the NPC is the higher of the two legislatures. Moreover, while the NPC has the power 'to enact and amend basic laws' (Article 62, clause 3), the NPCSC is authorised only 'to enact and amend laws, with the exception of those which should be enacted by' the NPC and, when the NPC is not in session, 'to partially supplement and amend' those basic laws enacted by the NPC, 'provided that the basic principles of these laws are not contravened' (Article 67, clauses 2 and 3). It is commonly understood that these provisions set the legislative boundary between the two chambers, with the NPC solely responsible for enacting basic laws, even though it is somewhat ambiguous whether it is *limited* to enacting these laws.

In practice, however, there are plenty of reasons to believe that the NPCSC is the much more powerful and effective of the two chambers. Although the NPCSC is limited to enacting ordinary (non-basic) laws, it has to power to 'supplement and amend' these laws during the period when the NPC is not in session, which means most of the year. The supplements or amendments may not contravene the 'basic principles of these laws', but such a general prohibition is so vague as to render it useless for limiting the Standing Committee's amendment power, not to mention that the NPCSC itself is in charge of interpreting all laws, including basic laws. In reality, the NPCSC has often amended the basic laws made by the NPC, particularly the criminal law. For example, following the terrorist attack on 11 September 2001, it inserted provisions in the Criminal Law to crackdown on those who organise, lead, fund or participate in terrorist activities. Other amendments are more disputable. The General Principles section of the Criminal Law provides, for example, that 'any act is not to be deemed criminal or given punishment without explicit stipulations of law deeming it a crime' (Article 3). According to the Standing Committee's supplements to Articles 121 and 291 of the Criminal Law, however, the SCC and SPP broadened criminal acts to include 'funding terrorist activities', 'placing dangerous substances' and 'fabricating and intentionally propagating false terrorist information'.[13] It is at least debatable whether the broadening of these crimes violated one of 'basic principles' stipulated in Article 3 of the Criminal Law.

More problematically, the NPCSC occasionally revises laws that regulate the NPC, its supposed constitutional superior. In October 2010, for example, it amended the Law on Deputies to the NPC by inserting a provision that requires deputies to stay with their own occupations and to 'participate in uniformly organised activities for the performance of their duties when they are not in session', a move that was widely understood to target active local deputies who set up individual studios in order to promote communication with their electorates.[14] Despite strong

---

[13] Supplementary Provisions regarding the Enforcement of Criminal Charges Determined in the Criminal Law of the PRC (2002) Legal Interpretation 7, 26 March 2002. See (2002) 3 *The Supreme People's Court Gazette* 80–81.

[14] 'The Deputies Law Revised for the First Time, Prohibiting Individual Studios', *Southern Weekend* (25 August 2010).

academic protests that it is illegal to amend laws that regulate the NPC itself, the Standing Committee nevertheless passed the amendment when the NPC was not in session. And it is practically difficult if not impossible for the NPC to repeal or amend any inadequate Standing Committee amendments, given the paucity of NPC sessions and the inefficiency of running such a massive congress.

Even more fundamentally, although the NPCSC is supposedly elected by and responsible to the NPC, the reality is very much the reverse. To begin with, it is true that the NPCSC is elected by a newly formed NPC, but the election of the incoming NPC itself is 'conducted' by the outgoing Standing Committee (Constitution, Article 59). Both the number of the NPC deputies and the procedures of election are 'prescribed by law' (Article 59), but there is surely no NPC 'law' that fixes the number of NPC deputies; what the NPC normally does is to pass a decision that defines the maximum number of deputies in the next election and generally authorises the Standing Committee to allocate the number of deputies for each province.[15] The NPCSC then enacts a master plan that actually allocates the number of deputies for all provinces, municipalities, autonomous districts, the SAR and the Taiwan region, as well as detailed numbers of minority deputies.[16] Indeed, it is the positive duty of the Standing Committee to 'ensure the completion of election of deputies' to the succeeding NPC two months prior to the expiration of the term of the current NPC (Article 60).

Although neither the NPC elections nor the NPCSC elections are worth serious examination, since both are heavily manipulated by the CCP, such provisions do illustrate the controlling role of the Standing Committee in the NPC formation. Only when a new NPC is elected and actually meets in March does it elect its own Presidium to conduct its session, thereby potentially gaining some independence from the Standing Committee of the previous term (Article 61). But even then, the NPC does not run entirely on its own, since the NPCSC still con-

---

[15]   See, eg, the Decision with respect to the Issues of Number of Deputies to the 11th Congress of the National People's Congress and Their Election, Fifth Session of the 10th Congress of the National People's Congress, which set the maximum number of deputies to be 3000.

[16]   See, eg, the Plan for Allocation of Number of Deputies to the 11th Congress of the National People's Congress, and the Plan for Allocation of Number of National Minority Deputies to the 11th Congress of the National People's Congress, 27th Session of the 10th Congress of the Standing Committee of the National People's Congress, held on 27 April 2010, *NPCSC Bulletin* 2010 (No 4).

trols its operation. While the regular NPC session is 'convened by its Standing Committee', an extraordinary session 'may be convened at any time the Standing Committee deems it necessary' (Article 61), though such a session has never yet been deemed 'necessary'. Finally, when the NPC is not in session, the NPCSC, through the conferences of the Standing Committee chairs, is also in charge of directing and coordinating all special committees, which play an important role in drafting legislation.

Overall, the NPC, a giant of nearly 3000 members who meet only 10 days a year, appears more like an extraordinary legislature fit only for unusual occasions, while its Standing Committee – much smaller, more effective and meeting much more frequently – is the regular legislature responsible for enacting most ordinary laws.

B. Constitutional Functions of the NPCSC

As China's regular lawmaker, the NPCSC not only shares legislative power with the NPC but also exercise other powers ordinarily not available to the NPC. One primary function is 'to interpret the Constitution and supervise its enforcement' (Constitution, Article 67, clause 1), even though it has never formally made use of this power. The Sun Zhigang case would have provided the perfect occasion to exercise such a power, but the Standing Committee chose to remain silent as usual. It has made rather frequent use, however, of its power to interpret ordinary laws (clause 4), particularly with regard to the Criminal Law. On 28 April 2002, for example, the NPCSC released an interpretation of Article 294 of the Criminal Law, which involves the term 'organisations of triad nature'.[17] In 2000, the SPC defined such organisations as ones that are tightly organised for acquiring economic interest by violent means and under the illicit protection of government officials. The propriety of requiring the last element, commonly dubbed 'black umbrella' (黑保护 伞, *hei baohusan*), was widely debated, since a number of prosecutions against 'organisations of triad nature' were rejected for a lack of sufficient evidence relating to any 'black umbrella'.[18] The SPP charged that

---

[17] See (2002) 3 *The Supreme People's Court Gazette* 76.
[18] Zhang Jie, 'The Legal Problem Provoked by the "Black Protective Umbrella"', *Southern Weekend* (9 May 2002).

the judicial interpretation was too strict to allow for crime control at an earlier stage, and proposed that the NPCSC interpret this provision. The legislative interpretation of the Standing Committee removed 'black umbrella' as a constitutive element of the crime, listing it merely as one form of criminal organisation. Unlike supplementation or amendment of laws, legislative interpretation is essentially a new gloss on an old law and thus in principle can be applied retroactively, although principles of fairness and legal predictability counsel against such application.

The second important function of the NPCSC is to supervise the work of the State Council, the CMC, the SPC and the SPP (Constitution, Article 67, clause 6). Like the NPC, the NPCSC may also submit written questions addressed to the State Council and its ministries or commissions if a group of 10 or more members do so during session (Organic Law of the NPC, Article 33). In addition, the NPCSC has the power 'to annul those administrative regulations, decisions or orders of the State Council that contravene the Constitution or a law' and to annul local regulations or decisions made by a provincial LPC that contravene these superior laws or an administrative regulation (Constitution, Article 67, clauses 7–8).

Finally, when the NPC is not in session, the NPCSC may to a certain extent exercise powers normally reserved for the NPC, including the power to make major decisions. When the NPC is not in session, the Standing Committee may review and approve 'partial adjustments to the plan for national economic and social development or to the state budget that prove necessary in the course of their implementation' (Article 67, clause 5). It may even proclaim 'a state of war in the event of an armed attack on the country or in fulfilment of international treaty obligations concerning common defence against aggression' (clause 18). In fact, exclusively reserved to the NPCSC are the powers to ratify or abrogate treaties and important agreements concluded with foreign states (clause 14); to decide on general or partial mobilisation (clause 19); and to declare a state of emergency for the whole country or for a province (clause 20). Likewise, the Standing Committee may also appoint or remove chief officials of the state when the NPC is not in session, except the President of the state, the Premiers and Vice-Premiers, the State Councillors, the CMC Chairman and the Presidents of the SPC and SPP (clauses 9–12).

Like the NPC, the Standing Committee is not limited to powers enumerated in Article 67 of the Constitution but may 'exercise such other functions and powers as the National People's Congress may assign to it' (clause 21).

C. Structure and Legislative Procedure

The legislative procedure of the Standing Committee is somewhat simpler than that of the NPC, though more elaborate than that of the LPCs and their standing committees. According to the Law on Legislation, 10 or more NPCSC members may jointly propose a bill to the Standing Committee, and the caucus of chairpersons shall decide whether to put the bill on the agenda of the current session or to refer it to the relevant special committees for deliberation and comment (Article 25). In general, a bill put on the agenda is to be deliberated three times in the NPCSC sessions before being put to a vote (Article 27). The first deliberation is for the Standing Committee to hear the statements of the bill sponsor and refer the bill to its plenary session for preliminary deliberation. The Legislative Committee of the NPC is obliged to formulate a report concerning amendments or the result of deliberation, which includes a statement of the major differences in views, and to amend the draft law (Article 31). During the second deliberation, the Standing Committee hears the report of the Legislative Committee concerning the amendment of and major issues in the draft law, and refers the bill to seminars for further deliberation. During the third deliberation, the Standing Committee hears the report of the Legislative Committee about the result of the deliberation over the draft law and refers the amended draft law to the seminars for deliberation. The revised version of a draft law will then be amended by the Legislative Committee based on comments made by the Standing Committee, in order to formulate a version endorsed by the caucus of chairpersons, to be voted upon in the NPCSC plenary session (Article 40). A bill may be brought to a vote after two deliberations, and a bill that partially amends a law may be brought to vote after only one deliberation, if a general consensus has been reached (Article 28).

The daily work of the Standing Committee is assisted by several subcommittees, in addition to the General Office, and these include the Legislative Affairs Committee (LAC), Budget Work Committee, Deputies Qualification Review Committee and the Hong Kong and Macao Basic Laws Committees. As the 'working office' of the NPCSC, the LAC is composed of over 140 professional staff, who are divided into several areas of law. Although most of the staff are neither Standing Committee members nor NPC deputies, they are in charge of daily law-making and review activities. The LAC is responsible for drafting the NPCSC's legislative proposals and proposals for interpreting laws. It is also the LAC that filters the citizen complaints made to the NPCSC against the constitutionality or legality of national and provincial regulations.[19]

IV. LOCAL PEOPLE'S CONGRESSES (LPCS)

Below the national legislature are the local legislatures in the provinces (including the municipalities and autonomous regions), cities, counties, municipal districts, towns and townships. Article 96 of the Constitution provides that the LPCs at various levels are 'local organs of state power', and only LPCs at and above the county level can establish standing committees. The role and functions of these LPCs and their standing committees vis-à-vis local governments at the same level are largely parallel to those of the NPC and NPCSC vis-à-vis the national government, except that the LPCs are obliged to 'ensure the observance and implementation of the Constitution and the law and the administrative regulations in their respective administrative areas' (Constitution, Article 99).[20]

A. The Structure and Functions of LPCs

LPC deputies are elected either directly or indirectly by local constituencies. While deputies to LPCs at the county level or below are directly elected by their constituencies, deputies to LPCs above the county level are elected by the LPCs at the next lower level (Constitution, Article 97). This leads to a cascading election scheme: the NPC deputies are elected by deputies to their respective provincial LPCs, who are elected by deputies to the LPCs of cities, divided into districts within their respective provinces, who are in turn elected by deputies to the LPCs of districts and counties within those city jurisdictions, who are directly elected by

---

[19] See above ch 3.
[20] See above ch 3.

the local constituencies. Like the NPC, each LPC is elected for a term of five years (Article 98) and is subject to supervision by its electors (Article 102). Like the NPC, LPCs at various levels meet in session at least once a year, and a special session may be convened at any time upon the proposal of one fifth of the deputies (Organic Law on the LPC and LPG, hereinafter 'Local Organic Law', Article 11).

An LPC above the county level may establish special committees, such as legislative (political and law) committees, finance and economic committees, and education, science, culture and public health committees (Local Organic Law, Article 30). Candidates for the director, deputy directors and members of each special committee are nominated by the presidium from the deputies and are subject to the LPC's approval. When an LPC is not in session, the special committees shall work under the direction of its standing committees, which may appoint or dismiss the deputy directors and members of a special committee. The special committees shall discuss, examine and draft relevant bills and resolutions, make investigations and put forward proposals on matters within the scope of functions and powers of the respective LPC and their standing committees (Article 30).

Overall, LPCs exercise the following powers, with the peculiarity that the scope of powers is slightly different for LPCs at different levels (eg, compare Articles 8 and 9 of the Local Organic Law). First, there are electoral and removal powers. LPCs at their respective levels elect and have the power to recall governors and deputy governors, mayors and deputy mayors, or heads and deputy heads of counties, districts, townships and towns (Constitution, Article 101). LPCs at and above the county level also elect and have the power to recall court presidents and chief procurators at the corresponding level, while the election or recall of chief procurators must be reported to the LPC standing committees at the next higher level for approval (Article 101). When an LPC at or above the county level is in session, its presidium, its standing committee or a joint group of at least one tenth of its deputies may submit a proposal to remove from office members of its standing committee or members of the government, the court president or the chief procurator at the corresponding level. When an LPC at township or town level is in session, the presidium or a group of at least one fifth of the deputies may submit a proposal to remove from office its chairman or vice-chairmen, the head or deputy heads of the township or town. The presidium will refer the proposal to the congress for deliberation, and persons proposed to be removed from office have the right to defend themselves at a meeting of the presidium or at the plenary meeting of a session, or to submit a written defence (Local Organic Law, Article 26).

Second, LPCs have policymaking powers. LPCs adopt and issue resolutions and examine and decide on plans for local economic, cultural and public service development within the limits of their authority prescribed by law; LPCs at and above the county level examine and approve plans for economic and social development and the budgets of their respective administrative areas, as well as reports on their implementation (Constitution, Article 99). When an LPC is in session, its presidium, standing committee and special committees and the government at the corresponding level may submit bills and proposals within the scope of the LPC's functions and powers; the presidium can decide to refer such bills and proposals to a LPC session for deliberation or to simultaneously refer them to relevant special committees for deliberation and reports before submitting them to the session for a vote. 10 or more LPC deputies at or above the county level, or five or more LPC deputies at township or town level, may jointly submit a bill or proposal to the LPC at the corresponding level, within the scope of its functions and powers; the presidium must decide whether to place it on the agenda or to first refer it to a relevant special committee for deliberation and recommendation (Local Organic Law, Article 18).

Third, the LPCs also have supervisory and corrective powers. LPCs hear and examine the reports of their standing committees, the governments, the courts and procuratorates at the corresponding levels (Local Organic Law, Article 8, clauses 8–9). They also have the power to alter or annul inappropriate resolutions of the standing committees and the governments at the corresponding levels (clause 10). When an LPC is in session, a group of at least 10 deputies may submit a written proposal for addressing questions to the government or any of its departments, the court or the procuratorate at the corresponding level. The presidium must decide whether to refer the proposal to the organ addressed either for an oral reply at the meeting of the presidium, at the plenary meeting of a session or at the meeting of a relevant special committee, or for a written reply (Article 28).

Some LPCs are more active than their national counterpart in exercising their powers. In February 2001, for example, the majority of the LPC of Shenyang (the capital of Liaoning province) declined to approve the work report of the Shenyang Middle Level Court, due to rampant

corruption and dereliction of duty within the Court. The LPC reconvened in August to hear and review the court report for a second time.[21]
In January 2003, deputies to the Guangdong provincial LPC examined,
for the first time since 1949, the government budget proposal that listed
by each item the expenses of 102 provincial departments in 600 pages;
not surprisingly they found many unexplained problems.[22] In February
2012, the LPCSC of Zhuhai (Guangdong province) declined to approve
the nomination for director made by the mayor because many committee members found the nominee's presentation 'empty' (空洞,
kongdong).[23]

B. The Structure and Functions of LPCSCs

Standing committees are established only within LPCs at or above the
county level. The relationship between a local standing committee and
its local congress is similar to that at the national level. An LPC at or
above the county level elects and has the power to recall members of its
standing committee, which is responsible and reports its work to the
relevant LPC (Constitution, Article 103). Like their counterpart at the
national level, however, LPCSCs are also empowered to 'direct or conduct the election of deputies' and to 'convene sessions' of its LPC
(Local Organic Law, Article 44, clauses 2 and 3). In practice, since LPCs
are much smaller than the NPC, they tend to play a more important role
than their national counterpart vis-à-vis their standing committees; at
least, they are institutionally capable of doing so if they choose to.

LPCSCs are likewise proportionally smaller than their national counterpart (Local Organic Law, Article 41). While the average size of a provincial LPC is about 50 members (with a maximum of 85), that of an
LPC for a city divided into districts is about 30 (with a maximum of 51),
and that of a county LPC is around 20 (with a maximum of 35). Similar
to the NPCSC, an LPCSC meeting is convened by its chairman and held

---

[21] Cheng Peng, 'Applause Rang when the Work Report Failed to be Approved',
Sina.com news (9 August 2001), http://news.sina.com.cn/c/2001-08-09/324307.
html.
[22] Zhang Li, 'How to Spend the 22 Billion Yuan Government Expenditure',
Southern Weekend (23 January 2003).
[23] 'Director Nomination Made by Zhuhai (Guangdong) Mayor Failed to Acquire
LPC Approval', *Guangzhou Evening News* (23 February 2012).

at least once every other month (Local Organic Law, Article 45). It exercises similar supervisory powers as exercised by the NPCSC over the government, court and procuratorate at the same level, and shares similar constitutional problems in exercising some of these powers. For example, an LPCSC is authorised to revoke 'inappropriate' resolutions passed by the LPC at the next lower level (Local Organic Law, Article 44). Keep in mind, however, that an LPCSC is elected by its LPC, which is in turn elected by the LPC at the next lower level. In terms of democratic accountability, it would undoubtedly odd for an LPCSC to be able to revoke a decision made by its own LPC, to which it should be held directly accountable; and it is no less odd for the LPCSC to be able to revoke a decision made by an LPC at one level below, to which the LPC (and ultimately, the LPCSC itself) at the upper level should be held accountable by election.

Members of an LPCSC exercise legislative and investigatory functions similar to those exercised by their national counterparts, though arguably with more efficacy. Besides the council of chairmen of an LPCSC and local government, five or more members of an LPCSC above county level and three or more members for an LPCSC at county level may jointly submit a bill or proposal to the LPCSC within the scope of its functions and powers (Local Organic Law, Article 46). And the council of chairmen or a group of at least one fifth of the standing committee members may submit a proposal for organising an investigation committee on specific questions, to be submitted to the plenary meeting for decision (Article 52). Although the NPCSC has so far never established a special investigation committee, despite several public calls to do so,[24] local committees have been established, though rarely, to investigate specific issues. For example, the LPCSC of Xingcheng (Liaoning province) established a special committee in 2003 to investigate the dereliction of the city court in enforcing a law, which resulted in significant loss to the state grain storage. The LPCSC passed a resolution that openly criticised two vice presidents and ordered the court to correct its mistake.[25]

---

[24] The most recent example was the major railway accident that took place on 23 July 2011. The press release regarding the cause of the accident failed to gain public confidence since the investigation was carried out in a closed process, conducted by the Ministry of Railway alone, without participation of an independent agency. In fact, the exact number of casualties has never been disclosed.

[25] Fu Ke et al, 'Scholars Appeal NPCSC to Establish Special Investigation Committee', *Southern Metropolitan Daily* (28 July 2011).

V. HOW TO MAKE DEMOCRACY WORK

The institutional design of the People's Congresses is, to be sure, far from perfect, but it *could* work to some extent if the constitutional rules were given minimal respect and some efforts at enforcement were made. Besides the institutional arrangements outlined above, the 1982 Constitution also provides for quite a few procedural rights for individual deputies that are not unusual in a democratic constitution. For example, deputies may not be held legally liable for their speeches or votes (Constitution, Article 75; Organic Law of the NPC, Article 29). No deputy to the NPC or an LPC at or above the county level may be arrested, placed on criminal trial or subjected to any other restrictions of personal freedom without the consent of its Presidium or, when the Congress is not in session, without the consent of its Standing Committee (Constitution, Article 74; Organic Law of the NPC, Article 30). If a deputy to the LPC of a township or town is arrested, placed on criminal trial or subjected to any other restrictions of personal freedom, the executing organ is required to immediately report the matter to its LPC. The effects of these provisions are rendered nugatory, however, by the political control of deputies' activities, the institutional impediments to the effective performance of their capacities and, most importantly, ubiquitous meddling in electoral processes, which will be discussed in chapter eight.

A. From Supremacy to Rubber Stamp

With a constitutional mandate to exercise the supreme state powers for the people, deputies to the People's Congresses are given many legislative and supervisory functions. The freedom of their activities is severely limited, however, by the leadership of their own institutions, and one can glean the intent of such limitations from Article 19 of the Organic Law of the NPC, which provides that the Standing Committee shall 'organise deputies' of LPCs at or above the county level to carry out activities when they are not in session. Deputies of LPCs at or above the county level may, 'in line with the unified arrangements made by the standing committee', carry out inspections of the work of state organs and relevant units at the same or lower levels; and the standing committee shall, upon request by deputies, 'make arrangements for deputies' of the People's Congresses at the same or higher levels to conduct on-site inspections in their respective localities, and they may put forward proposals, criticisms or opinions to the units inspected 'but shall not deal with the problems directly' (NPC Organic Law, Article 21). With most off-session activities prearranged by their standing committees, deputies of the People's Congresses at all levels are reduced to mere symbolic roles, and 'inspections' have become occasions for sham displays of local achievement, even opportunities for tourism and banquets.

To be sure, there are active deputies who refuse to limit themselves to the official arrangements and exercise the constitutional functions on their own. Yao Lifa, a deputy to the LPC of Qianjiang city (Hubei province), was a good example.[26] After he was elected in the late 1990s, he quickly activated the local political atmosphere. In 1998, he discovered through his own investigation that local teachers were being denied subsidies of more than RMB¥100 million and organised 4,000 teachers to petition the city government for a remedy. The next year, he was informed by his constituency that the city education commission intercepted relief donations for the Yangtze River flood, which were forwarded to the appropriate recipients only after the misconduct was exposed. In 2000, he organised several city deputies to inspect the taxi system, as a consequence of which the city government was found to have exacted over RMB¥2 million in illicit user fees. In a session in the same year, he drafted a proposal against the proposed consolidation of three cities, which would have created positions for cadres retired from the provincial departments at the expense of wasting a huge amount of financial and agricultural resources. Yao's counter-proposal was co-signed by over half of the city deputies and sent directly to the State Council, effectively putting an end to the consolidation plans.

Although Yao did precisely what a competent deputy is expected to do for his constituents, the LPC leaders increasingly saw him as a 'controversial figure' because he acted on his own initiative rather than limiting himself to officially organised activities. They reminded him of the duty of deputies, which in their minds was 'to help the government to resolve difficulties and reduce worries, not to add troubles to it'.[27] In

---

[26] Huang Guangming, 'The Reality of a Plebeian Deputy', *Southern Weekend* (16 January 2003).

[27] Ibid.

December 2002, after Yao had failed to follow their advice and the locality was in the middle of a villagers' committee election, he was physically assaulted for making public a document that explained relevant policy from the city bureau of civil affairs. He edited and printed a brochure entitled 'Villagers should Decide who should be Elected Village Officials', essentially a popular explanation for the Organic Law of Villagers' Committee, and distributed it among the local peasants, all at his own expense. The city press and publication bureau denounced it as an 'illegal publication', punished Yao with a fine of RMB¥8,000 and ordered him to recall all copies of the brochure and hand them over for destruction.

Eventually, Yao was denied the opportunity to stand for re-election. No sooner had he left than the LPC of Qianjiang city fell back into 'rubber stamp' mode. With the recent revision of the Law on Deputies of the NPC, which explicitly spells out the limited number of acceptable 'organised activities', the already small number of active deputies such as Yao will further decrease, and the already rather dysfunctional People's Congresses will be further enervated.

B. Toward a Professional Legislature?

The passivity of deputies in China is attributable not only to political control by the ruling party but also to institutional impediments that deprive them time and energy in exercising their constitutional powers. In essence, the People's Congress is an anachronistic institution reminiscent of the House of Lords in medieval England, except without the honour and status that the House derived from its nobility. Most deputies and standing committee members, with the exception of a very few leaders, undertake their legislative obligations in a part-time capacity and are thus necessarily preoccupied by their primary occupations, from which their salaries are derived. The Organic Law of the NPC does require that 'the unit to which a deputy belongs must ensure him the time needed' to participate in the arranged activities (Article 31); moreover, the performance of the deputy's functions should be 'regarded as normal attendance' for his wage and benefit purposes (Article 32). 'Funds for deputy activities shall be included in the financial budget of the governments at the corresponding levels' (Article 33), and 'the state shall, as necessary, provide them with round-trip travelling expenses and requisite material facilities or subsidies' (Local Organic Law, Article 36). But such allowances are obviously insufficient to overcome the disincentives for deputies to perform their constitutional duties in anything but a passive manner.

Take again, as an example, Yao Lifa, who had to halt his regular occupation at the city education commission in order to actively engage in his congressional duties and even opened a small gas station in order to supplement his livelihood.[28] Every year he spent several thousand Yuan on travel, telephone expenses, publications and guest receptions, all at his own expense. He once applied to be a professional deputy with a state salary, but his application was firmly rejected. Although there *are* active personalities of his type in China, the part-time and nonprofessional nature of the position of deputy makes such a job extremely unattractive for anyone except those who wish to make use of the political connections it may bring for their own benefit. To make deputies duly perform their obligations as prescribed by the Constitution, the nature of the deputy's position must undergo fundamental change.

In 2003, the new regime headed by Hu Jingtao and Wen Jiabao briefly experimented with a limited 'professionalisation' (专职化, *zhuanzhi hua*) of the NPCSC. 20 Standing Committee members quit their primary occupations and became full-time members in charge of legislation. Yet this reform was not followed up, and the scope of a professional NPC and Standing Committee has not been expanded or explored under the leadership of a conservative Chairman (吴邦国, Wu Bangguo). More progress has been made at the local levels, but this progress was abruptly halted by the NPCSC. In summer 2010, Luojiang county of Sichuan province openly experimented with local professional deputies, who were to establish personal studios for receiving constituent complaints, but such apparently benign local experiments were speedily brought to halt by the conservative NPCSC, which revised the Law on Deputies of the NPC as a restrictive response to the individual initiatives of active local deputies.[29] Apparently, the professionalisation of People's Congresses, which is vital for democracy to work in China, still has long road to travel.

---

[28]   Chen Chuyue, 'The Legislative Path of Legislator Yao', *Xici Alley* (16 January 2003), http://www.xici.net/b26696/d8497520.htm.

[29]   'The First Studio of Full-Time Congressional Deputy Was Halted', *The First Finance Daily* (31 August 2010).

On the whole, the People's Congresses in China remain 'rubber stamps', incapable of efficient law-making or vigorous supervision of government officials in ways that are stipulated in vain in the Constitution and relevant laws. Without effective representation, the people find no way to exert their voices, integrate their interests and oblige the governments at various levels to be accountable to them; without pressure from the people and their deputies, officials everywhere tend to fall into corruption, and the supposedly 'public' policies they enact run against the public interest. The Custody and Repatriation Measures, which were enacted by the State Council and caused Sun Zhigang's death,[30] is but one example of many that have resulted from an inept representative system, which can be held responsible for almost all evils recurring in contemporary China. Nevertheless, the People's Congresses are also the key to the badly needed political reform. As long as increasing numbers of ordinary people come out to vote or even stand as independent candidates in congressional elections, there is no reason why the institution of People's Congress cannot become more effective at representing and vindicating the people's interest.

FURTHER READING

H (A) Chen, *An Introduction to Legal System of the People's Republic of China*, 4th edn (Hong Kong, LexisNexis Butterworths, 2011) ch 6.

Young Nam Cho, *Local People's Congresses in China: Development and Transition* (Cambridge, Cambridge University Press, 2010).

PH Corne, 'Creation and Application of Law in the PRC' (2002) 50 *American Journal of Comparative Law* 369.

MW Dowdle, 'The Constitutional Development and Operations of the National People's Congress' (1997) 11 *Columbia Journal of Asian Law* 1.

Jiang Jinsong, *National People's Congress of China* (Beijing, Foreign Languages Press, 2003).

Lin Feng, *Constitutional Law in China* (Hong Kong, Sweet and Maxwell Asia, 2000).

KJ O'Brien, *Reform without Liberalization: China's National People's Congress and the Politics of Institutional Change* (Cambridge, Cambridge University Press, 2008).

---

[30] See above ch 3.

5

Administration of the State According to Law

——◦◦◦——

THE CENTRAL GOVERNMENT – State President – The Central Military Commission (CMC) – State Council: Structure – State Council: Powers – **LOCAL GOVERNMENT** – Structure and Functions – Extensions: Villagers' Committees – **TOWARD ADMINISTRATIVE RULE OF LAW?** – Justifying Rule of Law: The Balance Theory – Landmark Development: Administrative Litigation Law of 1990 – Other Legislative Progress – Administrative Law Reform within Chinese Reality: A Brief Assessment

THE POWER OF administration (行政, *xingzheng*) is quintessential to China, a country that has remained an administrative state ever since its first unification in 221 bc. Whenever a conflict arises, power almost always prevails over the law, and the limits of administrative power, if any, are set by Confucian moral codes rather than by prescriptions of law. In 1999, a constitutional amendment added a clause to Article 5, which committed China to 'administration of the state according to law' and construction of a 'socialist state of rule of law'. Past experience has proved, however, that bringing administrative power under rule of law is an immensely difficult task in China.

This chapter will introduce the structure of administrative power in China, with a focus on administrative law developments in a constitutional context. I will describe the structure and powers of various agencies whose functions normally fall under the heading 'administrative' in Western literature (though China does not necessarily fit in well with such categorisation, as shown by the example of the Central Military Committee). I follow with an account of major administrative laws enacted since the 1990s and end the chapter with an evaluation of both China's efforts in establishing a 'socialist state under rule of law' as pledged in its constitutional amendment and the prospect of achieving constitutionalism via administrative law.

I. THE CENTRAL GOVERNMENT

While the 1982 Constitution establishes a unique unicameral legislature with two chambers and a dual judiciary,[1] the 'triplet' administrative structure it establishes is even more unusual, with three institutions sharing what are normally categorised as 'administrative' powers:[2] the head of the state, the chief executive, and the top military commander. Some countries amalgamate all three powers in one position (eg, the American presidency); others distribute them in their own ways. From 1982 until now, the pattern of distribution has been changing in China. The three powers used to be controlled by separate hands, but a stable pattern gradually emerged after 1989, when Jiang Zemin (江泽民) replaced Zhao Ziyang (赵紫阳) as the Secretary General of the Chinese Communist Part (CCP) in the aftermath of the Tiananmen Protests. Nowadays, the Secretary General is also the head of the state and military commander, forming a 'troika', as it were, with the National People's Congress Standing Committee (NPCSC) Chairman and the chief executive (Premier).

A. State President

Although the 1982 Constitution is in many ways an heir to the first constitution enacted in 1954, it differs remarkably from its predecessor in the institutional design of the state president. Analogous to the role of President in the United States, the President of the State (国家主席,

---

[1]   See below ch 6.

[2]   Some of these powers may be categorised as 'executive' in some constitutions (eg, the Constitution of the United States), but the Chinese translation of that term 执行 (*zhixing*) connotes the narrower meaning of 'enforcement', which can be misleading in the Chinese context. For this reason, the word 'administrative' is used throughout this book to embrace all powers relating to administration of the state and the execution of laws.

guojia zhuxi) in the 1954 Constitution was not only the commander-in-chief of the national military force and the chairman of defence commission but also chairman of the supreme state conference (国务会议, *guowu huiyi*) and had the power to recommend appointment and dismissal of the Premier. In fact, since the President would exercise most of his constitutional powers according to the decisions made by the National People's Congress (NPC) or its Standing Committee, they were together regarded as constituting a 'collective head of state'. The President of State was abolished in the 'revolutionary' constitutions of 1975 and 1978 but was restored in the 1982 Constitution, although the power of the new President has been dramatically curtailed. No longer burdened with administrative and military affairs, he has become almost a purely dignitary figure, as suggested by Article 79, which provides that a citizen can be elected to President or Vice President only at an age of 45 or above.

The powers of the President, defined in Articles 80 and 81 of the Constitution, are largely limited to authenticating the decisions made by the NPC and its Standing Committee. These include decisions to 'promulgate statutes'; to appoint or remove the Premier, Vice-Premiers, State Councillors, Ministers, the Auditor-General and the Secretary-General of the State Council; to issue special pardons; to declare war and states of emergency; to issue mobilisation orders; to appoint or recall plenipotentiary representatives abroad; and to ratify or abrogate treaties and important agreements concluded with foreign nations.

The apparent lack of substantial power is in sharp contrast to the real power exercised daily by the President – in the capacity of Secretary General of the CCP, as the two positions have merged since late 1989. This contrast between text and reality prompted a 2004 constitutional amendment that conferred upon the President 'the capacity of to conduct activities of national affairs'. Despite being somewhat vaguely expanded, the nature of presidential power remains symbolic.

B. The Central Military Commission (CMC)

The military power removed from the President of the 1954 Constitution was taken over by the newly formed Central Military Commission (CMC) (中央军委, *zhongyang junwei*), the most cryptic institution provided for in the 1982 Constitution, which regulates it through only two articles. Article 93 defines the CMC as the supreme military organ in charge of leading the national military force. It is headed by a Chairman, who is elected by the NPC and is responsible to the NPC and its Standing Committee (Article 94). Unlike the State Council or local governments, the CMC is not regulated by organic law or other types of statutes. The Law on Legislation 'Supplementary Provisions' does mention that the CMC must 'enact military regulations in accordance with the Constitution and other laws' (Article 93), but it specifies no mechanism for ensuring the conformity of military regulations with the Constitution and other laws.

The brevity of the constitutional and legal regulation of the CMC has left many questions unresolved. For one thing, there are in fact two CMCs – a state CMC and a Party CMC – even though they are essentially the same institution sharing the same chairman and staff. During regime transition, however, a 'paradox of two chairmen' may arise since the new Chairman for the Party CMC will be elected during the session of the Party Congress, which usually takes place several months earlier than the NPC session, during which the outgoing Chairman will give up his state CMC post. This occurred during the transition between the regimes of Jiang Zemin and Hu Jingtao in 2003.[3] Such a paradox merely highlights the uneasy relationship between the Party and the State in the military context. When the CCP maintains stable control over the State, nothing unexpected happens during the short transition period; if, however, the organisational strength of the CCP declines to the point that it can no longer bring about factional consensus, glitches may arise from the institutional dislocation of the two CMCs.

More significantly, although the CMC is in charge of military command and policymaking, daily business is run by the Ministry of Defence, under the State Council and led by the Premier; and there is no law or regulation that distributes powers between the CMC and the Ministry of Defence. Although all these institutions are supposed to be ultimately responsible to the NPC and its Standing Committee, this theoretical scheme is without any practical bearing since neither the NPC nor the Standing Committee is equipped to deal with military matters. Although the CMC Chairman is at the same time the Party Secretary General, who, as China's most powerful person, is above the Premier,

---

[3]   See Zhang Qianfan, *Introduction to the Study of Constitutional Law*, 2nd edn (Beijing, Law Press, 2004) ch 5.

this customary arrangement is at most an 'unwritten constitutional convention' premised on the absolute supremacy of the CCP. Although the CCP always claim 'party leadership over guns' (党指挥枪, *dang zhihui qiang*), it ultimately relies on the gun barrels to maintain its power over the state. Once its grip loosens, power grabs may break out between the Party and the State over the military, which may well be running on its own, unaccountable to either institution – and most importantly, unaccountable to the people. The intricate relationship between the military, the State and the Party remains unresolved at the constitutional level, bringing far-reaching consequences for China's peace and stability.

C. State Council: Structure

With the exception of the military and defence power, all other substantive powers of the central government are lodged in the most important administrative organ, the State Council (国务院, *guowu yuan*). In fact, the State Council *is* the Central People's Government (中央人民政府, *zhongyang renmin zhengfu*), 'the executive body of the highest organ of state power' and 'the highest organ of state administration' (1982 Constitution, Article 85). The State Council is composed of the Premier and Vice-Premiers, State Councillors, Ministers in charge of ministries or commissions, the Auditor-General and the Secretary-General. While the Premier assumes 'overall responsibility for the work of the State Council', the Ministers assume 'overall responsibility' for the specific areas of which they are in charge, and the State Councillors are entrusted by the Premier to take charge of special tasks or specific areas of work and may conduct foreign affairs on behalf of the State Council (Organic Law of the State Council, Article 6). Important issues are decided after discussions at plenary meetings attended by the whole Council or, more often, at the executive meetings (常务会议, *changwu huiyi*) attended by the Premier and Vice Premiers, the State Councillors and the Secretary-General (Article 4). All these meetings are chaired by the Premier.

The organisational structure of the State Council has undergone several rounds of institutional reform, most recently based on the Regulation of Establishment and Staffing of Administrative Agencies, which was enacted in 1997. The State Council now includes a General Office, component departments, affiliated agencies and other offices, under which bureaus and divisions are set up. While a proposal regarding the establishment, revocation or consolidation of component departments has to be decided by the NPC or its Standing Committee after it is discussed and approved at an executive meeting of the State Council, the State Council may directly make organisational adjustments to the affiliated agencies and other offices.

Basic administrative functions are exercised by the component departments of the State Council, which now includes 22 ministries, five commissions, the China People's Bank and the Auditor-General's Office. Examples of ministries and commissions are the Ministry of Foreign Affairs, the Ministry of Defence, the Ministry of Public Security, the Ministry of State Security, the Ministry of Supervision, the Ministry of Finance, the Ministry of Land and Natural Resources, the Ministry of Justice, the Ministry of Civil Affairs, the Ministry of Education, the Ministry of Culture, the Ministry of Transport, the Ministry of Agriculture, the Ethnic Affairs Commission, the Birth Control Commission, the Economic and Trade Commission and the Defence Science, Technology and Industry Commission.

Unlike most democratic countries in which audit offices are affiliated with Parliament, China's auditing office is established within the administrative branch itself, with the aim of 'supervising through audits the revenue and expenditure of all departments under the State Council and of the local governments at various levels, and the revenue and expenditure of all financial and monetary organisations, enterprises and institutions of the state' (Constitution, Article 91). To guarantee its independence and fairness, however, the Constitution does place the Auditor-General's office under the immediate direction of the Premier so that it may 'independently exercise its power of supervision through auditing in accordance with the law, subject to no interference by any other administrative organ or any public organisation or individual' (Article 91).

The affiliated agencies (直属机构, *zhishu jigou*) are somewhat similar to the 'independent agencies' of the United States, usually in charge of specific areas of regulatory functions. Examples are the Environmental Protection Administration, the General Administration of Civil Aviation, the General Administration of Customs, the State Administration of Taxation, the Industry and Business Administration, the Drug Supervision Administration, the General Administration of Sports, the State Bureau of Religious Affairs, the General Office of Press and Publications and the Administration of Radio, Film and Television.

The State Council is also assisted by a number of offices in charge of policy research and formulation, eg, the Press Office, the Office of Legal Affairs, the Foreign Affairs Office, the Hong Kong and Macao Affairs Office and the Taiwan Affairs Office. Unlike the component departments and affiliated agencies, these offices are without independent executive functions.

D. State Council: Powers

Like the American President or other modern chief executives, the State Council exercises powers of a mixed legislative, executive and adjudicative nature (Constitution, Article 89). First, it is in charge of bringing unity to national regulations by enacting legislation. The State Council enacts administrative regulations to be enforced throughout the nation, with legal effect below the Constitution and laws enacted by the NPC or NPCSC; in accordance with the laws and administrative regulations, the ministries and commissions issue orders and directives within their respective jurisdictions (Article 89, clause 1). The State Council is also a major initiator of law-making, since one of its important functions is to submit proposals to the NPC and the NPCSC (clause 2).

Second, the State Council is also in charge of leading and supervising administration throughout the nation. It not only formulates the tasks and responsibilities of the ministries and commissions and exercises 'unified leadership' over their work but also formulates 'the detailed division of functions and powers' between the central and provincial governments and exercises 'unified leadership' over the work of local governments at various levels throughout the country (Article 89, clauses 3 and 4). More specifically, it may 'alter or annul inappropriate orders, directives and regulations' issued by the ministries, commissions or local governments (clauses 13 and 14). It appoints or removes administrative officials, provides for their training, appraises their performance and rewards or punishes them accordingly (clause 17). It also approves the geographic division of provinces and the establishment and geographic division of autonomous places within an autonomous region (clause 15).

Third, the State Council is in charge of formulating important policies and decisions in the areas of socioeconomics, culture, defence, etc. It formulates and implements the state budget, as well as 'the plan for national economic and social development' (clause 5), an on-going legacy of the planned economy era. It directs and administers an array of matters, including the economy, urban and rural development, education, science, culture, public health, sports, family planning, public security, judicial administration, national defence, civil affairs and protection of equal rights of minority nationalities and the right to autonomy of the national autonomous areas (clauses 6–8 and 10–11). It also conducts foreign affairs and concludes treaties and agreements with foreign states (clause 9) and may declare a state of emergency for parts of provinces (clause 17).

Like the provisions enumerating the powers of the NPC and the NPCSC, the enumeration of the powers of the State Council in Article 90 of the Constitution is an exemplary exercise rather than a delimitation, since it ends with a catch-all clause that authorises the State Council 'to exercise such other functions and powers as the National People's Congress or its Standing Committee may assign to it' (clause 18).

II. LOCAL GOVERNMENT

In comparison to the central government, China's local governments are placed in a much more modest position in the Constitution, but they wield substantial power, as delegated by the central government, for the purpose of implementing laws and policies. Of course, unchecked local power can be no less dangerous to individual liberty than unlimited national power.

A. Structure and Functions

Article 105 of the 1982 Constitution defines local people's governments (LPGs) both as 'the executive bodies of local organs of state power' and as 'the local organs of state administration at the corresponding levels', by which local leaders are made responsible to the Local People's Congresses (LPCs) at the same levels.[4] LPGs report to the LPCs at the same levels and, when the latter are not in session, to the LPCSCs at the same levels (Constitution, Article 110). As 'executive bodies' in the over-

---

[4] For discussion of LPCs, see above ch 4.

all state structure, however, LPGs are also responsible to the governmental bodies at higher levels. Thus, LPGs also 'report on their work to the state administrative organs at the next higher level'; and all LPGs are 'state administrative organs under the unified leadership of the State Council and are subordinate to it' (Article 110).

The functions of local governments are defined in Article 107 of the Constitution. LPGs at and above the county level conduct administrative work 'within the limits of their authority as prescribed by law', and this work can cover the economy, education, science, culture, public health, sports, urban and rural development, finance, civil affairs, public security, ethnic affairs, judicial administration, administrative supervision and birth control. They also have the authority to issue decisions and orders; to appoint and remove local administrative functionaries; to provide for their training; and to appraise their performance and reward or punish them accordingly. While the primary function of LPGs at the lower levels (eg, at the town or township level) is to execute the resolutions of an LPC at the same level and the decisions and orders of the LPG at the next higher (eg, county) level, they also 'conduct administrative work in their respective administrative areas' (Constitution, Article 107).

The local governments at various levels may also establish 'extended agencies' (派出机关, *paichu jiguan*) if 'necessary' and with the approval of the governments at the next higher level (Local Organic Law, Article 68). The provincial governments used to set up 'administrative agencies' (行政公署, *xingzheng gongshu*) to assist in the management of county governments, but these agencies gradually were phased out, particularly after the counties were effectively made subordinate to the cities that have districts. 'District offices' (街道办事处, *jiedao banshichu*), established by city governments at the lowest level (ie, municipal districts or cities not divided into districts), did survive. Although district offices are outside the four-level structure defined in the Constitution,[5] they do exercise a fair number of daily executive functions.

China's local government seems to be secondary in terms of its constitutional status, but this is valid only when a local official is in front of his superiors from the central government. In a top-down framework where the government is not held accountable to its electorate, a local official enjoys unchecked power over the people and may exploit such

---

[5] See above ch 3.

power to his own benefit and at their expense. Not only can he abuse his power through selective application of central laws and policies, but local regulations, policies and decisions are made to systematically favour the status quo. A typical example is found in the tremendous waste of government revenue on luxurious government buildings and 'three public expenditures' (三公消费, *sangong xiaofei*), namely government vehicles, lavish public banquets and publically financed tourism in the name of 'study' and 'investigation'. For example, the town of Huangjin (Chongqin municipality) modelled its government building on Tiananmen in Beijing and financed the building by deducting the compensation for the land taken from the peasants.[6] Similarly, Yingquan district of Fuyang city (Anhui province), an area known for its poverty, modelled its offices on the White House.[7] It is ironic that many luxurious government buildings have been erected in poverty-stricken areas that survive on subsidies from the central and provincial governments. On the other hand, local public goods, such as public schools and environmental quality, are often jeopardised by serious shortages of funds. During the massive earthquake in Wenchuan, Sichuan province, in 2008, many elementary school students and teachers died in classrooms of substandard construction.[8]

B. Extensions: Villagers' Committees

In the vast countryside of China, certain executive functions are not exercised by township governments but are instead delegated to villagers' committees (村民委员会, *cunmin weiyuanhui*), which can be viewed as extensions of township governments, even though they are characterised by the Constitution as 'mass organisations of self-management at the grass-roots level' (Article 111). In fact, Article 111 is the last provision in Section 5 of Chapter III (entitled 'The Structure of the State'), which deals with LPCs and LPGs. Although elections of villagers' com-

---

[6] Nei Xiaoxiao, 'Huangjin Town of Chongqin Borrowed Debt for Its Office Building, Appearance Similar to Tiananmen', *Chongqing Times* (29 December 2004).

[7] Chen Fei and Cheng Shihua, ' "White House Secretary" of Fuyang, Anhui, Was Sentenced to Death with Reprieve during First Trial', *Jinghua Times* (9 February 2010).

[8] Yuan Yue, 'Killer Is the Building, Not the Earthquake', *Southern Weekend* (22 July 2010).

mittees were regarded as the first genuine democratic experiments in the People's Republic when they were initiated in 1988, developments in the following two decades have largely ended in failure, rendering most villagers' committees no more than extended executive arms for implementing such unpopular policies as tax or fee collection and birth control.

The Organic Law of the Villagers' Committee (OLVC) was formally adopted by the NPCSC in 1998 and most recently revised in 2010. Article 2 defines villagers committee as:

> the primary mass organisation of self-government, in which the villagers manage their own affairs, educate themselves and serve their own needs and in which election is conducted, decision adopted, administration maintained and supervision exercised by democratic means. The villagers' committee shall manage the public affairs and public welfare undertakings of the village, mediate disputes among the villagers, help maintain public order and convey the villagers' opinions and demands and make suggestions to the people's government.

Like a local government, a villagers committee is elected by and made responsible to the local assembly, which is composed of villagers aged 18 or above, whose decisions are adopted by a simple majority vote of the villagers present (OLVC, Articles 21 and 22). A villagers' assembly (村民会议, *cunmin huiyi*) reviews the annual work report of the villagers' committee, evaluates the performance of the members of the villagers' committee and has the power to cancel or modify any inappropriate decision made by the villagers' committee or the villagers' representatives' assembly (Article 23). Such important issues as change of land use must be discussed and decided by the villagers' assembly before they are dealt with by the villagers' committees (Article 24). Since a whole assembly usually involves more than a thousand villagers and is convened by the villagers committee itself (Article 21), however, most villagers' assemblies seldom convene to examine the performance of their villagers' committees. The revision of the OLVC in 2010 minimally strengthened 'villagers' representative assemblies' (村民代表会议, *cunmin daibiao huiyi*), elected by village households (Article 25) as 'parliamentary substitutes', as it were, for direct village democracy. The term of office of the villagers committee and representative assembly was debated during the revision, but unlike local governments, these village institutions remain elected for terms of three years (instead of five years, which is the case for all other levels of government), partly out of fear that unifying the terms of offices would further undermine village democracy and diminish already meagre village autonomy.[9]

In practice, most villagers' committees are supervised not so much by villagers as by township governments. The Organic Law of Villagers' Committees prohibits township governments from 'interfering with the affairs that lawfully fall within the scope of self-government by villagers', but at the same time, it authorises them to 'guide, support and help villagers' committees in their work' and requires the latter to 'assist the work' of township governments (Article 5). If the boundary between 'interference' and 'guidance', 'support' or 'help' is necessarily vague, Article 4 of the Organic Law makes it perfectly clear that 'the grassroots organisations of the CCP in the countryside shall 'play its role as the leading core, guide and support villagers' committees' exercise of functions and powers'. Indeed this is the only provision in the entire Chinese legal system in which the ruling Party is mentioned at all, and its specific role to 'guide and support' villagers' committees was emphatically asserted in the 2010 revision, casting an ominous shadow over China's village democracy and rule of law.[10]

III. TOWARD ADMINISTRATIVE RULE OF LAW?

Although rule of law has been the theme of China's reform for the past three decades, it is unsurprisingly a challenging task for a country with millennia of political despotism. In a country where officials used to be nicknamed 'parents' (父母官, *fumuguan*) and litigation against one's actual parents would amount to a felony punishable by death, the words 'administration' and 'law' had never been joined together as one expression, much less could 'administrative litigation' (行政诉讼, *xingzheng susong*) have been imagined as even a remote possibility. Despite sporadic trials during the Nationalist period, administrative law and litigation were swept into limbo by revolutionary ideology that regarded the very rule of law as a 'bourgeoisie remnant'. The economic reform period after the Cultural Revolution rehabilitated rule of law as a constitutional principle, but exercising rule of law against the powerful official

---

[9] Cai Dingjian (ed), *A Report on China's Electoral Situations* (Beijing, Law Press, 2002) 593.

[10] See further discussion below ch 9.

administration is bound to be difficult in China's historical and political context.

The Sun Zhigang incident was in fact a typical administrative case, involving both illegal police actions and dereliction of official duty.[11] It was a mistake in the first place to categorise Sun as an illegal immigrant to Guangzhou and put him in detention. And it was a failure of the detention centre personnel to prevent the assault by other inmates that caused his death. In the existing framework of administrative law, Sun's family was entitled to bring administrative litigation both against the illegal actions of the Guangzhou police department and against the detention centre for failure to fulfil official duty, and they were further entitled to claim compensation from the state for Sun's wrongful death. Yet the each step proved to be more difficult than what the plain letter of the law suggests.

A. Justifying Rule of Law: The Balance Theory

The difficulty with China's administrative law begins with its philosophical underpinning. Consistent with the Confucian cultural assumption of 'virtuous government', which was discussed above in chapter one, and the historical deficit in institutional checks and balances, China after 1949 was heavily influenced by the 'statist model' (管理论, *guanli lun*) of its Soviet ally, which advocated the agglomeration of all powers in the hands of the state in order to aid rapid industrial modernisation. This obviously left little room for checks and balances on administrative power – an institutional prerequisite for the rule of law. The latter-day economic reforms opened China to Western theories on rule of law and models of checking administrative powers (控权论, *kongquan lun*). In 1983, the first textbook on administrative law was published[12] and was followed by rapid developments in administrative law scholarship, laying the theoretical foundation for the landmark Administrative Litigation Law.[13]

More fundamentally, the basic theory of governmental administration began to be revised. While it has been difficult for China to absorb

---

[11] For detailed discussion of the case, see above ch 3.
[12] Wang Lianchan, *Studies in Administrative Law* (Beijing, Law Press, 1983).
[13] Ibid, 11–12.

wholesale Western theories that highlight checks against administrative power, the old statist model was modified to suit the new consensus that rule of law is necessary for sustained economic and social development. This has led to a 'balance model' (平衡论, *pingheng lun*) gradually being established as the prevailing theory in China's administrative law.[14] As its name indicates, the crux of the theory is to 'balance' the oft conflicting needs for exercising administrative power on behalf of the public interest on the one hand and for protecting individual rights and interests provided in the laws on the other hand. According to the 'balance school', the purpose of administrative litigation is to balance the inherently unbalanced relationship between public power and private rights. While complete individualism is neither possible nor desirable in China, individual rights are now at least weighed on one side of the balance; as their weight increases over time, they play an increasingly important role in drafting major administrative legislation.

B. Landmark Development: Administrative Litigation Law of 1990

In March 1989, the NPC passed landmark legislation aiming, for the first time in Chinese history, to put an end to administrative lawlessness: the Administrative Litigation Law (ALL). Unprecedentedly, it took 18 months for it to take effect. The ALL encompasses a new philosophy based on the balance theory, which is clearly reflected in its General Provisions (Chapter 1). Article 1 defines the goal of the ALL as 'protecting the lawful rights and interest of citizens, legal persons and other organisations, and upholding and supervising the exercise of administrative power in accordance with law'. It is now generally agreed, however, that the primary role of the ALL is to provide judicial safeguards to legitimate rights and interests against the official abuse of power. Article 2 provides that those who 'consider that a concrete administrative act by administrative organs or personnel infringes their lawful rights and interests' may bring administrative litigation to the courts.

[14] For a representative contribution, see Luo Haocai, Yuan Shuhong and Li Wendong, 'The Theoretical Foundation of Modern Administrative Law: On the Balance of Rights and Obligations between the Administrative Organ and Its Counterpart' (1993) 1 *Chinese Legal Science* 52–59.

Article 7 further underlines the equal legal status of the parties in an administrative litigation.

The provision that most obviously reflects the influence of the balance theory is Article 32, which is widely interpreted to have 'reversed' the burden of proof for administrative litigation: 'The defendant shall have the burden of proof for the concrete administrative act he has undertaken and shall provide the evidence and regulatory documents in accordance with which the act has been undertaken.' Article 33 further prohibits the defendant from collecting (as opposed to merely 'supplementing') evidence, on its own motion, from the plaintiff or witnesses once litigation has been initiated.

Major debates arising from ambiguities or apparent inconsistencies in the ALL pertain to the scope (受案范围, *shou'an fanwei*) of judicial review. While a literal reading of Article 2 seems to suggest that the violation of *any* 'lawful right or interest' by a concrete administrative act may constitute sufficient ground for bringing an administrative action, Article 11 imposes specific restrictions by listing seven categories of administrative acts against which a party may challenge at the court,[15] ending with a catch-all clause that authorises judicial review of acts that infringe 'other personal and property rights'. The last clause apparently excludes such non-personal and non-property rights as political and religious rights. Article 12 further excludes four types of actions from litigation, including 'internal decisions' (内部决定, *neibu jueding*) of an administrative organ regarding awards for or punishment of its personnel or regarding the appointment or relief of duties of its personnel, effectively barring civil servants from bringing litigation. In a few innovative judgments, however, the courts have appeared willing to extend the coverage of the ALL to include 'the right to receive education',[16] which is neither a 'personal' nor a 'property' right if rigorously construed. Although the Administrative Reconsideration Law, promulgated in 1999, does afford the 'reconsideration' (复议, *fuyi*) of such right, the ALL itself is yet to be revised to explicitly authorise such judicial extension.

---

[15] The seven categories include four types of positive acts, such as 'administrative penalties' (行政处罚, *xingzheng chufa*), and three types of negative acts, such as refusal (or failure) to protect personal and property rights as part of the legally defined duties.

[16] See, eg, Zhan Zhongle et al., '*Liu Yanwen v Beijing University*' (2000) 4 *Peking University Law Journal* 1.

Another perennial source of debate is the cryptic distinction made between 'concrete' (具体, *juti*) as opposed to 'abstract' (抽象, *chouxiang*) administrative acts, an area over which the courts lack jurisdiction, as Articles 11 and 12 of the ALL make clear. Although the Supreme People's Court (SPC) has issued judicial interpretations to clarify this distinction,[17] they are unlikely to succeed in settling the line-drawing debates that are pervasive in so many laws. Furthermore, Article 5 of the ALL explicitly limits the judicial review of concrete administrative acts to their legality (合法性, *hefa xing*) as opposed to their reasonableness (合理性, *heli xing*). As a result, a judgment usually takes only one of two forms: either sustaining a lawful act or annulling an unlawful concrete act and, if necessary, sending the case back to the same administrative organ for a second decision. As a matter of rule, a court cannot modify a decision on its own motion and based on its own judgment of the best alternative; only in exceptional cases where administrative penalties are found to be 'manifestly unjust' may courts modify the degree of the penalties (Article 54).

Consistent with its limited jurisdiction to review the legality of concrete administrative acts rather than abstract norms, much less the constitutionality of laws enacted by the NPC and the NPCSC, a court may ground its judgment only in laws or administrative and local regulations (ALL, Article 52). Administrative rules enacted by the ministries or commissions of the State Council or by provincial governments serve as 'references' (参照, *canzhao*) for deciding administrative cases (Article 53). According to common understanding, the vast number of normative documents (规范性文件, *guifanxing wenjian*) issued by the lower governments are also treated as 'references' in such cases, though the precise legal effect of a 'reference' is unclear.

Conspicuously missing among 'grounds' (or even 'references') is the Constitution. Although the Constitution is 'the fundamental law of the state with supreme legal effect' (according to the Preamble), its provisions are *not* to be applied by judges in deciding cases. A judicial interpretation in 1954 reasoned that constitutional provisions shall not be used as grounds for criminal conviction and sentencing, and another judicial interpretation in 1986 opined that constitutional provisions shall

---

[17]   (2000) 3 *Supreme People's Court Gazette* 87. See further below ch 6.

not be cited as grounds for civil judgments.[18] Although these interpretations were justified in themselves (constitutions are not generally directly applied in ordinary civil and criminal cases), they have been unjustifiably extended to exclude the application of the Constitution from *all* cases. Such a misunderstanding has not been changed by the ALL and was suspended only briefly by the Qi Yuling case in 2001, which will be discussed further below in chapter six.

C. Other Legislative Progress

The 1990s was a productive decade for Chinese administrative law. The ALL was but one major achievement, and an appreciation of the scope of the reforms is incomplete without reference to other legislative innovations, which are briefly introduced here in chronological order.

Administrative reconsideration (行政复议, *xingzheng fuyi*) was established initially as a regulation by the State Council in 1994 and enacted as law in 1999 through the Administrative Reconsideration Law (ARL). Unlike in the American administrative system, which requires plaintiffs to 'exhaust administrative remedies' before bringing litigation, a party in China may initiate an action under the ALL without going through the administrative appeal process, unless a law specifically provides otherwise. Administrative reconsideration can be a more effective device for protecting legal rights and interests since, unlike judicial review, an administrative review is not limited to the legality of a challenged act but may touch on the reasonableness of the act and modify any unreasonable acts. Furthermore, the ARL allows a party to bring collateral attack on a normative document that serves as the ground for the challenged concrete administrative act. For the first time, 'red-tape documents' (红头文件, *hongtou wenjian*) can be challenged for contradicting higher legal norms.[19] Finally, the ARL broadens the scope of administrative

[18] Supreme People's Court, 'Reply Regarding the Impropriety of Citing the Constitution as the Ground for Crime Sentencing in Criminal Law Judgments', Research Note No 11298 (1956); Supreme People's Court, 'Reply regarding How the People's Courts Cite Legal Normative Documents in Writing Law Opinions', Research Note No 31 (1986).

[19] For the first review of such a document, which was jointly issued by four ministries and commissions of the State Council with respect to the prohibition of operating computer games in internet cafes, see 'State Council's First Review of Red-Tape Produced Result', *Computer Global Daily* (24 February 2000).

review, allowing for the reconsideration of 'other concrete administrative acts that infringe lawful rights and interests', in contrast to the ALL, which is limited to reviewing only acts that infringe personal and property rights.

In 1996 the NPCSC enacted the Administrative Penalty Law (APL), a carefully drafted statute that balances the need for administrative efficiency with the protection of lawful rights and interests. This is important given the enormous number of penalties imposed by various levels of government in China. The APL carefully distinguishes six types of penalties and requires severe penalties to be regulated by higher legislation. For example, only laws enacted by the NPC or NPCSC may provide for administrative penalties that restrict personal freedom (Article 9), a principle reaffirmed in the Law on Legislation in 2000. Further, Article 31 of the APL explicitly requires that as a general principle, an administrative organ must consider the 'fact, reason, and ground' of an administrative penalty *before* it is actually made. This principle can help to cultivate a more reason-oriented and less imperious bureaucracy in China. Third and related, the Administrative Penalty Law provides for three types of procedures tailored to various penalties according to their severity; and it establishes, for the first time in China's administrative history, the right to hearing for severe penalties: if a case involves an order to cease production and management, or revocation of permits or licenses, or a 'relatively large amount' of monetary penalty, the aggrieved party may demand a hearing (Article 42). The hearing is to be open and chaired by a person appointed by the administrative organ but not directly associated with the investigation of the same case.

Obviously, administrative litigation would produce little effect without due compensation being available for victims of illegal administrative acts. Although the ALL empowers plaintiffs to seek compensation as part of administrative litigation, a more systematic framework is provided in the State Compensation Law (SCL), which was enacted in 1994 and revised in 2010. It requires the State to compensate for injuries suffered from both illegal administrative acts and criminal investigations. However, it limits compensation to injuries of personal and property rights (Articles 3 and 4), although Article 2 generally provides rights to all whose 'lawful rights and interests are injured' by the 'illegal exercise of administrative power'. In practice, not only did victims often find it difficult to win state compensation, but even if they won, the amounts of compensation were usually so meagre that the SCL was dubbed the

'No State Compensation Law'. The SCL was subsequently revised in 2010, resulting in easier procedures for claiming compensation and a broader scope for the award of damages.[20]

Having joined the World Trade Organization (WTO) in 2001, China is obliged to observe the rule of law and market principles by reducing its pervasive licensing scheme, the hallmark of a planned economy, and by increasing transparency. In 2004, the NPCSC therefore enacted the Administrative License Law, which is another systematic effort to curtail excessive and arbitrary administrative actions. It declares, for the first time, the general principles of protecting legitimate expectations and, more important, of establishing a limited government that respects market rules (Articles 12 and 13). The only drawback to this law is the apparently 'soft' enforcement mechanism, which reduces its effectiveness. Still, within two weeks after the law took effect, a case was brought that struck down the license review and approval power of the Industry and Commerce Administration.[21] In 2007, the State Council enacted the Regulation on the Disclosure of Government Information, which makes open government a fundamental principle (Articles 5 and 6). Failure to disclose may be challenged in administrative review or litigation, though winning a case has proved to be extremely difficult.[22]

D. Administrative Law Reform within Chinese Reality: A Brief Assessment

Since the promulgation of the ALL in 1989, Chinese administrative law has seen phenomenal growth, as reflected even in the number of the cases initiated, decided and appealed in the years since. Although the number of administrative cases (less than 100,000 by 1999) is still far behind the number of civil and economic cases (3.5 million and over 1.5 million, respectively, by the same year), it has clearly been rising at a much higher rate. In the decade of 1990s, while the number of civil cases almost doubled and that of economic cases increased over 1.5 times, the number of administrative cases rose more than seven times.

---

[20] Song Shijing, 'Interpreting Four Highlights of the SCL Revisions', *Procuratorate Daily* (30 April 2010).

[21] *Nanjing Knowledge Law Firm v ICAB* (2004).

[22] Wang Lin, 'Where Lies the Difficulty of the Litigating Government Information Disclosure?' *Oriental Morning Post* (16 September 2011).

Even excluding the number of withdrawals, which has been unusually high for administrative litigation, the net number of cases decided has still increased by six times. The quantity of cases does not speak to the quality of judgments, but it does suggest that administrative litigation has made headway in China, and the public has become increasingly conscious of their own rights and are increasingly willing to defend them through legal institutions.

On the other hand, these achievements cannot conceal the many conspicuous problems within China's administrative rule of law. First, although the amount of administrative litigation has multiplied, it is still a tiny proportion of the massive number of administrative decisions that affect the daily lives of ordinary Chinese people and, even among this small group of cases brought to the courts, a significant portion is 'voluntarily' withdrawn (撤诉, *cheshu*) for a variety of reasons; a plaintiff may simply withdraw her case when the government approaches her with a deal, which may be accepted out of fear of retaliation.[23] The rate of withdrawal once reached as high as 70 per cent of the administrative cases filed, although it has since declined to 30–40 per cent.[24] The ALL explicitly prohibits 'settlement' (调解, *tiaojie*) of administrative litigation precisely to prevent government coercion (Article 50), but the prohibition has been ignored in practice, particularly since the third judicial reform, which is discussed below in chapter six, has taken settlement as a major function of China's courts. Second, the primary institutional cause for the rarity of administrative cases as compared to other cases is the excessively narrow limits on the courts' jurisdiction. The limitation of scope of review to 'concrete' administrative acts was perhaps a cautious attempt to prevent a flood of litigation, but it has proved entirely unnecessary in retrospect. Another unnecessary restriction is the scope of legal interest protected, which excludes those outside 'personal' and 'property' rights.

[23] See, eg, 'What Is So Difficult with Civilians Suing Officials?' *Southern Weekend* (31 May 2001).

[24] Zhang Qianfan, 'From Administrative Rule of Law to Constitutionalism: The Changing Perspectives of Chinese Public Law' in Nak-in Sung (ed), *Constitutionalism and Constitutional Adjudication in Asia* (Seoul, Seoul National University College of Law and Korean Legislation Research Institute, 2005) 3–32. Once a plaintiff has passed through the trial process and lost, the rate of withdrawal in the appellate process is reduced to less than 10 per cent.

Ultimately, of course, China's administrative rule of law is limited by the narrow capacity of the courts to review the legality of administrative acts in the existing political framework. This problem is particularly important in administrative litigation, which pits the courts directly against the powerful state defendant. Unfortunately, the latter controls both judicial appointments and funding, raising serious doubts about judicial capacity to control administrative power.

FURTHER READING

Wang, Canfa, 'Chinese Environmental Law Enforcement: Current Deficiencies and Suggested Reforms'(2007) 8 *Vermont Journal of Environmental Law* 159.

Hand, K, 'Watching the Watchdog: China's State Compensation Law as a Remedy for Procuratorial Misconduct'(2000) 9 *Pacific Rim Law & Policy Journal* 95.

He, Haibo, 'The Dawn of the Due Process Principle in China' (2008) 22 *Columbia Journal of Asian Law* 57.

Leung, CSC, 'Chinese Administrative Law Package: Limitations and Prospects' (1998) 28 *Hong Kong Law Journal* 104.

Lin, Feng, *Administrative Law Procedures and Remedies in China* (Hong Kong, Sweet and Maxwell, 1996).

Peerenboom, R, 'Globalization, Path Dependency and the Limits of Law: Administrative Law Reform and Rule of Law in the People's Republic of China' (2001) 19 *Berkeley Journal of International Law* 161.

Zhang, Q, 'From Administrative Rule of Law to Constitutionalism: The Changing Perspectives of Chinese Public Law' (2006) 3 *Asia Law Review* 47–75.

6

De-politicising the Judiciary

————•————

INTRODUCTION: ESTABLISHING JUDICIAL REVIEW? – A Ground-breaking Mistake? The *Qi Yuling* Case of 2001 – The Failure of 'Constitutional Judicialisation' – JUDICIAL STRUCTURE AND FUNCTIONS – Traditional Deficits in Judicial Independence – Judicial Structure in the 1982 Constitution – Jurisdictions and the Role of the SPC – A Dual Judiciary? The Procuratorates – JUDICIAL REFORM: NECESSITIES, POSSIBILITIES, LIMITS – The Chinese Judicial Syndrome – Toward a More Professional Judiciary: The First and Second Five-Year Outlines of Judicial Reform – The Third Outline: 'Judicial Populism' or Back to Political Control? – The Brighter Side: The Rise of a Professional Legal Community and 'Public Interest Lawyers'

SINCE ITS FIRST experiment with 'reform and opening' in 1978, China has made a 'great leap forward' on the road toward rule of law. In the span of three decades and while recovering from the trauma of the Cultural Revolution, the National People's Congress (NPC) and its Standing Committee (NPCSC) have made 236 laws; the State Council has issued some 690 administrative regulations; and local authorities have made over 8600 local regulations.[1] The legislative frame-work seems moreover to have successfully buttressed a burgeoning economy, which so far has been the major driving force of the Chinese

---

[1] Report of the NPC Standing Committee, the Fourth Conference of the 11th National People's Congress, 10 March 2011. See also Cai Dingjian, *History and Evolution: The Historical Course of the Construction of the Legal System of New China* (Beijing, China University of Politics and Law Press, 1999) 179–97.

reforms. In early 2011, the NPCSC Chairman was confident enough to declare that China had established a 'socialist legal system'.[2]

It is commonly known, however, that the enactment of laws is not to be confused with rule of law and that having a constitution is not the same thing as making it work. Mainland China exemplifies this conventional wisdom. Although Chinese lawmakers at all levels have enacted a wide variety of laws and regulations, the country is still grappling with applying these laws to reality.[3] With regard to China's Constitution, the disparity between words and deeds is even greater for a simple reason: although civil and criminal laws are enforced by the courts, and although administrative litigation can even be entertained against officials since 1990, the 'supreme law of the land' has ironically been left undefended, at least judicially. China's constitutionalism and rule of law are surely limited by the functioning of its judiciary, which has been excessively politicised at least since 1949. And the much needed judicial reform was initiated only in 1999, twenty years after economic reform was inaugurated in Xiaogang Village in Anhui province,[4] and has so far achieved only limited progress. A depoliticised and impartial judiciary is something taken for granted in developed countries, but it is still a remote objective for China today.

This chapter will begin with a discussion of an unexpectedly bold move made by the Supreme People's Court (SPC) in 2001, when it cited the Constitution as grounds for legal interpretation for the first time in its history. This approach was not followed by later cases, however, and was formally abandoned by the end of 2008. This came as no surprise given the traditional outlook of Chinese courts, which will be discussed next, together with the structure and functions of the courts, as well as of the procurator offices, which are defined by the Chinese Constitution as another part of the judicial branch of government. The chapter will end with a discussion of China's 'judicial syndrome', a term used here to describe a series of related symptoms that keep Chinese courts from delivering impartial justice, and a series of judicial reforms aimed to cure the syndrome, though with only limited success. The brighter side of the picture is that the judicial reforms have helped to foster a group

---

[2] Chen Baocheng, 'Wu Bangguo Declares that the Chinese Legal System Has Been Established', *Southern Metropolitan Daily* (10 January 2011).

[3] See above ch 3.

[4] See above ch 2.

of 'public interest lawyers' who are ready to promote China's rule of law and human rights within the existing constitutional framework.

I. INTRODUCTION: ESTABLISHING JUDICIAL REVIEW?

For a country governed neither by democracy nor by rule of law for millennia, the absence of judicial review is nothing extraordinary; nor is China alone among the 'socialist camp' in rejecting judicial review. Leftist ideology in socialist countries typically hyperbolises popular sovereignty in opposition to any institutional control, not least against a judiciary commonly viewed as part of an 'elite' minority. Somewhat extraordinary was China's bold experiment with judicial review in 2001, two years after the inauguration of the ambitious judicial reform, which aimed to fundamentally transform the status and role of judges. That reform ultimately failed, however, even though it was followed by secondary 'judicial reforms', which departed significantly from its original direction.

A. A Ground-breaking Mistake? The *Qi Yuling* Case of 2001

The case of *Qi Yuling v Chen Xiaoqi and Others* has now become a desolate milestone in the constitutional history of China.[5] In 1990, Qi Yuling passed the entrance examination for specialised secondary professions (中专, *zhongzhuan*) and was admitted by Jining Commercial School (Shandong province). Yet her admission letter was stolen by her classmate, Chen Xiaoqi, who then studied under her name and went on to take a good job in a bank upon graduation. Qi found out about the whole affair only a decade later, during which she had unsuccessfully sought to find a decent job, owing to her lack of technical education. After she initiated litigation, the middle-level court of Tengzhou (Shangdong province) ordered the defendants to pay RMB¥35,000 for the emotional damage caused by the infringement of Qi's right to her name, which is protected by civil law;, but the court declined to provide a remedy for the alleged violation of her right to education, which is protected in Article 46 of the 1982 Constitution.

---

[5] 'Right to Education Is Not to be Violated: The Topic Introduced by the First Case on Violation of Right to Education', *Guangming Daily* (4 September 2001).

During appeal, in an extremely succinct reply to the request of the Shandong High Court for judicial interpretation, the SPC held that the plaintiff's 'basic right to education as provided by the Constitution' was violated.[6] This was the first case in which the SPC explicitly cited a constitutional provision as the legal ground for a judicial decision or interpretation. The Shandong High Court went on to order the defendants to pay RMB¥100,000 for the loss that Qi suffered from the infringement of her constitutional right to education. The decision, often hailed as China's 'first constitutional case' since it formally 'judicialises' the Constitution,[7] shocked the legal community and generated a large body of academic literature debating the propriety of 'constitutional judicialisation'.[8]

Despite minor technical problems, the first constitutional case did offer some bright hope, not only for the right to education specifically but also for the promotion of constitutionalism as a whole. Western experiences almost unanimously suggest that the words of a constitution do not count unless it is somehow 'judicialised' – in the United States by ordinary courts, in France by the special Constitutional Council and in Germany by federal and state constitutional courts. Had it been allowed to develop under its own momentum, China's constitutionalism could have travelled along a similar path, and the *Qi Yuling* case might now be known as China's *Marbury v Madison*.[9]

B. The Failure of 'Constitutional Judicialisation'

Unfortunately, subsequent developments quashed the prospect of developing constitutionally enforceable rights. Chinese judges have not taken any steps to consolidate their power in the aftermath of the *Qi Yuling* case; on the contrary, they have chosen to avoid invoking the

---

[6] 'Reply regarding whether One who Violated the Constitutionally Protected Basic Right to Education of the Citizen should Bear Civil Obligation' (2001) *Judicial Interpretation* 25.

[7] To be precise, this was not the 'first case' in which the Constitution was cited as ground for a judicial decision, since several local civil courts had done so in their judgments before; but it was the first time the SPC explicitly affirmed that constitutional provisions can be cited as independent grounds for judgment.

[8] 'The Admission Theft Event Triggered the First Case of Constitutional Judicialisation', *Southern Weekend* (16 August 2001).

[9] (1803) 137 US 5.

Constitution. Since 2001, there has not been a single 'constitutional case' to speak of. This is not to say that the People's Republic has not made any progress on constitutional issues. Indeed, in recent years there have been several cases on equality in which the plaintiffs won, either in or outside the courts, but none were decided on constitutional grounds.[10]

More fundamentally, judicial application of the Constitution has been viewed as potentially threatening to the leadership of the Chinese Communist Party (CCP). It was rumoured that the SPC circulated an internal directive forbidding courts from following the *Qi Yuling* decision, which might have explained the de facto demise of the potential precedent. In any case, the new SPC president who assumed the post in 2007 seemed to be dissatisfied even with its dysfunctional existence and moved to explicitly delete the *Qi Yuling* case from the case book. In December 2008, the SPC published a document that officially voided the legal effect of several out-dated judicial explanations, among which the *Qi Yuling* case was the only one so voided without even a brief explanation.[11] In retrospect, the demise of the *Qi Yuling* case came as no surprise. It was the product of Huang Songyou, the then progressive chief judge of the civil section of the SPC; he was under investigation for corruption by 2008,[12] and the constitutional progress he helped to initiate came to an end along with his judicial career.

The failure of the judicial experiment with constitutional review illustrates vividly the powerless and dependent status of China's judiciary and particularly of individual judges. While rank-and-file judges are obliged to follow the direction of their court presidents, lower courts are obliged to follow the direction of higher courts, and the SPC is dominated by its President. The SPC President himself is but a cadre of middle rank in the power echelon of the Party and is under the leadership of the Central Politics and Law Commission, the Secretary of which is a member (among nine) of the Politburo Standing Committee (PSC) headed by the Secretary-General of the CCP, the most powerful

---

[10] See further below ch 7.

[11] 'The Seventh Decision of the Supreme People's Court to Repeal Relevant Judicial Interpretations Released before 2007', 18 December 2008. Most of these judicial interpretations were voided either because their effective period had expired or because the circumstances in which they were enacted had changed.

[12] Recently he was sentenced to life imprisonment: Zhu Yan, 'Disagreeing with the Trial Sentence, Huang Songyou Will Appeal', *New Beijing Daily* (29 January 2010).

decision-making institution in China today. The SPC President, who is in charge of drafting and implementing plans for judicial reform, merely executes the will of the PSC. And when the President changes during a shift in the political leadership, so does the direction of judicial and constitutional reform. The lack of institutional independence thus preordained the premature death of the judicially initiated experiment with constitutional review.

II. JUDICIAL STRUCTURE AND FUNCTIONS

The lack of judicial independence is of course nothing new in Chinese history. In many ways the functioning of a judiciary is determined by its structure, and the very lack of a separate judicial structure in traditional China was telling enough. Although courts were established in modern China, the traditional lack of judicial independence has remained – indeed, it has been aggravated by the revolutionary movements that demanded a docile judiciary and eliminated any judicial impediment to the achievement of political goals.

A. Traditional Deficits in Judicial Independence

In traditional China, the judiciary was always a neglected branch of government,[13] subordinate to and often directly assumed by the same executive officer. In a local government, the 'judge' was the very same person as the executive head; whenever his authority was challenged, he would be the judge of his own cause, subject to review by the superior government. The lack of a judicial branch separate from the executive was a major source of bias, injustice and corruption. In the central gov-

---

[13] There arguably are exceptions to this categorical statement. The legendary figure Gao Yao seemed to enjoy a high status, owing to his ability to decide cases fairly. See 'The Counsels of Gao Yao' in *The Book of History* (尚书, Shangshu); for an English translation, see C Waltham, *Shu Ching: A Modernised Edition of the Translations of James Legge* (Chicago, Henry Regnery Co, 1971) 28. Legends remain legends, however, and cannot substitute for reality. The most famous judge was Lord Bao (包拯, Bao Zheng), a real figure of the Song dynasty. Sometimes called Bao Qingtian ('blue sky'), referring to the heavenly integrity that enabled him to rectify all grievances and injustices caused to the common people, he was made widely known among ordinary folk by popular theatrical performances.

ernment, the highest court was maintained as a separate institution but was subordinate to the highest executive officer.[14] In any case, judicial independence remained unknown to China until the late Qing dynasty, when Western jurisprudence was brought to China.

After the 1911 Revolution, the Nationalist government established a judicial system based on Western models and experimented with genuine judicial independence. Although wars, national exigencies and one-party dominance proved to be less than propitious for establishing a mature modern judiciary, the Nationalists did achieve some success, which has been inherited and carried forward by Taiwan following the Nationalist retreat in 1949. After the murder of the Nationalist leader Song Jiaoren in 1913, for example, the district prosecutor in Shanghai was courageous enough to summon the Premier to question him about his role in the plot.[15] Although the latter failed to appear in the court, citing illness as an excuse, the event demonstrated a considerable degree of judicial independence that is unthinkable today.

The Western-type judicial developments were too short-lived to take root in China before they were pushed aside by the Communist revolution that succeeded in 1949. If the judiciary was kept relatively independent under the Nationalist one-party rule, it has consistently been treated as ordinary state machinery under Communist rule, essentially no different from other state organs that are primarily executive in nature. For example, it shares with the public security bureau and the procuratorate the common role of enforcing the 'proletarian dictatorship'. A directive of the central government in 1950 declared that 'the people's judicial work is just like the people's army and the people's police; it is one of the important tools of the people's government.'[16] As a result, China's judiciary was seen as the functional equivalent of the army and police force – the 'knife handle' (刀把子, *daobazi*) of the ruling party.[17] It is thus hardly surprising that until recently, Chinese judges

[14] During the Qing Dynasty, for example, the top judiciary, Dalisi (大理寺), was subordinate to the prime minister (宰相, *zaixiang*). Of course, it was also subject to direct intervention by the Emperor. See Qu Tongzu, *Chinese Society and Chinese Law* (Beijing, Zhonghua Shuju, 1981).

[15] Yuan Weishi, 'The Historical Experience of Political Strategy and Early Republican Constitutionalism' (2000) 6 *Strategy and Administration* 1.

[16] The Central Government's Directive for Strengthening the Work of the People's Judiciary, 3 November 1950.

[17] He Rikai, 'The Judicial Reform: From Power to Authority' (1999) 4 *Law Science* 30–38.

looked remarkably similar in appearance to soldiers and police officers, wearing military-style uniforms with starred epaulets.[18]

The judicial reform in 1952 further consolidated Party leadership over the judiciary. By 1957, however, Party control was under serious attack within the Chinese judicial circle. The protest backfired and intensified the political control, leading to the purge of over 6,000 'old law officers' (旧法人员, *jiufa renyuan*), ie, those Nationalist judges and clerks who remained on the mainland after 1949 and contributed to the pool of extremely scarce judicial resource in Communist China. In the civil division of the Shanghai second middle-level court, for example, eight out of 20 judges were declared 'rightists' (右派, *youpai*),[19] and their vacancies were filled by revolutionary activists who had little if any legal training. Such a 'purified' judiciary could not, of course, be expected to present itself as even a minimal impediment to grave human catastrophes like the Great Leap Forward and the Cultural Revolution.

B. Judicial Structure in the 1982 Constitution

Recovering from the lawless destruction of the Cultural Revolution and recognising the importance of law, the 1982 Constitution reaffirms the courts as 'judicial organs of the state' (Article 123). They are comprised of the SPC, local courts at various levels, military courts and other special courts. As heirs of the revolutionary tradition, these courts are not independent but subject to the supervision of the People's Congresses at the same levels (Article 128). Article 126 of the Constitution does provide that 'the people's courts exercise judicial power independently, in accordance with the provisions of the law, and are not subject to interference by any administrative organ, public organisation or individual'. But the significance of this provision has been questioned on at least two grounds. First, it excludes interference from the government, individuals, organisations and possibly political parties, if they are interpreted to be a form of 'public organisation', but it is silent about People's Congresses

[18] On 1 July 2000, judges nationwide began to wear the uniform specially designed for them as civil officers, yet the new uniform apparently failed to bring about a new judicial culture among Chinese judges.

[19] Tie Li and Lu Jingbi, 'A Defective Judicial Reform: A Study of Important Events in the Legal Community since the Establishment of the State' (1998) 6 *Legal Science Monthly* 2–5.

and the Procuratorates. In fact, it is these institutions that are in charge of supervising the courts – the former through the election of the judges and supervision of court performance as a whole, and the latter through the protestation procedures used against individual judgments, which means that those judgments can simply be deemed wrong.

It was once debated whether the People's Congresses could supervise individual cases (个案监督, *ge'an jiandu*), and this question has been answered in the negative; deputies may, according to the Constitution and other laws, investigate or remove judges who improperly performed their functions, but such power does not authorise them to inquire into cases they found wrongfully decided.[20]

Second and more profound, Article 126 of the Constitution provides for 'court independence' rather than the independence of individual judges. Literally understood, a court enjoys institutional protection against interference from other institutions or individuals, but individual judges do not enjoy the same protection in daily judicial practice; in other words, they may be subject to the direction and supervision of court leaders, and in fact they are. The Organic Law of the People's Courts (OLPC) establishes the so-called 'president responsibility system' (院长负责制, *yuanzhang fuzezhi*), by which a court president, assisted by the judicial committee (审判委员会, *shenpan weiyuanhui*), is held responsible for all the judgments made by that court. If the president finds 'definite error in the determination of facts or application of law' in a legally effective judgment of his court, he is obliged to submit the judgment to the judicial committee for disposal (OLPC, Article 14). Presided over by the court president and staffed by the vice presidents, the Party secretary, the chief judges of divisions and senior judges, the judicial committee is a 'court' within the court whose major task is to practice 'democratic centralism' by 'summing up judicial experience and discussing important or difficult cases' (OLPC, Article 11). In fact, such committees directly decide cases and can replace different judgments made by presiding judges, even though none of the committee members may have heard the cases.

Against this background, Article 8 of the Judges Law – which lists a number of judges' rights, among which is 'to brook no interference

---

[20] Cai Dingjian, 'The Current Status and the Reform of the People's Congress's Individual Case Supervision' in Cai Dingjian, *Supervision and Judicial Fairness: A Study and Case Report* (Beijing, Law Press, 2005) 69.

from administrative organs, public organisations or individuals in trying cases according to law' (clause 2) – must be understood as a heedless slip of the pen. In fact, the same law establishes a more rigorous assessment and reward/punishment scheme for judges, whose performance is evaluated by a 'commission of examination and assessment' headed by the court president (Articles 48 and 49). Judges are also divided into twelve 'grades', to be 'determined on the basis of their posts, their actual working ability and political integrity, their professional competence, their achievements in judicial work and their seniority' (Article 19). In such a tightly regulated scheme, an individual judge can hardly find any space for independent judgment based on her own conscience, free from interference of her own court. And judges with enough courage to insist on independent judgments will sooner or later be purged. For example, Wang Guangya (王光亚), a judge at Fuping county court (Shaanxi province), was officially denounced and removed for arguing with the judicial committee and 'adamantly refusing to admit his errors'.[21] Jia Tingrun (贾庭润), the former president of the Lulong county court (Henan province), was also removed for refusing to follow the direction of the 'superiors' and suffered from reductions in rank and salary.[22] These painful 'lessons' served sufficient deterrent to independent judges, making 'judges' independence' impossible.

Nor is the constitutional provision for the institutional independence of the courts implemented in practice. The *Luoyang Seed* Case, discussed above in chapter three, clearly illustrates how a court is controlled (or 'supervised') by its Local People's Congress (LPC) and the superior courts, which are ultimately all controlled by the ruling party. The seemingly reasonable judgment in that case, which defended the supremacy of the national Seed Law against a local regulation, sparked unexpectedly strong reaction from the Henan LPC Standing Committee (LPCSC), which had enacted the disputed regulation and had the power to supervise the Henan provincial high court and the Luoyang city LPC, both authorised to 'supervise' the Luoyang city court. Denouncing the court judgment as 'serious illegal act' that 'essentially constituted legality review of the local regulation enacted by the provincial LPCSC, and

---

[21] 'It's No Crime to Decide Cases according to Law', *People's Daily* (22 February 2001); Huang Guangming, 'A Judge's Cost for "Disobeying the Superior" ', *Southern Weekend* (22 March 2001).

[22] Guo Guosong, 'How Difficult Is It for Judge to Abide by His Conscience', *Southern Weekend* (5 December 2002).

violated the People's Congress institution of our country and the authority properly belonging to the organ of state power', it pressured the provincial high court to 'treat seriously' and the city LPCSC to 'correct' the 'illegal act' and to take actions against the 'directly responsible judge and leaders in charge'.[23] According to these harsh demands, the leading Party group of the city court decided to revoke the status of presiding judge and the assistant judgeship of Li Huijuan (李慧娟), the trial judge, as well as the position of the vice division chief who issued the judgment. Only under sharp national criticism, particularly from the legal community, did the city court withdraw the disciplinary decision and restore Li Huijuan's judgeship.

C. Jurisdictions and the Role of the SPC

Although the entire judiciary is under the name of 'people's court', China's courts resemble not so much the American courts of general jurisdiction as the German courts of special jurisdiction. Although jurisdictional divisions shift and vary by levels and locations, an ordinary court is usually divided into the following substructures: civil divisions for civil, commercial and intellectual property cases; a criminal division for criminal cases; an administrative division for administrative litigation; a filing (立案, *li'an*) division in charge of filing of cases; a judicial supervision (审监, *shenjian*) division for reviewing cases that either superior courts order for retrial or the procuratorates at the lower level protest; and an enforcement division.[24] For practical purposes, a division operates as a separate court; eg, the administrative division within a court is tantamount to an administrative court for hearing administrative litigation. A 'division' is not identical to a 'court', however, especially if one takes into account that a judicial committee, which plays a decisive role in important cases, is composed of leaders from the whole court.

Vertically, China's courts are divided into four levels: the SPC, the 'highest judicial organ' in the nation (Constitution, Article 127); a high court for each province, municipality and autonomous region; middle-level courts

---

[23] Guo Guosong, 'The Judge Struck Down a Local Regulation: Is She Violating the Law or Vindicating the Law?' *Southern Weekend* (20 November 2003).

[24] Conspicuously absent is a constitutional court, since the Constitution is not legally enforceable. Here China departs from the Continental model, the legal system to which it generally adheres.

for the cities that are divided into districts; and basic-level (基层, *jiceng*) courts for counties, city districts and cities that are not divided into districts (OLPC, Articles 18, 23 and 26). The level of court to which a specific case should be brought depends on the importance of the case. Usually the trial process is initiated at a basic-level court, but important cases can be moved to higher courts upon the lower court's petition (Articles 21 and 25). In administrative litigation, for example, the higher courts are responsible for trying the 'major' (重大, *zhongda*), 'complex' (复杂, *fuza*) and 'difficult' (疑难, *yinan*) cases within their respective jurisdictions or other cases specified by law (Administrative Litigation Law, Articles 14–16).[25] The administrative division of a middle-level court is also responsible for trying cases that involve custom disputes or identification of patents, as well as cases in which the defendants are provincial governments or ministries or commissions of the State Council (Article 14). The judgment of a trial court can be appealed once to its superior court, where the judicial process normally ends.

The SPC, composed of over 250 judges divided into special jurisdictions, is the highest authority for review cases appealed from the lower courts; it can even serve as a trial court in exceptional cases (eg, in the public trial of the 'Gang of Four' in 1980[26]). In reality, however, the SPC rarely decides concrete cases except in the approval of death sentences, an area for which a special section has been created, essentially to act as an extra review as a final appellate judgment.[27] The main function of the SPC is to issue 'judicial explanations' (司法解释, *sifa jieshi*) of statutes or regulations and a variety of advisory opinions to the lower courts. Its bimonthly publication, the *SPC Gazette*, does contain exemplary decisions made mainly by lower courts, but the legal effect of these decisions is unclear, since China, in following the Continental legal tradition, does not recognise the binding effects of 'precedents'. Although the recent judicial reform highlights the SPC role in establishing a 'case guidance system' in order to improve uniformity and certainty of judicial decisions, that system is a far cry from the full-fledged common law system of precedent. The exemplary judgments in the *SPC Gazette* at best represent approval by the nation's highest court and may serve as signposts for the lower courts to follow in deciding similar cases. But

[25] As Art 16 of the ALL provides, even the SPC will sit as a trial court for 'significant and complex' administrative cases of 'national scope'.

[26] See above ch 2.

[27] See below ch 7.

since these decisions are not 'precedents' in any sense, lower courts are not obligated by law to follow them, and there is no evidence that any of them are consistently followed at all.

The lower courts are obliged, however, to follow the judicial interpretations of the SPC, which are in essence pieces of secondary legislation that specify how provisions in primary legislation should be applied to specific cases. For example, Article 12 of the Administrative Litigation Law prohibits courts from reviewing abstract acts with 'general binding force' (clause 2), and the SPC has interpreted that clause to mean 'normative documents directed to non-specific parties and capable of repeated applications'.[28] In certain circumstances, judicial interpretations serve to supplement or extend the provisions in the original laws. Article 25 of the Administrative Litigations Law, for example, seems to limit the defendants in administrative litigations to organisations 'authorised to undertake an act by the law or regulations', without including rules (规章, *guizhang*) made by local governments or departments in the State Council. By interpreting that provision to mean organisations authorised not only by laws and regulations but also by rules, the SPC extended the scope of defendants against whom administrative litigation can be legally brought.[29]

That a *court* is empowered to establish binding abstract norms raises serious questions about judicial legitimacy. In fact, Article 42 of the Law on Legislation explicitly provides that the 'power to interpret law' belongs to the NPCSC, apparently negating the long-standing tradition of judicial interpretation. Yet, untouched by the enactment of this law in 2000, the tradition of judicial interpretation is vital as ever today – and necessarily so, since the NPCSC interpretations rarely go beyond the area of criminal law, making the SPC an indispensable institution for interpreting laws in general.

D. A Dual Judiciary? The Procuratorate

Finally, one must be reminded that China's 'judiciary', when spoken of in a broad sense, is not just the courts; it is also the procurators, the

---

[28] Supreme People's Court, 'Interpretation of Several Problems regarding the Implementation of the PRC Administrative Litigation Law' (2000) 8 *Law Interpretations* 3.

[29] Ibid, 20. See (2000) 3 *Supreme People's Court Gazette* 87–93.

equivalent of prosecutors, who are usually treated in the West as having an administrative rather than judicial function, although there is debate about the issue.[30] The procuratorate figured prominently throughout the imperial period in China, when the country could rely neither on popularly elected parliaments nor on law courts to check against abuses of public power. Han Yu (韩愈, c 768–824), a famous poet of the Tang dynasty, for example, served as imperial procurator (御史台, *yushitai*), who had the power to impeach high court officials and even to criticise the Emperor himself.[31] In many ways the procuratorate of the People's Republic ranks higher in power and importance than the courts, though lower than the public security bureaus (PSBs). The 1982 Constitution places both the procuratorate, 'the state organ for legal supervision' (Article 129), and the courts under section 7 in Chapter 3 and provides a similar institutional structure for both branches, including protection for procutorial independence against administrative interference (Article 131). Hence the constitutional structure of 'one government, two chambers' (一府两院, *yifu liangyuan*), each separate and independent from the other and both under the supervision of the People's Congresses.

Article 5 of the Organic Law of the People's Procuratorates provides for five types of powers, three of which are most commonly used. First, the procuratorates may directly conduct investigations of criminal cases, usually involving malfeasance or corruption of state officials (clause 2). An 'anti-corruption bureau' (反贪局, *fantanju*) has been established within each procuratorate to work together with the Party's 'commission for discipline inspection' (纪律检查委员会, *jilu jiancha weiyuanhui*) to investigate rapidly rising corruption over the past decades. Second, the procuratorates' primary function is to review cases investigated by the PSB and 'determine whether to approve arrest, to prosecute or to exempt from prosecution', and to 'exercise supervision over the investigatory activities' of the PSBs to ensure their legality (clause 3). Third, for those criminal cases that have been approved for prosecution, the procuratorates are responsible for conducting the public prosecutions and, somewhat peculiarly, 'exercising supervision over the judicial activities of people's courts' in order to ensure the legality of the judicial

[30]   See, eg, the debates in the American context about the constitutionality of 'special prosecutors': *Morrison v Olson* (1988) 487 US 654.

[31]   But Han Yu himself was demoted for offending the Emperor with his unsparingly critical words. See He Chengxuan, *The History of Southern Extension of Confucianism* (Beijing, Peking University Press, 2000) 186.

judgments (clause 4). If a local procuratorate discovers any error in the judgment of a case of first instance, it shall lodge a 'protest' (抗诉, *kangsu*) and appeal the case to the higher court (Article 17).

For criminal investigations and trials, the Constitution requires the courts, the procuratorates and the PSBs 'to divide their functions, each taking responsibility for its own work, and to coordinate their efforts and check each other to ensure the correct and effective enforcement of the law' (Article 135). A PSB investigates, takes into custody, arrests and conducts the pre-trial of a criminal case; the procuratorate is in charge of approving the arrest and prosecution and conducting the prosecution; and the court shall decide the case according to law. Although the Criminal Procedure Law defines the procedure and timing of each stage, these safeguards have often been evaded, resulting in rather frequent extortion for confessions (刑讯逼供, *xingxun bigong*) and extended detentions (超期羁押, *chaoqi jiya*).[32] The courts, usually the least powerful if not 'the least dangerous' branch of the three, are simply too weak to protect suspects from illegal treatment by the PSBs or the procuratorates.

III. JUDICIAL REFORM: NECESSITIES, POSSIBILITIES, LIMITS

After the great devastation of the Cultural Revolution, China's judicial system recovered beginning from the ground level, and over the past three decades, the judicial system has grown phenomenally. By 1997 the number of judges and procurators exceeded 290,000 and 210,000 respectively.[33] In the meantime, the number of lawyers reached 100,000; notary public offices had been established across the country; and legal aid centres mushroomed in the cities.[34] Since then, the number of judges and procurators has remained largely steady, but the number of lawyers has continued to increase and by 2011 exceeded 200,000. Decades of politicisation have mired China's judiciary, however, in a 'judicial syndrome' that

---

[32] See below ch 7.

[33] One problem is that the Chinese definition of 'judge' is much broader than the Western definition, so that the reform has to deal with so many 'judges' of low professional quality.

[34] For a review of the contribution of the nongovernmental sector (the 'NGOs') to the rule of law in China, see CD Lee, 'Legal Reform in China: A Role for Nongovernmental Organizations' (2000) 25 *Yale Journal of International Law* 363.

both calls for and sets limits to judicial reform. With regard to this 'syndrome', the 'judiciary' is to be understood in the narrower sense – as the courts, since they are commonly expected to be the last guardians of rule of law, and their individual and institutional independence must be carefully protected against administrative and political encroachment.

A. The Chinese Judicial Syndrome

The Chinese judicial syndrome is an interlocking combination of dysfunctional symptoms: (1) local protectionism that seriously undermines the uniformity of law; (2) overall low professional and moral quality of judges, making them prone to corruption and unfit for impartial administration of justice; (3) bureaucratic management of the courts and political control of the judges, which are at odds with the generally recognised principle of judicial independence and impartiality; and (4) the lack of adequate material provisions (salary, funding and working conditions) for the effective functioning of the courts.[35]

These symptoms result from both personal and institutional dysfunctions. At the institutional level, China's judges are too many in number and too poorly paid, lacking sufficient salaries and funding for properly carrying out judicial functions. It is perhaps a peculiar 'Chinese phenomenon' to define 'judges' so loosely that they number over 300,000, – greatly exceeding the number of lawyers,[36] even though only a portion of the 'judges' actually participate in *judging* cases. A large body of non-professional 'judges' means that each of them is unlikely to be adequately paid. In poor areas, courts hardly find enough funding to maintain basic operation and a dignified external image;[37] court presidents have even been nicknamed 'Mr Public Relations' or, more scathingly, 'beggars carrying a scale (of justice)' for soliciting funds.[38]

---

[35] Q Zhang, 'The People's Court in Transition: The Prospects of the Chinese Judicial Reform' (2003) 12 *Journal of Contemporary China* 69.

[36] Wang Chengguang, 'Judicial Efficiency and the Reform of Internal Operating System of the Courts' (1998) 10 *Legal Science Monthly* 46–51.

[37] For a widely cited report that the acute lack of funding had led the Chinese courts to take various forms of profit-seeking behaviour, see 'Serious Shortage of Judicial Funding in the Basic-Level Courts in the Poor Areas' (1993) 7 *May People's Court Daily*.

[38] Hao Tiechuan, 'On Governing the State according to Law in the Transitional Period of Chinese Society' (2000) 2 *Chinese Legal Science* 7.

On the other hand, the local control of judicial finances and appointments has made China's courts excessively responsive to local demands, at the expense of judicial integrity and the national uniformity of laws. Added to that, administrative control within the courts further depresses judges' independent spirit and distorts their moral personalities, turning them into 'yes-men' of the court presidents and, in some cases, even into willing abettors and beneficiaries of judicial corruption. Nowadays corruption of individual judges no longer constitutes 'news'; only collective corruption of entire courts raises eyebrows.

A poor institutional environment contributes to the deteriorating professional quality of China's judges by making it difficult for the courts to attract young talent. Many 'judges' lack the proper legal training and analytical ability that is necessary to hear and decide cases; even among competent judges, the number of those who have graduated from various extension training programs greatly exceeds those who are formal law graduates.[39] According to a survey conducted in the late 1990s, only 5.6 per cent of judges nationwide had earned formal undergraduate degrees, and only 25 among a thousand judges had earned graduate degrees.[40] Even in Beijing, where the education level of judges is among the highest in the nation, only 10 per cent had obtained formal undergraduate degrees and, among this small number, it was unclear what percentage were formally educated in law.[41]

The overall low quality of the judges, poor working conditions and a restrictive institutional environment have combined to produce the 'judicial syndrome' that has made China's courts easily corruptible places, which in turn hamstrings any attempt at judicial reform. After all, a genuine judicial reform must begin by removing some of the political and bureaucratic controls over individual judges, instead giving them more independence, trust and freedom. If, however, the judges are already corrupt and prove to be corrupt even when they are overseen by various supervisory mechanisms, can China really afford to grant them more independence? While more independence may well provide extra opportunity for judicial corruption, tightening supervision to curb

[39] See Li Hanchang, 'An Overview of the Judges' Quality and Judicial Education in the Background of Judicial Institutional Reform' (2000) 1 *Chinese Legal Science* 49.

[40] Ma Junjü and Nie Dezong, 'The Existing Problems in Our Current Judicial System and the Strategies for Improvement' (1998) 6 *Legal Science Review* 25–30.

[41] Cai Dingjian, 'Preliminary Comments on the Reform of the Court System' (1999) 1 *Strategies and Management* 97–102.

corruption may simply take China's judiciary back to the pre-reform era, when the courts were simply a political instrument for the ruling party.

B. Toward a More Professional Judiciary: The First and Second Five-Year Outlines of Judicial Reform

Is it possible, then, to cure the judicial syndrome? The Chinese legal community answered affirmatively in October 1999 with a blueprint for a fundamental reform. For the first time in its five-decade history, the SPC published an Outline of Five-Year Reform for the People's Courts (hereafter 'First Outline'). A result of years of academic criticism and local experimentation, the Outline vowed to improve the existing judicial structure in China, to enhance the power and autonomy of individual judges and to guarantee judicial efficiency and fairness. Undertaking to make China's judges 'real judges',[42] this ambitious reform aimed to professionalise the hitherto politicised courts and did successfully change the outward appearance of the judicial figure from army uniform and starred epaulets to black robes and gavel. Furthermore, judges were to be more carefully selected from the existing stock of judicial tribunals and lawyers who had established records of good performance.[43] In the meantime, those judges unable to meet the professional standard would be laid off.

The reform also aimed to improve the quality of reasoning in judicial opinions. Chinese judicial decisions had been notoriously sparse on legal reasoning; the so-called 'reasoning' is more often than not a pretext for prejudged conclusions.[44] The situation was exacerbated by a lack of transparency: judicial opinions are normally available only to the specific parties rather than to society at large. Such shelter from the public exposure only encourages shoddy opinions and secret deals. To remedy this problem in criminal trials, the SPC drafted in 1999 the Model Format for Judicial Opinions in Criminal Trials, which emphasises a need for

---

[42] Words expressed by the former SPC president, Xiao Yang, who was instrumental in hammering out the first five-year plan for the judicial reform. See *Xinhua Daily* (25 October 1999).

[43] *Xinhua Daily* (25 October 1999) B1.

[44] See Wang Yong, 'The Reversed and the Neglected Legal Reasoning', *Legal Daily* (27 February 2000) 3.

legal reasoning in all types of judgments.[45] From June 2000, the SPC also began to publish judicial opinions of 'particularly important and typical' cases in the *SPC Gazette*, the *People's Court Daily* and on the Internet.[46] The publication of opinions has so far been highly selective, however, and it is impossible to say if ordinary opinions will ever be publically accessible.

The First Five-Year Outline did relatively little with respect to the institutional structure of the courts, local protectionism and judicial corruption. It did modernise the trial process by explicitly separating the filing, trial, enforcement and supervision stages of cases. These measures helped to prevent ex parte contacts with judges and to eliminate the egregious 'three-together' (三同, *santong*) phenomena, whereby a judge would travel, dine and lodge together with the plaintiff at the latter's expense under the pretence of conducting investigation outside his jurisdiction.[47]

The SPC also fashioned an institutional mechanism to reduce local protectionism by requiring provincial high courts to establish special enforcement divisions or bureaus.[48] The mechanism was expected to streamline the overall enforcement process and reduce the pervasive 'enforcement difficulty' (执行难, *zhixing nan*), which became even more conspicuous when unfavourable judgments had to be enforced in other provinces, where a losing party could easily collude with local authorities to resist enforcement. Rather than making a court directly enforce its judgment outside its jurisdiction, the new mechanism delegated the task to the enforcement bureau of the province in which the judgment was to be enforced. Of course, to root out local protectionism, court financial structures needed to be overhauled, and local courts could no longer rely on the local governments to provide for their necessities but instead were to receive funding directly from the central treasury.[49] Although

---

[45] Li Yanfeng, 'Xiao Yang Teaches Students at the Judge Institute, Emphasising Active and Stable Push for the Court Reform', *People's Court Daily* (2 June 2000).

[46] http://www.court.gov.cn. See Supreme People's Court, 'Method for Administering the Publication of Judicial Opinions' (2000) 4 *SPC Gazette* 118; *Xinhua Daily* (20 June 2000); and *Beijing Youth News* (28 November 2000).

[47] Wan Exiang, 'Deepening Judicial Reform, Guaranteeing Judicial Fairness' (1999) 3 *Law Review* 1–2.

[48] See reports in *People's Court Daily* (2 November 2000); and *People's Daily* (6 November 2000).

[49] For supporting arguments made by the former president of the SPC, see Zheng Tianxiang, *On Governing the State according to Law* (Beijing, People's Court Press, 1999).

there was talk of making court financing more 'vertically' dependent (on the central government as opposed to the 'horizontal' dependence on local government), these words have not been converted to policy actions.

The First Outline aroused many expectations on badly needed judicial reform. In retrospect, however, its achievements were limited at best. While China's judges now wear robes and hold gavels, the opinions they write suggest that the extent of change in their minds has been far less than the change in their appearance. An increase in the number of law schools and, consequently, the number of law graduates has resolved the problem of professional quality for courts in urban centres such as Beijing and Shanghai, but the problem persists for courts in less developed areas, particularly poor rural areas that are unable to provide any attractions to talented candidates.

Fundamentally, in the same institutional structure that stifles free inquiry and independent reasoning, legal knowledge and techniques can be more easily used to conceal corrupt minds than to serve justice, and professionally qualified legal minds can easily be converted into moral delinquents who hide behind the camouflage of legal language. This point was well illustrated in the infamous case of Li Zhuang (李庄), a defence attorney who was victimised in the 'strike-mafia' (打黑, *dahei*) campaign in Chongqing.[50] The presiding judges defended the obviously defective criminal procedure in their judgment (eg, the failure to cross-examine the defendant's witnesses), despite the fact that some of them had doctoral degrees in law and had published in law journals. Like other forms of power, legal knowledge can be gravely misused in the wrong institutional context.

What the First Five-Year Outline left unaccomplished should have been picked up by the next wave of reform, but the momentum generated by the first Outline seems to have subsided considerably by 2005, when the Second Outline of Five-Year Reform of the People's Courts (2004–08) was published and implemented by the SPC under the same President, Xiao Yang (肖扬). Compared to its predecessor, the Second Outline was much more cautious in goal-setting and limited itself to technical reforms, such as the establishment of a unified bar examina-

---

[50] Li Zhuang was the defence attorney for one of the allegedly corrupt officials prosecuted in the Chongqing campaign, and was charged for, among other things, instigating the defendant to provide false testimony. Zhao Lei, 'The Li Zhuang Case: Contests In and Outside the Court', *Southern Weekend* (6 January 2010).

tion scheme and a 'case guidance system'; the prohibition of extortion for confession and extended detention; and the withdrawal of the provincial high courts' power to review death sentences.

C. The Third Outline: 'Judicial Populism' or Back to Political Control?

More than a decade after its inauguration, judicial reform in China had reached a crossroad, apparently having lost both momentum and direction. By the end of period covered by the Second Outline, the SPC was led by a new president, who had a new philosophy of reform. While professionalisation had been the goal, the new SPC allied with several legal scholars in advocating 'judicial populism' (司法大众化, *sifa dazhonghua*) for the people's courts and returned to an out-dated mass trial model that was once practiced in the Communist base of Yan'an during the 1940s. In effect, far from inviting ordinary people to participate in the 'people's courts', this line of judicial reform – if worthy of that name at all – seems like only to further undermine judicial fairness and invite even more political interference in activities that properly belong to courts. If the revocation of the legal effect of the Qi Yuling decision at the end of 2008 indicated the departure from the Western line of judicial reform initiated by the previous SPC, the Li Zhuang case in 2009 simply reminded the Chinese people of the damage that a complete retreat to the old revolutionary days can do to rule of law.

The main thrust of 'judicial populism' is to ensure that judgments will 'satisfy the people' (让人民满意, *rang renmin manyi*) and reduce social conflict in order to 'maintain stability' (维稳, *weiwen*), an overriding theme repeatedly emphasised by the Central Politburo Standing Committee. The official position is supported by a minority of legal scholars who advocate 'popular trials' (民意审判, *minyi shenpan*) and insist that judicial decisions should be made by the people rather than by judges.[51] Such a proposition confuses the judicial process with law-making, a democratic process that ultimately should 'satisfy' the public interest. In China, where the democratic law-making process has been

---

[51] Zhang Qianfan, 'Judicial Populism Is a False Proposition', *Economic Observer Daily* (26 July 2008); and He Bing, 'Is Judicial Democracy a False Proposition?' *Economic Observer Daily* (28 August 2008).

institutionally impaired, however, such a proposal has considerable appeal, since neither the NPC nor its Standing Committee keeps up with amending laws to adapt them to the changing demands of a fast developing society.

The Xu Ting case is telling evidence of this point. In April 2006, Xu Ting (许霆) made over 170 withdrawals from a malfunctioning ATM in Guangzhou, illegally obtaining a total of RMB¥170000 (roughly USD$25,000), which constituted an 'extraordinarily large sum' under a provision of the Criminal Law enacted in 1979. As a result, he was sentenced to life imprisonment. Like the Sun Zhigang case, the judgment excited strong public protest; although that sum may have been 'extraordinarily large' three decades ago, it is unthinkable today that this amount deserves such a disproportionate penalty as life imprisonment. The failure of the NPCSC to update the law – or, more precisely, to update its interpretation of the law – obliged the people to step out, express their disapproval and demand the court adjust its application of an out-dated law to specific cases. After requesting instruction from the SPC, which was apparently concerned with the mounting public pressure, the middle-level court of Guangzhou changed the sentence to five years' imprisonment.[52]

Although the Xu Ting case can be counted as a victory for 'judicial populism', such a process may lead both to sensational media coverage that fails to thoroughly examine stories and to demands by society at large for the government to take action. Under these circumstances, the court will likely be ordered to render whatever judgment will preserve the government's image and appease the public. Nor can ad hoc popular intervention promise any consistency of judgments in similar cases. A similar case, for example, occurred in Yunnan province, where an undergraduate illegally obtained over RMB¥400,000 and was sentenced to life imprisonment even though he had returned the money to the authorities, and he had already been in prison for seven years by the time the Xu Ting case was publically debated in 2008.[53]

More importantly, the 'people' are not always right. In April 2002, Liu Yong (刘涌), a rich merchant and the leader of a gang that was respon-

---

[52] Li Zhaotao et al, 'Xu Ting's Lenient Sentence Provoked Amazements on the Court, which Explained that Special Cases Should Receive Special Sentencing', *Information Times* (1 April 2008).

[53] See 'The Yunnan Version of the "Xu Ting Case" may Change its Sentencing', *Chutian Metropolitan Daily* (16 April 2008).

sible for one killing and 16 serious injuries in Shenyang city, was sentenced to death for murder. The judgment was quashed on appeal for lack of sufficient evidence and for suspicion that the confession was obtained by torture. Although most jurists in criminal law approved of the appellate judgment, the decision excited strong public protest out of hatred of criminal gangs. In December 2003, the SPC unprecedentedly took over the retrial and reverted the judgment back to a death sentence in order to appease public anger, despite the serious procedural breaches revealed by the appeal.[54]

In April 2008, the new SPC President expressed in a public speech that courts shall consider the nature of an unlawful act, its social harm and the people's 'feelings' in deciding whether a death sentence should be issued. Such an arbitrary standard can serve only to undermine justice and rule of law and to invite arbitrary political inference, out of a desire to 'maintain stability' and 'satisfy the people', much in the same way as the courts were used as the 'knife handle' for pursuing political ends at the expense of justice in the pre-reform past.

Moreover, the result-oriented approach proved unable to 'satisfy the people' in the famous Deng Yujiao (邓玉娇) case in 2009.[55] Deng, a hotel servant in Badong county, Hunan province, killed a local official while allegedly resisting attempted rape. Although the case excited enormous public attention, the Badong authority denied the rape attempt, harassed the defendant's family and attorneys, and refused to disclose the exact details of the case. At the end of the trial, Deng was essentially acquitted by the court, which apparently yielded to the public pressure. Since there was insufficient evidence for self-defence, however, the court had difficulty justifying the acquittal. Such an unconvincing judgment did not excite another wave of public anger but neither did it earn respect for the court from the public and 'satisfy the people', so to speak.

The retreat of the third reform, if still a meaningful 'reform', merely illustrates the inherent limits common to all judicial reform. Ambitious as it was, the very first reform failed to change the judges' thinking and, more fundamentally, the power structures both within and outside the courts – particularly the relationship between the courts and the ruling

---

[54] 'Supreme Court Brings "Liu Yong Case" to Trial Today with Two "Anticipations" ', *Beijing Morning Post* (18 December 2003).

[55] 'Deng Yujiao's Mother Suddenly "Fired" Lawyer', *Oriental Morning Post* (24 May 2009).

party. Just as judges are under the leadership of their court presidents, court presidents are under the leadership of the CCP, making the judicial structure as a whole prone to political interference. In fact, the First Five-Year Outline explicitly declared 'Party leadership' as a guiding principle of the reform. This might be a wise strategy for diverting political challenges from conservatives, but it also highlighted the bottom-line beyond which no reform has been allowed to proceed.

The Party may intervene in the judicial process in many ways.[56] First and most obviously, the presidents and vice presidents of a court are usually Party members and subject to Party discipline. Since the president is held responsible for the whole court, the Party can easily control the entire court through the presidential responsibility system and judicial committee system,[57] by which it can supervise any judicial judgments that involve 'important', 'complicated' or 'difficult' cases. Second, it is common for the Party secretary of the Politics and Law Committee (政法委, *zhengfawei*), usually the same person as the chief of the PSB, to coordinate the policies and case load of the PSB, the procuratorate and the court at the same level, and to ensure the conformity of all three institutions to Party principles. Finally, the Party is in fact responsible for initiating and carrying out all major reforms. The constitutional amendment on 'rule of law', for example, was first enacted in the CCP Charter during the 15th Party Congress before it was copied verbatim into the Constitution. Nor could judicial reform be launched without approval of the major Party leaders. Since any judicial reform must be initiated by the Party itself, it will inherently be limited by the Party's imperatives, especially when impartial justice runs into conflict with the personal interests of Party leaders. Thus it is perhaps impractical to expect that judicial reform will make the Chinese judiciary into real 'judges' by Western standards, as no reform will be allowed to go beyond the ultimate political limit: the Party, which is essentially above the law.

---

[56] See A Nathan, *China's Transition* (New York, Columbia University Press, 1997) 240–42.

[57] He Rikai, 'The Judicial Reform: From Power to Authority' (1999) 4 *Law Science* 30–38.

D. The Brighter Side: The Rise of a Professional Legal Community and 'Public Interest Lawyers'

Since the heyday of politicisation during the first three decades of the People's Republic, the Chinese legal community has travelled a long way on its march toward rule of law. The CCP may keep the courts in check and stall reform efforts, but the courts and procuratorates are merely the official components of the legal community; they operate alongside more independent professionals, namely lawyers and legal scholars. And the Party no longer controls everything as it wishes now that three decades of economic, legal, and social reform have passed, during which public consciousness for individual rights and rule of law has risen continuously. The Sun Zhigang case aptly illustrates the power of an awakened people when they have access to news coverage of a serious human tragedy caused by the abuse of public power. The three young legal scholars who petitioned the NPCSC to review the constitutionality of the Custody and Repatriation Measures[58] are part of a new generation of lawyers who have grown up in a legal community that is increasingly committed to rule of law and social justice.

Over the past three decades, law schools have mushroomed in China and now supply the legal expertise that was chronically absent during the lawless days of the Cultural Revolution. Legal scholarship recovered relatively quickly from the decade of revolutionary destruction, and frequent international exchanges have enabled it to surpass the levels reached earlier under more orthodox communist rule. Translations of Western legal classics have burgeoned since the early 1980s, and a flurry of foreign law books has introduced Chinese scholars and students to general legal principles and practices.[59]

In fact, the rounds of judicial reform beginning in 1999 were themselves a product of legal scholarship, which introduced the idea of the rule of law to contemporary China. Even if the reforms and experiments with constitutional review failed to fulfil their original promise, thousands of law graduates continue to walk out of schools every year and enter the law professions throughout the country. Although many of them quickly merge into the system to pursue their own interests, a growing number of lawyers are prepared to stand up to defend justice and public interest.

---

[58] For discussion of the Sun Zhigang case and the Measures, see above ch 3.
[59] For the evolution of China's constitutional jurisprudence, see above ch 2.

Many of these young devoted lawyers are following in the footsteps of Zhang Sizhi (张思之), a highly respected senior lawyer who defended the Gang of Four as vigorously as he defended the dissidents Wei Jingsheng (魏京生) and Wang Juntao (王军涛). Among the relative newcomers are a few notables who are courageous enough to involve themselves in politically sensitive cases: Chen Youxi (陈有西) and Si Weijiang (斯伟江), attorneys for the Li Zhuang case; Pu Zhiqiang (浦志强), who defended Chen Guidi (陈桂棣) and Chuntao (春桃), writers who were sued for 'libel' over their report of a county CCP secretary who seriously abused his power; Xu Zhiyong (许志永), whose NGO, Public Alliance, has defended many victims of public power abuse; Zhou Ze (周泽), who successfully defended Xie Chaoping (谢朝平), an author detained by the police for reporting about reservoir resettlements;[60] Hao Jingsong (郝劲松), who has challenged many state regulations in the courts; and Yang Jinzhu (杨金柱), who demanded, among other things, the resignation of the new SPC President for turning the judicial reform backward. These and other legal activists are still largely marginalised by the existing system in China, but they have won public confidence, and if one day the voice of the people is heard , they will readily serve as the backbone of the future legal community.

FURTHER READING

Hung, VM-Y, 'China's WTO Commitment on Independent Judicial Review: Impact on Legal and Political Reform' (2004) 52 *American Journal of Comparative Law* 77.

Liebman, BL, 'China's Courts: Restricted Reform' (2007) 21 *Columbia Journal of Asian Law* 1.

Orts, EW, 'The Rule of Law in China' (2001) 34 *Vanderbilt Journal of Transnational Law* 43.

Peerenboom, R, 'One Hundred Flowers Bloom, One Hundred Schools Contend: Debating Rule of Law in China' (2002) 23 *Michigan Journal of International Law* 471.

Zhang, Q, 'The People's Court in Transition: The Prospects of the Chinese Judicial Reform' (Spring 2003) 12 *Journal of Contemporary China* 69.

Zhu, Suli, 'Political Parties in China's Judiciary' (2007) 17 *Duke Journal of Comparative & International Law* 533.

---

[60] See below ch 8.

7

The Contemporary Rights Revolution: Life, Liberty, Property and Equality

---

INTRODUCTION: BACK TO THE SUN ZHIGANG MODEL – EQUALITY – Reforming the Household Registration System and the Treatment of Peasant Workers – Remedying Other Forms of Discrimination **– LIBERTY –** Improving Criminal Justice – The Right to Life and Reform of Capital Punishment – Abolishing the Labour Education Programme? **– PROPERTY –** Constitutional and Legal Developments – Consequences of Unjust Compensation – Regulatory and Law Reforms

I. INTRODUCTION: BACK TO THE SUN ZHIGANG MODEL

HAVING SUFFERED FROM serious violations of human rights and dignity during the Cultural Revolution, the drafters of the 1982 Constitution provided a rather comprehensive list of rights in Chapter II on the Fundamental Rights and Duties of Citizens. The fact that the rights provisions, previously Chapter III in the 1954 Constitution, are now placed before the chapter on the Structure of the State attests to the drafters' heightened consciousness of human rights and their recognition that the protection of fundamental rights is the very purpose for which the state exercises its power. Protection of rights is more than mere provision of rights, however. Without an independent judiciary able to actively vindicate individual rights against government encroachment, constitutional provisions remain empty words. The failures of judicial reform and the experiment with judicial review in the Qi Yuling decision merely verify the conventional wisdom that rights are by no means a free gift bestowed by the government but rather are to be earned by the people through hard-won cases. While the protection of rights cannot be effective without proper institutions, it likewise cannot come without the people demanding both their own rights and the establishment of the institutions in the first place.

The most significant constitutional events of the past three decades have been the rise of public consciousness regarding human rights and the enactment of relevant measures by the central government in response to popular demand, as vividly illustrated by the Sun Zhigang incident (2003), which was discussed above in chapter three. That incident was, of course, a typical human rights case in itself. It involved the right to freedom of movement, the lack of which had tied Chinese peasants to the land on which they toiled for decades; it involved the right to be free from search and seizure without probable cause and the right to humane treatment while in custody; it also involved equality of treatment between city residents, peasants and peasant-workers (ie, those who work in the cities with 'peasant' status). More important, the Sun Zhigang incident established a model in which an aggrieved party and the media (most notably on the Internet) can ally together to create such a powerful national impact that the central government takes action against offending local officials.

This chapter covers the rights that have been gained more or less through the Sun Zhigang model, which has so far been the dominant method to attract official attention for public grievances. It will review the major advances in the areas of protecting life, liberty, property and equality and will point out the inadequacies that still remain.

II. EQUALITY

Equality is the very bedrock of any socialist constitution, and it is variously provided for in the 1982 Constitution. Besides the general provision in Article 33, which states that 'all citizens . . . are equal before the law', Article 4 provides for equality among all nationalities; Article 5 for personal equality ('No organisation or individual is privileged to be beyond the Constitution or the law'); Article 48 for gender equality, which entitles women to 'enjoy equal rights with men in all spheres of life, in political, economic, cultural, social and family life'; and Article 34 for political equality. The last guarantees that:

[All citizens] who have reached the age of 18 have the right to vote and stand for election, regardless of ethnic status, race, sex, occupation, family background, religious belief, education, property status or length of residence, except persons deprived of political rights according to law.

In practice, however, as the Sun Zhigang case partly reveals, the Chinese have long received disparate treatment with respect to their residence (namely whether they are from cities or from rural areas), gender, age, political status, physical characteristics (eg, appearance, even height) and health condition, based on dubious justification. Since 2000, with the rise of public consciousness of rights, victims of this sort of pervasive discrimination have been increasingly active in vindicating the rights that belong to them. Although Article 33 of the Constitution was once thought to prohibit only irregular application of a law to similarly situated persons defined in the law rather than unjustifiable distinctions in the law itself,[1] it is now commonly understood to stand for substantive equality of law.

This section focuses primarily on regional and occupational discrimination, which has affected millions of Chinese people and with which China has been grappling in recent years, even though other forms of discrimination are also prominent. Despite years of Communist campaigns for gender equality, for example, gender discrimination has remained pervasive in the once Confucian-dominated society, where women were kept in subjugation. It is usually more difficult, for instance, for female college graduates to find employment than it is for their male classmates. But such discrimination is often rendered covert by unwritten policies, which are more difficult to discover and remedy.

A. Reforming the Household Registration System and the Treatment of Peasant Workers

The Custody and Repatriation Measures that led to the Sun Zhigang tragedy was but an instrument for enforcing a deeply rooted dualist structure that strictly separates Chinese cities from rural areas, where over two thirds of the population reside. The intent was to promote modernisation and industrialisation in the cities, but these objectives

---

[1] See Material Office of the CASS, *Everyone is Equal before the Law* (Beijing, Social Science Literature Press, 2003).

were carried out at the expense of peasants. To prevent the latter from fleeing from the agricultural land to the cities to seek better lives and thereby disturb the social order (by, eg, increasing urban unemployment), a rigorous household registration (户籍, *huji*) system was established during the 1950s.

In 1953 and 1956, the State Council issued two directives that prohibited cities from hiring labourers from 'blind flows' (盲流, *mangliu*) from the countryside. In 1958, the National People's Congress Standing Committee (NPCSC) enacted the Regulation on Household Residence Registration (户口登记条例, *hukou dengji tiaoli*), which formally established the urban–rural divide, which has persisted to this day.[2] The household registration system essentially restricts every person to his or her abode as recorded in the household registration files; any extended stay (more than three days) outside the registered place is to be reported to and approved by the local People's Security Bureau (PSB). Once someone has been identified as a 'peasant' by his or her 'agricultural household residence' (农业户口, *nongye hukou*), that person is not permitted to be in the cities without justification; those who work in cities must obtain temporary residence permits (暂住证, *zanzhu zheng*) from the city PSBs – and Sun Zhigang was detained precisely because he left home that fateful night without carrying such a permit.

The urban–rural dualist structure, which had been maintained by the house registration system and enforced by the Custody and Repatriation Measures, was obviously a living monument of discrimination against peasants. Not only was their physical freedom severely limited, but they continued to be impoverished by discriminatory treatment and a deprivation of employment opportunities. According to the *Yearbook of China Statistics*, the ratio of urban–rural income was 3.48 in 1957 and 2.36 in 1978, a level that remains constant today.[3] The public anger triggered by the Sun Zhigang incident could not be appeased by the mere abolition of the Custody and Repatriation Measures, which was only the means to

---

[2] For survey studies and historical analysis of the household residence system, see Tian Bingxin, *China's First Certificate: Survey Manuscript of Chinese Household Residence Institution* (Guangzhou, Guangdong People's Press, 2003); Lu Yilong, *Transcending Household Residence: Interpreting Chinese Household Residence Institution* (Beijing, China Social Science Press, 2004); and Wang Weihai, *Historical and Political Analysis of the Chinese Household Residence Institution* (Shanghai, Culture Press, 2006).

[3] Xie Haiding, 'The Causes for the Urban–Rural Wealth Difference: From the Perspective of the Household Residence Legal System' (2004) 3 *China Legal News* 38–43.

realise an invidious discriminative end; the very root of the entire urban–rural divide and the household registration system would have to be eradicated in order to cure the inherent injustice suffered by Chinese peasants. After half a century of relentless enforcement, what had become an iniquitous social and cultural institution eventually began to crumble.

Some cities began to reform their household registration and subsidiary systems. In July 2003, the PSB of Shenyang city (Liaoning Province) abolished the temporary residence permit system. A non-resident to the city now needs only to register at a local PSB by providing personal identification and a residential address. Once so registered, he or she should enjoy the same personal freedom as the city residents do; the police should neither conduct disturbing searches nor adopt compulsory measures to restrict personal freedom. Following Shenyang, over 20 other cities have abolished the temporary residence permit system. Those cities that still retain the system have fundamentally transformed its functions: a permit no longer serves as a restriction of personal freedom but merely affords proof of status for enjoying equal right as residents.

Other cities have undertaken more radical reform by reducing the threshold requirements for city residence applications. The most dramatic example is Zhengzhou, the capitol of Henan province, which now grants approval for applications if an applicant has bought a house, invested in the city or acquired a higher education credential. The new policy has proved so attractive that, within a year of promulgation, the city added 100,000 new residents. The city government then allowed those relatives who lived with the residents to apply for residency, a policy that quickly added another 150,000 residents. Confronted with such problems as transportation congestion and shortage of education resources, however, the city was forced to limit the beneficiaries of the second reform to the direct relatives of residents.[4] Most cities and provinces are more conservative and limit themselves to the first type of reform adopted by Zhengzhou. In July 2004, for example, the new registration measures of Nanjing, the capitol of Jiangsu province, abolished the distinctions between household registrations and established a uniform registration system.[5]

---

[4] 'Sharp Increase in Population Brings Pressure, Zhengzhou Household Residence "New Deal" Partially Suspended', *China Youth Daily* (15 September 2004).

[5] 'Nanjing Abolishes Rural Household Residence', *China Youth Daily* (25 June 2004).

Local reforms have been buttressed and facilitated by corresponding reforms of the central government. The NPCSC revised the Organic Law of the Urban Residents Committee so that it guarantees that non-residents, upon living in a fixed abode for three years, shall enjoy the same rights as residents, including the right to vote and to stand for election. The Ministry of Public Security has drafted a plan to abolish the urban–rural distinction in the registration system and establish a uniform registration system nationwide, which will gradually reduce restrictions on migrations from rural to urban areas.[6] However, the plan has met with considerable resistance from local governments. Given the enormous disparity between urban and rural conditions, any uniform reform is likely to be more formal than substantive at this stage. However, the most recent Chengdu plan in Sichuan province provides hope for the future of China's reform of the household registration system. Initiated in November 2010, it aims to abolish substantive discrimination against peasants and establish a uniform medical insurance and social protection programme by 2012.[7]

Nor is it sufficient to remedy discrimination against 'peasants' narrowly defined, since a large group of them have become 'peasant workers' (农民工, *nongmin gong*), ie, they come to work in the cities, many for long terms or even permanently. This group, which now number more than 200 million, carries their discriminated status into the cities. Although restrictions to their physical mobility have been removed, they are handicapped by other types of institutional discrimination against 'non-residents'. Unlike the urban residents they rub shoulders with every day, most peasant workers do not enjoy, for example, medical insurance, unemployment protection or other types of social welfare; nor can they send their children to the same schools attended by urban children and receive compulsory education of the same quality, which is a basic right in the 1982 Constitution (Article 46). In 2010, Beijing finally allowed the children of peasant workers to attend the primary and middle schools near their homes,[8] but the Beijing reform remains the lone exception rather than the rule, and peasant children in most cities are still barred from entering the standard city schools. These substantively

---

[6] *Legal Daily* (26 October 2005).

[7] Tong Haihua, 'A "Giant Step" in Chengdu Household Residence Reform Is Not Achieved in One Day', *China Economic Herald* (20 November 2010).

[8] Zhang Ling, 'The Non-resident Population in Beijing Will Be Allowed to Enter the Nearest Schools Without Examinations', *Beijing Times* (16 April 2010).

discriminatory measures have, among other things, created millions of 'left-behind' (留守, *liushou*) children who stay with their grandparents in the countryside and who can meet with their parents only once a year during the short interval of the Spring Festival, casting a huge shadow over the environment in which a significant proportion of China's next generations grow.

B. Remedying Other Forms of Discrimination

The household registration system is simply the most egregious example of discrimination against peasants, but it is by no means the only form of discrimination in China. Nor is discrimination against peasants limited to the explicit form of household registration. In September 2010, a joint letter co-signed by over 10,000 non-resident parents who had worked in Beijing for many years demanded that the Beijing Education Commission allow their children to take the college entrance examination (高考, *gaokao*) in Beijing (rather than in the provinces where their households were registered). Since then, parent activists have gathered before the Ministry of Education to petition their cause on more than 20 occasions, with total signatories approaching 100,000. In October 2011, 15 legal scholars also petitioned the State Council to review the legality of the Working Regulation issued by the Ministry of Education that required examinees to register at the place of their household registration.[9] During the NPC convention in March 2012, the Minister of Education stated that this limit will be lifted in a matter of months, following a pilot programme in Shandong province.[10]

These events help to reveal what is hidden behind the bizarre undergraduate admission system in China, which has long accorded disproportional benefits to the residents of Beijing, other municipalities and rich provinces. Under the current admission scheme, an obstinate remnant of the planned economy era, each university allocates admission quotas for every province. In 2010, for example, Peking University

---

[9] Xu Tian et al, '15 Scholars Petitioned the State Council to Eliminate Household Registration Limit on Entrance Examinations', *Legal Evening News* (24 October 2012).

[10] Guo Shaofeng, 'Scheme for Reforming Entrance Examination Will Be Published in 10 Months, Requiring Parents Be Local Workers', *New Beijing Daily* (4 March 2012).

allocated 368 admissions spaces for a total of 81,000 Beijing examinees, and a mere 60 admissions spaces for 660,000 Shandong examinees, 78 for 950,000 Henan examinees, and 30 for 615,000 Guangdong examinees. The admission ratio (the quota divided by the total number of examinees of that province) for applicants whose parents are Beijing residents is 50, 55 and 93 times greater than the same ratio for applicants from Shandong, Henan and Guangdong, respectively.[11]

Peking University and other 'national universities' in Beijing are far from the worst discriminators in admission, since the Beijing students in these universities normally constitute about 15 per cent of the entire student body, while public national universities in other metropolises used to allocate over half of the total admission quotas to local residents and gradually reduced the ratio of local students only under the pressure exerted by the Ministry of Education. Such ratios may not appear so high from an American or Canadian perspective, where most public universities are 'local' in the sense that they are financed by the state or local governments. Keep in mind, however, that Peking University and other 'national universities' are subordinate directly to the Ministry of Education and other departments of the central government and are financed mostly by taxpayers across the nation. They are thus obliged to observe the constitutional principle of equality, an ideal that is belied by the extremely uneven distribution of these higher education resources, which are concentrated in large cities and affluent provinces.

The regional discrimination of the admission schemes puts applicants from agrarian provinces at a serious disadvantage when competing for higher education opportunities, which used to be reflected in a much higher admission score when all examinees across the country took the same entrance examinations. From 2002, however, Beijing and other 15 provinces and municipalities began to implement their own entrance examinations (自主命题, *zizhu mingti*) to be taken by their own residents. Not surprisingly, the Beijing examinations are considerably easier than those of many provinces, and this is one reason that non-resident parents petitioned for their children to take the examination in Beijing.

---

[11] Zhang Qianfan and Yang Shijian, 'University Admission and Constitutional Equality' (2009) 11 *Legal Science Monthly* 15–19; and the accompanying articles in the same issue.

In 2001, three students from Qingdao (Shandong province) brought litigation against the Ministry of Education for maintaining the discriminatory university admission scheme, but the court declined to review the case.[12] Successes have been achieved, however, in the area of occupational equality, where academics like Professors Cai Dingjian (蔡定剑) and Zhou Wei (周伟), practitioners and nongovernment organisations (NGOs) have joined efforts to bring several cases to court, specifically on the equality clause in Article 33 of the Constitution, even though ultimately none of the cases were decided on constitutional grounds. In the *Bank Employment Advertisement Case* (2002),[13] the Chengdu Branch of the People's Bank of China put out an employment advertisement that required, among other things, both male and female applicants to be above certain heights. Jiang Tao, a male applicant and a law student at Sichuan University who fell short of the height requirement, challenged the bank advertisement for infringing his equal opportunity to public posts as guaranteed by the Constitution. The court of Wuhou district, Chengdu decided that the employment practice failed to constitute an 'administrative act', which would involve the exercise of administrative power, and thus declined to review the substance of the case. The rationale given by the court was dubious since there was little reason to exclude the employment process of a state bank from the purview of 'administrative acts', though the defendant bank did revise its advertisement and delete the height restrictions during the litigation.

Most recently, women have become active in vindicating their equal rights with regard to employment practice. After the Communists took over in 1949, gender equality became a priority on the policy agenda; women were allowed to retire earlier than men and to receive as pension 80 per cent of their full-time salaries. The implications of the early retirement policy changed over the years, however; what used to be a privilege soon turned out to be a disadvantage, since bonuses now constitute a major portion of income not included in salary and sometimes even exceed salary, and such bonuses are lost after retirement. A woman employee who had reached the retirement age of 55 (men normally retire at 60) challenged the differential retirement policy of the China

---

[12] 'Admission According to National Uniform Exams Resulted in Disparate Admission Grades; Three Examinees in Qingdao Sued Ministry of Education', *Qilu Evening News* (22 August 2001).

[13] *Jiang Tao v People's Bank of China, Chengdu Branch*. See Zhang Qianfan, *Introduction to Studies of Constitutional Law* (Beijing, Law Press, 2004) 503–4.

Construction Bank, which was based on the State Council's Provisional Method for Allocating Old, Weak, Sick and Handicapped Cadres, enacted in 1978. In the case she brought to the court in Pingdingshan (Henan province), she argued that she was in good health and could conduct her professional activities with competence; thus, the women's early retirement policy violated both Article 33 of the Constitution and the gender equality provisions in the Labour Law. In July 2006, after the trial court rejected her claim, she petitioned the NPCSC, the State Council and the China Women's Federation to review the constitutionality of regulation, but there has not been any reply from these institutions.

Employment of civil servants in China has been subject to a variety of discriminatory restrictions. Frequent complaints were made against a common criterion that excluded the carriers of the non-infectious hepatitis-B virus, which resulted in a tragedy in 2001 when a Zhejiang applicant who had been rejected on that ground killed, out of sheer fury, a local admission official and seriously wounded another.[14] In the *Hepatitis-B Virus Case* (2004),[15] the government of Anhui province was challenged for maintaining such a restriction in admitting civil servants. The victim charged that such a health criterion constituted discrimination prohibited by Article 33 of the Constitution. The court of Wuhu city invalidated the decision to refuse admission in this particular case for 'insufficient evidence', but it declined to comment on the constitutional grounds. The chief judge of the administrative division of the Anhui High Court was apparently under the belief that Article 33 of the Constitution applies only to the irregular application of law in administrative processes rather than the classification of laws themselves, a clear misunderstanding, which might have influenced the judgment of the lower court.

The favourable court decision further prompted the central government to eliminate the discrimination against Hepatitis-B virus carriers in the civil service[16] but stopped short of putting an end to Hepatitis-B discrimination in general. In college admissions, for example, examinees

---

[14] Shen Ying, 'Zhou Yichao Killed for Hepatitis-B Discrimination', *Southern Weekend* (7 August 2004).

[15] See Zhou Wei, *A Study of Judicial Remedies of Constitutional Fundamental Rights* (Beijing, China People's Public Security University, 2004) 100.

[16] See Wei Mingyan, 'Healthy Hepatitis-B Virus Carriers May Be Admitted as Civil Servants', *New Beijing Daily* (1 August 2004).

were still required to undertake health examinations, which included testing for Hepatitis-B; a positive test result constituted sufficient ground for rejection.[17] It was only after continuous efforts by such NGOs as Yirenping (益仁平), led by Lu Jun (陆军) and other activists, that the Ministry of Hygiene eventually moved to abolish Hepatitis-B discrimination in the educational and occupational fields altogether.[18] Notably, the NGOs did not bother to go to court, though they have occasionally used litigation as a threat to initiate policy changes or to implement desirable policies. Since neither the courts nor the People's Congresses are reliable guardians of constitutional equality, it is often more effective in practice to directly petition the relevant administrative agencies to reform discriminatory policies.

III. LIBERTY

The impact of the Sun Zhigang case has gone beyond dismantling the restrictions on free movement, the house registration system and the urban–rural barriers that affected large numbers of China's population. It has also brought in the broader question of how the government should treat its people, especially in matters of life and death as dealt with by criminal procedure and the death penalty, both of which have been substantially reformed in recent years.

A. Improving Criminal Justice

Unlike the constitutions of many Western countries (eg, the United States) and perhaps under the influence of the revolutionary ideology that demanded merciless treatment of criminal 'enemies', the 1982 Constitution does not require due process for criminal justice, with the exception of a general provision that personal freedom (人身自由,

---

[17] Usually the examinees were advised to spend some time for recovery, during which the qualification for admission was reserved; but after the grace period (eg, one year), if the examinee failed to recover, the qualification was generally revoked.

[18] Yang Wenyan, 'China Will End Educational and Occupational Discriminations against Hepatitis-B Carriers', *NetEase News* (29 December 2009), http://news.163.com/09/1229/11/5RMQRFIF0001124J.html. For more details, see the Yirenping website: http://www.yirenping.org.

renshen ziyou) is 'inviolable' (Article 40). The Constitution does require arrests to be approved by the procuratorate, however, and does prohibit 'unlawful' searches, detention and restrictions of freedom. The Criminal Procedure Law prohibits extortion for confession and extended detention, but these acts were nonetheless common practice within criminal justice until recently.

Partly out of a need to maintain social order and an image of government efficacy, China had long rejected the presumption of innocence. In reality, criminal suspects were presumed guilty, and the major task of the PSBs and the procuratorate was to make suspects confess to the crimes committed. Even if evidence fell short of 'proof beyond reasonable doubt', a suspect was not to be acquitted, since there was still a fair chance that he had committed the crime, but the sentence would be reduced to some extent – as if to compensate for the insufficiency of evidence. Such practices, coupled with the lack of modernised technical means for legally conducting criminal investigation, necessarily led to widespread torture and extended detention.

The most dramatic example of procedural abuse was a case involving She Xianglin (佘祥林) that, like the Sun Zhigang event, received overwhelming public attention. In January 1994, She's mentally ill wife disappeared. Three months later, a woman's body was found in a river near a neighbouring village. The body was identified as his wife by her relatives. She Xianglin immediately became the suspect and was forced to confess after he was severely tortured by the police, who painstakingly 'guided' him to make the confessed 'plot' consistent with the crime scene. He initially received a death sentence, which was later reduced to imprisonment for 15 years when the upper court found his criminal file suspicious. The story took a dramatic turn in 2005, after he had served eleven years of his sentence: his supposedly murdered wife resurfaced, alive.[19] She Xianglin eventually received RMB¥450,000 as compensation, which set the record at the time for state compensation in such cases. Although money can hardly compensate for what he and his family had suffered, She Xianglin is considered much luckier than another victim, Nie Shubing (聂树斌), who was wrongfully executed and whose family is still fighting for his innocence today.[20]

---

[19] 'She Xianglin Was Wronged for 11 Years; the Chief Culprit Is Presumption of Guilt?' *New Beijing Daily* (14 April 2005).

[20] Zhao Lei and Deng Jiangbo, 'Supreme Court Retries the Nie Shubing Grievance as "Most Important Case" ', *Southern Weekend* (8 November 2007).

Closely tied to extortion for confession is extended detention, which is widely used in the context of unresolved criminal cases. Although the Criminal Procedure Law explicitly defines the maximal periods for detention during police investigation, prosecution and court trial, the timetable for each stage has often not been strictly followed in practice. In Quyang county (Hebei province), for example, Yang Zhijie (杨志杰) was detained for 12 years without sentencing. He and his wife were extorted to confess that he set a bomb to kill his neighbor, but since the police could not find direct evidence for conviction, he was detained until they could either collect enough evidence to convict him or identify a different suspect.[21] In another record-breaking case, Xie Hongwu (谢洪武), a peasant from Guangxi province, was illegally detained for 28 years.[22]

Egregious procedural violations frequently occur in the pre-trial stage, when a suspect is placed in a detention centre (看守所, *kanshou suo*) under the sole control of the PSB for prolonged periods. The Criminal Procedure Law authorises PSBs to detain 'major suspects' for three days, which can be ultimately extended to one month, prior to the procuratorate's approval for arrest (Article 69); after approval, 'custodial investigation' will be carried out initially for no longer than two months but may be extended to a maximum of seven months in special cases (Articles 124, 126 and 127). Unlike many Western countries, China lacks the right to habeas corpus; a suspect can be held in a police station for investigation, usually without the presence of lawyers, instead of being handed over to the courts promptly after arrest. In fact, habeas corpus has been rejected explicitly in the PRC to facilitate police investigation since, unlike prison, detention centres are charged with the important function of 'digging deeply into extra crimes' (深挖余罪, *shenwa yuzui*), by which the police may discover accomplices or related crimes through surveillance and informants. Such an environment is necessarily bereft of due process and instead full of police and inmate violence. The Detention Centre Regulation, enacted by the State Council in 1990, seems to be an unrevised product of the 1950s, treating suspects as

[21] Huang Guangming, 'Put Behind Bars for Twelve Years without Clear Reason', *Southern Weekend* (29 January 2003). For a similar incident, see 'Five Youths were Wrongly Detained for 11 Years; Two Died in the Ward', *Yanzhao Metropolitan Daily* (17 October 2005).
[22] 'Xie Hongwu: The "Record Keeping Victim" of the Illegal Extended Detention', *Procuratorate Daily* (25 July 2008).

'prisoners' (人犯, *renfan*), who are obliged to study, labour and receive moral and political education (Articles 3, 33 and 34). In fact, a detention centre can be a great deal worse than a prison in terms of conditions, and the irregular deaths of detained inmates have figured frequently in the headlines of national news.[23]

The She Xianglin case and similar events have prompted the Chinese government to take criminal justice more seriously. Since July 2003, the courts, the procuratorate and the PSBs began to clean up extended detention cases. In early August, the court in Baofeng county (Henan province) sentenced a police officer to six months' imprisonment for illegal detention, the first time that a police officer has been punished for this sort of abuse. In November 2003, the Supreme People's Court (SPC), the Supreme People's Procuratorate (SPP) and the Ministry of Public Security jointly adopted a 'Circular on Strictly Abiding by the Criminal Procedure Law and Earnestly Redressing and Preventing Extended Detentions'. Two years later, the Second Five-Year Outline of judicial reform[24] reaffirmed the principle of presumption of innocence and identified the prohibition of extortion as a top priority for the reform. These efforts seem to have had a substantial impact on China's criminal justice. In 2005, the courts found 2162 criminal suspects innocent,[25] and the procuratorate investigated 110 torture cases, while the instances of extended detention were reduced to 271.[26] The seriously out-dated Detention Centre Regulation must still be revised, however, before China's criminal procedure is brought truly under the rule of law.

B. The Right to Life and Reform of Capital Punishment

The right to life is not explicitly provided for in the 1982 Constitution. This is not surprising alongside a longstanding birth control policy that

---

[23] In the most notorious incident, an inmate who died of torture was said to have died during a hide-and-seek (躲猫猫, *duomaomao*) game: 'Man in Detention Centre Died of Hide-and-Seek', *China Youth Daily* (28 February 2009).

[24] For the Five-Year Outlines for judicial reform, see above ch 6.

[25] Report of the Supreme People's Court, presented to the National People's Congress, 10 March 2006.

[26] The SPP Report, presented to the NPC in March 2006, *New Beijing Daily* (12 March 2006).

requires compulsory abortion and foetus destruction in some circumstances. Nor has China abolished the death penalty, although the issue has been vigorously debated since an undergraduate received the death penalty in 2011 for cruelly killing the victim of a car accident that he caused.[27] In 2012, the SPC repealed a death sentence that had been handed down to Wu Ying (吴英), a young Zhejiang entrepreneur who had committed 'financial fraud' (集资诈骗, *jizi zhapian*).[28] It remains to be seen whether the judicial move will become a precedent for abolishing the death penalty for crimes that do not involve physical violence or official corruption. Thousands of criminals are still executed each year in China, though the exact number has been kept a matter of 'state secrecy'.

Notwithstanding the high numbers, compared to ordinary sentences in China, the death penalty is generally accorded extra caution and procedural gatekeeping: history records that in imperial China, emperors personally reviewed and approved every death sentence. Article 48 of the Criminal Law limits death sentences to 'crimes of extremely serious nature', and if it is unnecessary to execute immediately, a death sentence can be given a reprieve (缓期, *huanqi*) of two years, after which it is usually reduced to life imprisonment. Both the Criminal Procedure Law (Article 144) and the Organic Law of the People's Courts (Article 13) require that a prosecutorial petition for the death sentence may be initiated only at a middle-level court, and all death sentences must be reported to the SPC for review and approval (核准, *hezhun*).

As the crime rate climbed rapidly in the wake of economic reform, the NPCSC authorised, by a resolution in 1980, provincial high courts to approve death sentences for crimes seriously jeopardising social order. In 1983, the NPCSC revised Article 13 of the Organic Law of the People's Courts to allow the SPC to authorise the provincial high courts to approve, 'when necessary', death sentences for certain crimes that seriously endanger public order and security. As a result, the SPC authorised the high courts to approve death sentences for serious crimes, except for 'counter-revolutionary crimes' (abolished in 2004) and serious economic crimes. The delegation of approval power made the approval process meaningless, since it meant that a charge for death sentence, which had to be initiated at a middle-level court, could be

---

[27] Zhang Han, 'The Change of Yao Jiaxin from (Car) Hitting to Killing', *New Beijing Daily* (6 December 2010).

[28] 'Supreme Court Took the Wu Ying Case; Will She be Spared from Death?' *China Management Daily* (15 February 2012).

appealed only to the provincial high court, which would be the same court for approving its own sentence.[29]

The appearance of prejudice in such a self-approving process is clearly illustrated in the following questionable case. In 2002, Dong Wei (董伟) was convicted for a murder committed during a brawl and received a death sentence, which was sustained by the Shaanxi provincial high court. Minutes before the execution, however, he was saved by an emergency directive from the SPC demanding a second review. Four months later, the high court simply reaffirmed the original sentence in a closed meeting, the panel deciding that 'the facts were sufficiently clear', and Dong was finally executed. Dong's relatives alleged that, among the five judges in charge of the final review, three had participated in the first review, and the relatives had demanded their recusal, but this apparently reasonable request was not granted.[30]

The Dong Wei case and other reports of wrongful executions prompted the SPC to withdraw the approval power delegated to the provincial high courts. The Second Five-Year Outline of judicial reform identified trial and approval procedures for death sentences as top priorities. Its very first paragraph required the appellate process for death penalty cases to be open to the public, and the second paragraph explicitly reverted approval power back to the SPC. Besides reducing erroneous judgments, the reversion of the approval process aimed to reduce the number of death sentences, not only because the SPC would exercise more care and prudence but also because the Court is limited in capacity to review and approve a number of death penalties each year, notwithstanding the three new sections within the Criminal division that were established for just that purpose. According to a recent report, the SPC has refused to approve as many as 40 per cent of death penalties handed down by provincial high courts.[31]

---

[29] For a review of problems in death sentencing, see Chen Xingliang, *A Memorandum of Death Penalties* (Wuhan, Wuhan University Press, 2006).

[30] Zeng Min: 'Save a Person under the Gun', *Southern Weekend* (18 July 2002); and 'Reinvesting the Life-Saving Case', *Southern Weekend* (19 September 2002).

[31] 'Supreme Court Judges Revealed that about 40 per cent of Death Sentences Failed to be Approved', *South Metropolitan Daily* (18 October 2010).

C. Abolishing the Labour Education Programme?

Finally, one should not be misled to conclude that only convicted criminals suffer deprivations of freedom in China. In fact, Sun Zhigang himself was detained by the Guangzhou police not under any criminal statute but on the authority of an administrative regulation. Not only does the Regulations on Administrative Penalties for Public Security authorise detention as a form of 'administrative penalty' up to fifteen days for a variety of activities that disturb public order, but a person may be sentenced to 'rehabilitation through labour' (劳动教养, *laodong jiaoyang*) programme for up to three years, extendable for one more year, during which both physical freedom and political rights are deprived. Moreover, such sentences are decided by administrative boards rather than courts. The Sun Zhigang case did not merely result in the abolition of the Custody and Repatriation Measures; it also prompted the Chinese public to impugn the constitutionality of the equally longstanding rehabilitation through labour programme, since both programmes restricted personal freedom without authorisation by law and were plainly contrary to Article 8 of the Law on Legislation.[32]

Like household registration and the related custody and repatriation system, the rehabilitation through labour programme has existed in China for over half a century. In 1956, the Chinese Communist Party (CCP) Central Committee issued a directive that required local governments to establish rehabilitation through labour institutions. The programme was formally established in 1957 when a NPC resolution approved the State Council's Decision on Rehabilitation through Labour Programme. In 1979, the State Council issued a Supplementary Provision, which established the commission of rehabilitation through labour and defined the scope and supervision methods of the programme.

Compared to 'transformation through labour' (劳动改造, *laodong gaizao*), which is a principle applied to sentencing for serious crimes, rehabilitation through labour is designed to punish and reeducate those who have committed misdemeanors that are too minor to constitute crimes. The original purpose of the programme was to make inmates useful to society through labour and education, to maintain social order

---

[32] See above ch 3.

and to reduce unemployment. Over the years, however, local regulations and rules gradually extended the scope of application. The programme currently applies to six types of activities that are considered socially or politically unacceptable but insufficient to warrant criminal punishment. A large portion of the programme resources are used for the rehabilitation of drug addicts, but the programme is also used to contain political dissidents and to punish whistleblowers and repeated 'petitioners' (上访户, *shangfang hu*), who personally appeal to the superior governments for their grievances allegedly caused by local officials.[33] According to a survey in 1999, China had at that time roughly 310 rehabilitation through labour centres, with more than 310,000 inmates.[34]

Like the Custody and Repatriation programme, the rehabilitation through labour programme provided ample opportunity for official corruption and violence. In September 2002, Zhang Bin (张斌), a resident of Chaoyang city (Liaoning province) who had committed larceny, was sent to a rehabilitation through labour camp for three years. On 16 April 2003, he died as a result of repeated battery and month-long mistreatment by other inmates. Like the Sun Zhigang incident, which had occurred just a month earlier, Zhang Bin's death shocked the senior leaders of the central government, who ordered a special investigation of the case.[35]

In fact, the legality of the rehabilitation through labour programme had been under attack even before these events. In the NPC session of March 2003,[36] 127 delegates had proposed four bills that were opposed to such a system. A year later, fuelled by the Sun Zhigang and Zhang Bin controversies, as many as 420 delegates proposed 13 bills challenging the programme for its lack of legal authorisation, vague scope of applicability, disproportional punishment, procedural irregularities, lack of transparency and, above all, conspicuous absence of court enforced due process. Decisions to assign someone to a rehabilitation through labour programme are made by PSB-dominated commissions and *can* be chal-

[33]   *Chongqing Morning Post* (29 March 2006).
[34]   Chu Huaizhi, 'On the Reasonableness of the Education Treatment' (1999) 3 *China Education through Labour* 40.
[35]   Wei Wenbiao, 'Rehabilitee through Labour Died of Beating in Hulu Island, Liaoning', *Shenyang Today* (11 July 2003).
[36]   Sun Zhan: 'The Labour Education Program that Operated Nearly 50 Years Was Challenged, Fundamental Reforms Put on Agenda', *News Weekly* (23 March 2004).

lenged by administrative litigation, but the courts are normally so deferential to board decisions as to make such challenges meaningless.

To cure these institutional defects, the drafting of the Law on Correction of Illegal Activities was placed on the national legislative agenda in 2005. Like the reformed relief programme that replaces the Custody and Repatriation Measures, the reformed rehabilitation programme will also be more humane insofar as it will provide inmates with more freedom, flexibility and public supervision. Unlike the voluntary relief programme that took effect several months after the Sun Zhigang event, however, the legislation on rehabilitation has dragged on without yet producing a formal bill.

IV. PROPERTY

By the very end of 2009, the Sun Zhigang tragedy seemed to have been repeated in a different context. On 23 December, Tang Fuzhen (唐福珍), a Chengdu resident who had forcibly resisted for hours a demolition team that was trying to tear down her house, lost control and poured petroleum over her body before setting herself on fire. Despite prompt rescue, she died in hospital several days later.[37] The news spread instantly on the Internet, fuelled by videotape footage taken by a neighbour using mobile phone, which vividly recorded the self-immolation. Like the Sun Zhigang event, the news created a massive public uproar, and it was followed by five law professors from Peking University petitioning the NPC Standing Committee to review the constitutionality of the Regulation on the Demolition of City Houses ('Urban Demolition Regulation'), which authorised urban renovation projects. Although the Regulation was not strictly applicable to Tang's house, which was allegedly an 'illegal construction' located in a 'village within the city' (城中村, *chengzhongcun*), minor details like these seemed to make little difference, and public pressure for abolishing the Urban Demolition Regulation became overwhelming.

The Tang Fuzhen case set the scene for the on-going property rights reform in China. Unlike equality, to which the socialist constitutions paid at least lip service, private property had very much been the principal

---

[37] 'A Relocatee in Chengdu Died of Self-immolation after Resisting the Urban Demolition Team for 3 Hours', *NetEase News* (2 December 2009), http://news.163.com/09/1202/10/5PH8QC3K00011229.html.

bourgeois evil to be eradicated in communist China. Above all, land ownership, the 'primary means of production' under orthodox Marxist ideology, must be firmly controlled by the state under a 'proletarian dictatorship'. Although the enterprises (also a 'means of production') of the 'national' and petit bourgeoisie, many of whom supported the Communist takeover in 1949, were spared from confiscation during the initial 'transition period', the urban land and enterprises were gradually taken over by the state; and the rural land, which the CCP had promised to the peasants to gain their support in the revolutionary border areas, was taken away and merged into the People's Communes almost overnight during the upheaval of the Great Leap Forward in 1957–58.

The economic reforms of the late 1970s and after dissolved the People's Communes and privatised many urban enterprises, but the land ownership never changed hands. In fact, the 1982 Constitution declares explicitly that 'land in the cities is owned by the state' (Article 10). Although successive constitutional amendments have gradually enhanced the status of the 'private economy',[38] which has long contributed more to China's gross domestic product (GDP) than the public sectors, public land ownership remains the ultimate touchstone for the 'socialist' character of a socialist constitution. And the potential for abusing public power hidden in the phantom of 'public ownership', coupled with the official imperative to promote 'development' (发展, *fazhan*) and the GDP figure from which the legitimacy of the ruling party is primarily derived, has given rise to a multitude of social conflict and innumerable tragedies of the Tang Fuzhen type.

A. Constitutional and Legal Developments

During the past three decades of economic reform in China, the rise of public consciousness regarding individual rights has been reflected above all in the rapidly reviving consciousness regarding property rights; with disenchantment over socialist ideology, ownership of private property is no longer a sign of a depraved bourgeoisie but a source of social recognition and personal pride. In the aftermath of the Sun Zhigang incident, the 2004 constitutional amendments not only generally required the State to 'respect and protect human rights' but declared

---

[38] See above ch 2.

more specifically that 'the lawful private property of citizens is inviolable' (Article 13), only a slight step below 'socialist public property' (Article 12), which is 'sacrosanct' (神圣不可侵犯, *shensheng buke qinfan*). And for the first time, private property can be taken for public use only if the State 'pays compensation in accordance with the law' (Article 13). Such a provision may seem less than impressive, even meaningless, since 'compensation' of some sort is almost always paid in land-taking or in the demolition of houses, as it was in the Tang Fuzhen case; it is 'just compensation' that should have been required, and it was the absence of such a requirement that caused Tang Fuzhen's death and many more similar tragedies. Nevertheless, the constitutional amendment does reflect an emerging public consensus on a vital principle for China's social harmony and provides an anchor, as it were, for further legal developments.

One of these major developments was the Property Law, enacted by the NPC in 2007, after a year's delay caused by Professor Gong Xiantian (巩献田) from Peking University, who challenged the provisions that confer largely equal protection for private and public property because they violate the 'socialist character' of the 1982 Constitution. The Property Law, essentially a part of a larger Civil Code to be enacted in the future, provides comprehensive protection for various types of property but has proven to be marginally useful for the protection of land rights against taking without just compensation. Article 42 reiterates the constitutional requirement for 'compensation in accordance with the law', but the legally defined compensation may well be below the fair market value of the land or property (eg, houses) on the land to be taken, not to mention that even a requirement for just compensation may not be effectively enforced by courts whose appointments and finances depend on local governments, which are inevitably the main driving force behind the taking of land in the first place. In February 2002, for example, over 10000 evicted residents in Beijing brought a class administrative action against the demolition of their homes, yet the court declined to review the case.[39] Although the SPC requires the lower courts to hear such taking cases, local courts often narrow the scope of review on their own initiative to avoid such 'sensitive' cases.

---

[39] Duan Hongqing, 'Waiting for Supreme Court's Judicial Interpretation of Demolition' (2004) 11 *Finance* 104–9.

B. Consequences of Unjust Compensation

Widespread non-compliance with the just compensation standard has made local governments even more inclined to appropriate property, since doing so is lucrative: a local authority can gain the difference between the buying and selling prices of property, thereby generating government revenue and opportunity for bribery. The incentive for taking property is further intensified by two factors: the top-down 'performance evaluation' (政绩考核, *zhengji kaohe*) scheme, whereby the 'local GDP' is the major indicator of both local development and each local official's 'performance'; and the depletion of local funds due to the 'divided-tax' (分税制, *fenshuizhi*) reform, which tilted the revenue distribution scheme in favour of the central government. Both schemes were set up in 1993–94, after Deng Xiaoping took his 'southern tour' (南巡, *nanxun*) to Guangdong province, where he underlined the theme 'development is the solid reason' (发展是硬道理, *fazhan shi yingdaoli*) in order to resuscitate the economic reforms during a time when political reform was suffocated in the aftermath of the 1989 Tiananmen Protests. Soon enough, these measures began to produce the expected effect of making officials (rather than the people) the driving force behind social development. During the two decades that China's GDP has been increasing at a rate close to 10 per cent each year – a 'China miracle' that has contributed to the 'solid' legitimacy of the ruling party – a 'Great Leap Forward' in land-takings and demolition under the name of 'development' has created massive dislocation and serious deprivation of property and livelihood to common people like Tang Fuzhen.

On the one hand, local officials at all levels are obliged to take land and property, both to augment local revenues and to improve their performances ratings, since urbanisation and urban renewal are always shortcuts to inflating local GDP. As a result, China has been converted into a grand construction site, in perennial demolition and rebuilding – so much so that the name 'China' itself has become the subject of a pun in Mandarin Chinese: '*chai'na'er?*' (拆哪儿) (Where to demolish next?). On the other hand, property-taking and demolition has long been the culprit for social conflict and instability. According to statistics provided by the Ministry of Construction, property-taking related grievances have consistently ranked top in the number of petitions in recent years. In the first half of 2004, over 18,000 petitioners went to Beijing to seek relief, the majority in large groups.[40] On 20 April, for example, several hundred peasants from Tianjin municipality went before the Ministry of Land and Natural Resources to complain about the loss of their contract land.[41] And the number of conflicts has risen over the years, producing countless 'nail houses' (钉子户, *dingzihu*) across the country, the owners of which are pitted against the government, refusing to sell their houses for the amounts of compensation offered.

To be sure, the people do make use of the Constitution and laws to protect their rights. On the same day as the NPC passed the Property Law, the court of Jiulongpo district (Chongqing municipality) issued an 'ultimatum' for final relocation to the residents of the most robust 'nail house', who had refused to move for years even though the surrounding houses had been long demolished, leaving the house as an isolated island, as it were, without water and power supply.[42] Benefitting from the propitious timing at the passing of the new Property Law, however, the residents succeeded in obliging the Chongqing government to make an offer to their satisfaction, after which they peacefully moved out. Unfortunately, such a happy ending remains the exception.

C. Regulatory and Law Reforms

Like the Sun Zhigang case, the Tang Fuzhen tragedy moved the central government to take prompt action. The Legislative Affairs Office (LAO), the State Council's legal department, responded quickly to public pressure. Following several meetings with legal scholars, who were invited to express opinions, the LAO published in early 2010 a draft revision of the Urban Demolition Regulation, eliminating a number of its constitutional flaws.[43] Unlike the Custody and Repatriation Measures, however, the revision of the Urban Demolition Regulation was a much

---

[40] Zhao Xiaojian, 'Political Economy behind the "Land New Deal"' (2004) 21 *Finance* 90–93.

[41] Chang Hongxiao, 'Toughening the Law on Land Contract' (2004) 14 *Finance* 110–12.

[42] See 'The Strongest Holdout Sticks to the Isolated House', *New Beijing Daily* (23 March 2007).

[43] For example, Art 4 of the draft new regulation requires taking and compensation should follow the principles of democratic policymaking, due process and just compensation, among others. Regulation on Taking of and Compensation for Houses on National Land, issued by the State Council in 2011.

more difficult task since it met serious resistance from local governments, which have derived a significant portion of their fiscal revenues from lucrative land-takings by paying compensation at sub-market values.[44] Although the LAO expressed its willingness to require just compensation and narrow the scope of justifiable 'public interest' in the new regulation, it did not appear confident enough to withstand the pressure of local governments, which are in charge of implementing most of the central laws and policies and thereby enjoy considerable discretion.

After a long delay, during which they apparently consulted with the local governments, the LAO came up with a second draft of the Regulation on Taking and Compensation for Houses on State-Owned Land, which made considerable concessions to the local governments. Although the new draft affirms the principle of just compensation and authorises compulsory taking only with court approval, it omits several important provisions that were in the first draft and that enabled interested parties to participate in the process of deciding whether a proposed appropriation is required by 'public interest' and whether compensation satisfies the just compensation criterion. Under the new Regulation, affected parties may challenge compensation decisions in court, but it remains unclear just how much protection the judicial system will provide, given its present status.[45]

Even if the new Regulation may somewhat reduce the number of contested demolition orders in Chinese cities, it is inapplicable to land-taking in rural areas, which is where the Tang Fuzhen tragedy took place. Article 10 of the 1982 Constitution not only provides for state ownership of urban land but also provides that 'land in the rural and suburban areas is owned by collectives' – presumed to be the villagers – thus instituting a dualist land ownership regime. Associated with the dualist regime is the common understanding (or more precisely, misunderstanding) that a change of ownership *requires* taking by the State. This (mis)interpretation has clear benefits for local officials, since urbanisation is now virtually a synonym for 'land-taking': whenever rural land is to be converted into industrial, commercial or urban residential property, the local government is constitutionally authorised to step in, and the land will in the end be sold for a much higher price. Unsurprisingly then, local officials

---

[44] See Zhang Qianfan, 'Just Compensation and the Constitutional Limitation on Takings Power' (2005) 2 *Chinese Journal of Law* 25–37.

[45] See further above ch 6.

are highly committed to this sort of 'development', resulting in millions of peasants who become landless petitioners with substandard compensation. Indeed, compared to urban demolition, rural land-taking has produced many more conflicts and tragedies. In Zhucheng (Shandong province), for example, the local government coerced peasants to move into storied buildings in exchange for their homesteads.[46] Having recognised the scope and severity these problems, the central government is in the process of revising the Land Administration Law.

* * *

China has not been the same since the open-door reforms began in 1978, but popular consciousness regarding rights remained largely dormant until the breakthrough controversy surrounding the Sun Zhigang incident in 2003. Since then, common Chinese people have become ever more conscious of their constitutional rights and are now actively working to protect them. From the Hepatitis-B virus case (involving rights to equality and anti-discrimination) to the She Xianglin case (involving criminal justice and personal freedom), and from the 'most robust nail house' in Chongqing to the Tang Fuzhen tragedy (which involved property rights), it has been ordinary people who have supplied the impetus to the subsequent institutional reforms. Perhaps it is this crucial difference that sets contemporary China apart from imperial Qing China, where intellectual elites like Kang Youwei and Liang Qichao represented the primary moving force for constitutional reform, while ordinary people remained silent and passive.[47]

However, if the Chinese people are becoming more conscious and active, the political system they confront today is as rigidly opposed to salutary change as it was a hundred years ago. The government today is even more prudent and effective than its imperial predecessors in banning rival parties, controlling the media and limiting the free development of all social forces, be they churches, associations or labour unions, lest they grow strong enough to challenge the political monopoly of the ruling Party. Without these fundamental freedoms, the Sun Zhigang model will prove to be of only limited use to the protection of life, liberty and equality.

---

[46] Tu Chonghang, 'Many Provinces and Municipalities Forcibly Abolish Villages to Exchange for Construction Land and Expand Land Finance', *New Beijing Daily* (2 November 2010).

[47] See above ch 1.

FURTHER READING

Brown, RC, 'China's Employment Discrimination Laws during Economic Transition' (2006) 19 *Columbia Journal of Asian Law* 361.

Huang, FX, 'The Path to Clarity: Development of Property Rights in China' (2004) 17 *Columbia Journal of Asian Law* 191.

Guo Luoji, 'A Human Rights Critique of the Chinese Legal System' (1996) 9 *Harvard Human Rights Journal* 1.

Hand, KJ, 'Using Law for a Righteous Purpose: The Sun Zhigang Incident and Evolving Forms of Citizen Action in the People's Republic of China' (2007) 45 *Columbia Journal of Transnational Law* 114.

Seay, PA, 'Law, 'Crime, and Punishment in the People's Republic of China: A Comparative Introduction to the Criminal Justice and Legal System of the People's Republic of China' (1998) 9 *Indiana International & Comparative Law Review* 143.

Huang, D, 'The Right to a Fair Trial in China' (1998) 7 *Pacific Rim Law & Policy Journal* 171.

Wang Chenguang and Zhang Xianchu (eds), *Introduction to Chinese Law* (Hong Kong, Sweet & Maxwell Asia, 1997) ch 17.

Mo Zhang, 'From Public to Private: The Newly Enacted Chinese Property Law and the Protection of Property Rights in China' (2008) 5 *Berkeley Business Law Journal* 317.

Xun Zeng, 'Enforcing Equal Employment Opportunities in China' (2007) 9 *University of Pennsylvania Journal of Labor & Employment Law* 991.

8

Still Dormant: Political and Religious Rights

<hr/>

INTRODUCTION: WHAT THE SUN ZHIGANG MODEL
CANNOT DO – FREEDOM OF SPEECH – Freedom of Speech,
the Internet Effect and Officials' Right to 'Reputation' – Freedom
of the Press and Its Regulation – Freedom of Assembly and Its
Regulation – Freedom of Association and Its Regulation –
FREEDOM OF RELIGION – Constitutional Protection, Legal
Restrictions – How to Distinguish 'Normal Religion' from 'Evil
Religion'? – The State–Religion Relationship – THE RIGHT TO
ELECTION – The Making of the People's Congresses: Election
or Selection? – The NPCSC Violation of the 'One-person One-
vote' Principle – Elections of the Villagers Committees: China's
Grassroots Democracy? – A One-Party-Dominant-Multiparty
System? –

I. INTRODUCTION: WHAT THE SUN ZHIGANG MODEL
CANNOT DO

THE SUN ZHIGANG incident was not only a case about freedom (of movement) and equality (between residents of cities
and those of the vast countryside) but also a case about free
speech. It would not have attracted the attention of the Chinese public
in the first place if the media had not reported the event, and it would
not have produced any institutional impact if citizens had not freely
expressed their reactions to the abuses of public power revealed by
the Sun Zhigang tragedy. As a successful example of civic participation
empowered by free expression and press coverage, the Sun Zhigang
model has helped, at least to a limited extent, to redress many individual
grievances caused by egregious abuses of public power.

The Sun Zhigang model is inherently limited, however, with regard to preventing such abuses. In fact, the Sun Zhigang incident was caused by a set of institutional dysfunctions that this model of activism is unable to resolve. At the institutional level, the tragedy was the result of unreasonable search and seizure, inhumane treatment by a detention centre and its inmates and, more remotely, the longstanding segregation policy that discriminated against peasants. But such discriminatory policies and excessive restrictions could be made and maintained only in the absence of public participation; the situation would have been quite unthinkable had the peasants, who constitute the vast majority of the voting population, been consulted and allowed to speak about these policies and regulations that so heavily discriminated against them. Fundamentally, the Sun Zhigang incident and many similar tragedies are caused by governments that are not held responsible through genuine elections, judicial review and other institutional mechanisms that oblige the governments to respect popular demands and rule of law.

The Sun Zhigang case was eventually resolved by massive public protests (mostly on the Internet), but the media reporting of the incident was somewhat exceptional in an institutional environment where public speech and the press are severely restricted. Indeed, the *South Metropolitan Daily*, an outspoken newspaper that reported the case, was later sanctioned for that and other reports which put the government in an awkward position. It was entirely uncertain whether the agitated public outcry would succeed in moving the central government to abolish the Custody and Repatriation Measures. In other words, the Sun Zhigang model of social and political change cannot work reliably without concurrent institutional guarantees such as representative democracy and freedom of speech. Unfortunately, these institutional rights have never been meaningfully protected in China, so they remain 'dormant', as it were. Using the Sun Zhigang model as a touchstone, this chapter explores the problems with political and religious rights in contemporary China.

Even in these politically sensitive areas, China is not completely without success. The people in Xiamen, for example, successfully pressed the city government to abandon plans to construct a paraxylene (PX) chemical plant near the city centre; they accomplished this by organising a 'collective walk' to the city hall without applying for a permit for demonstration.[1] But such successes are few and far between. This chapter

---

[1] See below s IIC.

examines the effect that the freedoms of expression and religion can have in promoting national unification and ethnic harmony, and it closes with a discussion of elections in contemporary China.

II. FREEDOM OF SPEECH

Article 35 of the 1982 Constitution states categorically that citizens 'enjoy freedom of speech, press, assembly, association, procession and demonstration'. Although none of these freedoms are institutionally protected in practice, one cannot gainsay the obvious fact that ordinary Chinese enjoy infinitely more free speech today than they did during the 'dark ages' of the 1950s and 1960s, when one could be executed for blasphemy against the 'supreme leader' (最高领袖, *zuigao lingxiu*), even if the sin was committed in one's private home. Nowadays people are essentially free to express any ideas in private conversation, even though phone lines may be tapped and mail (both postal and electronic) may be monitored. People are ordinarily free to speak even in public forums with limited audience numbers (eg, in classrooms with hundreds of students), even though such settings may be monitored by cameras and 'spies' of various sorts.[2] Most significantly, China, the most populous country in the world, also has the largest number of Internet users, which had grown to the size of 500 million by 2011 and is still growing. News that is tightly controlled in traditional media can easily leak onto the Internet and create surges of anger, sorrow or enthusiasm for public action in shocking cases like the Sun Zhigang and Tang Fuzhen tragedies.[3] On the other hand, public speeches of wide impact on forbidden subjects will be punished, as in the case of dissident Liu Xiaobo, the winner of the Nobel Peace Prize in 2010, who was sentenced to 11 years' imprisonment for initiating Charter 08, a manifesto that was widely circulated on the Internet.[4] In comparison to mere speech, the

---

[2] Two students of the East China Politics and Law University did inform the school authority that their teacher spread 'counter-revolutionary' views in the classroom, even though the crime under that name had long been deleted from the Constitution and the Criminal Law. Deng Yifu, 'Professor Criticised Government in Class, Accused by Female Students as "Counter-Revolutionary" ', *New Express Daily* (1 December 2008).

[3] For discussion of these cases, see previous chapters, especially chs 3 and 7.

[4] A Jacobs, 'Leading China Dissident Gets 11-Year Term for Subversion', *New York Times* (24 December 2009).

freedoms of the press, assembly and association are even more tightly restricted by specific laws and regulations.

A. Freedom of Speech, the Internet Effect and Officials' Right to 'Reputation'

Freedom of speech and the press provides a society with the essential information and tools for rational governance. In the past, the suppression of speech and the press brought grave tragedies to Chinese society. The Great Leap Forward and the People's Commune regime instituted in 1958 could have been halted in time to avoid the great famine that claimed a death toll of 30 million had the suffering peasants been allowed to freely air their grievances. The scale of the tragedy could have been reduced had Admiral Peng Dehuai (彭德怀), the Defence Minister at the time, been allowed to express his disagreement with these disastrous policies at the Mount Lu Conference (庐山会议, *lushan huiyi*), where Mao Zedong used his personal authority and political power to suppress Peng's open letter.[5] Likewise, China might not now be suffering from extreme overcrowding, which has led to an often inhumane birth control policy, had Professor Ma Yinchu (马寅初), then the President of Peking University, been allowed to freely publish his book *New Population Theory* rather than being denounced as a 'rightist'.[6] Both the dramatic reduction in population through famine and its even more dramatic rise in the following decades were the painful costs that ordinary Chinese people have borne as a result of institutions that positively suppress free exchange of information and opinion.

However, the Internet, mobile phones and other contemporary means of communication have allowed China's ordinary people to access information and to air their views, complaints and grievances on their own, without needing to rely on a media prone to government control. Indeed, major human rights abuses in recent years have been addressed almost exclusively as a result of public pressure brought by Internet exposure.

---

[5] Li Rui, *Record of the Lu Shan Conference*, revised edn (Zhengzhou, Henan People's Press, 1994) 12–14.

[6] See Xu Mei and Yi Jie, 'The Vision and Courage of Ma Yinchu', *Southern People's Weekly* (18 February 2011).

Although it is unfeasible for the government to impose prior restraints on these forms of expression, individuals may be penalised post hoc by allegedly 'defamed' officials. The first in this line of cases was the *Pengshui Poem* case in 2006. Qin Zhongfei (秦中飞), a local teacher, composed a poem that alluded to corruption in Pengshui county (Chongqing municipality), and it was circulated via mobile phone messages among friends.[7] The timing of the poem was less than propitious since the county leadership was about to be re-elected – more precisely, reappointed – and the Party committee of Chongqing municipality was therefore reviewing the county leaders' performance. No sooner was the county Party secretary made aware of the content of the poem then he ordered the local PSB to investigate the author. He then arranged for the PSB, the procuratorate and the Criminal Division of the court to sit in joint conference to 'study the case'. In order to prevent the poem from 'affecting social and political stability', the county Party leader instructed that the case be dealt with within five days using a 'ruthless hand'. Under such direction, the county PSB detained Qin Zhongfei for committing 'the crime of libel', and the county procuratorate immediately approved the arrest. Only after the case was exposed nationally, 'shocking' the Ministry of Public Security and the leaders of the central government, did the Chongqing authority reinvestigate the case, acquit Qin and provide him with state compensation.

Since the *Pengshui Poem* case, an array of cases have been reported in China, all involving 'libel' against local cadres through circulating mobile phone messages or electronic mail, or through regular mail sent to the superior government for the purpose of exposing local corruption. Most of the responsible parties were severely punished by the 'libelled' officials, who employed a full panoply of local investigatory, prosecutorial and judicial power. In 2007, for example, Zhang Zhijian (张志坚) was detained for nine months for simply posting an article on the Internet about the corrupt dealings between officials in the State Drug Administration and a drug company in Haikou city.[8] Only after the Chief Administrator of the State Drug Administration was convicted – indeed, he is among the few officials who have been executed during the contemporary era for serious malfeasance – did the procuratorate

---

[7] Zhang Qianfan, 'May a Citizen "Slander" an Official?' *New Beijing Daily* (13 May 2007).

[8] See reports in *New Beijing Daily* (9 April 2007).

withdraw the prosecution, by which time Zhang had already lost his job. Such misfortune is not limited to common people but may occur to officials as well. In the same year, the director of the Local People's Congress (LPC) Legal Affairs Commission of Jishan county, along with two other officials, mailed investigatory materials to the superior Party committee in Yuncheng city (Shanxi province), accusing the Party secretary of the county for failing to fulfil his obligations. Within 10 days, they were investigated and detained by police, and the director was convicted for committing 'libel'.

Internet exposure has transcended the limitations of traditional media like newspaper and television, which generally can provide only 'off-site supervision' (异地监督, *yidi jiandu*): a media outlet located in Beijing, for example, is generally effective in exposing only abuses of public power that occur in other jurisdictions, because the reporters will not have to fear retaliation from that local government. More recently, however, several local governments have been bold enough to engage in 'cross-jurisdiction pursuit' (跨省追捕, *kuasheng zhuibu*) by dispatching the local police force to arrest the 'libellants' residing in other provinces.[9] In March 2009, Wang Shuai (王帅) was taken away from his workplace in Shanghai by the police of his hometown, Lingbao city (Henan province), for exposing on the Internet the allegedly illegal land-taking by the local government, against which he repeatedly and in vain petitioned the land resource administration and Party disciplinary inspection departments at all levels . The Lingbao city government recalled him back home to 'teach him a lesson' and to make sure he would not 'repeat the same mistake' of humiliating the local government. The local procuratorate dropped the charge for insufficiency of evidence only after Wang's family reached a deal with the local government with respect to their land.

'Cross-jurisdiction pursuit' is not reserved for Internet users but may be used to catch authors and correspondents in other jurisdictions. In 2008, an entrepreneur was in Beijing petitioning for relief from the local persecution she had suffered in her home county of Xifeng (Liaoning province) when she was taken back from Beijing and convicted for 'libel'. The magazine *Law Person* (法人, *faren*) of the *Legal Daily* carried the story, which was widely circulated on the Internet. Alleging that the

---

[9] 'An Internet Post Invited 8 Day Imprisonment', *China Youth Daily*, 8 April 2009.

correspondent also committed 'libel', the Party secretary of Xifeng county sent the police to arrest her in Beijing as well and was forced to give up only under mounting public pressure after the news spread on the Internet.[10] In August 2010, Xie Chaoping (谢朝平), a Beijing author, published a book entitled *The Great Migration*, which exposed the suffering of migrants relocated from the Three Gate Gorges Hydropower project, a catastrophic failure that was constructed on the Yellow River in the 1950s, as well as detailing the local interdiction and misappropriation of central relief funds over the years. He was taken away from his Beijing home by plainclothes police dispatched by the offended government of Weinan city (Shaanxi province) and detained for 'illegally conducting business' (ie, publishing his book). After public pressure grew from public appeals by experts and extensive news coverage, which defied an official ban on reporting the case, the county procuratorate finally put Xie Chaoping on 'bail' (取保候审, *qubao houshen*), though they reserved the right to prosecute him for up to a year.[11]

B. Freedom of the Press and Its Regulation

Freedom of the press has never been embraced as an effective principle in China, where the First Emperor is widely known for having 'burned books and buried the Confucian scholars' (焚书坑儒, *fenshu kengru*) during the high tide of his Legalist reign (213–12 bc). Imperial China managed to control the private press primarily through post hoc penalties (which could be extremely harsh) rather than prior restraint. Even during the excessively severe 'literary inquisition' (文字狱, *wenziyu*) of the early Qing dynasty, censorship guidelines were unknown. Although censorship was sporadically set up during the late Qing and Republican periods, systematic control was established only after 1949, when both prior restraint and post hoc prosecution were routinely employed to ensure that media conformed to the Party line. More fundamentally, all forms of media became monopolised by the State; newspapers, magazines, books, radio and television are all run by entities of public nature, the leadership of which is directly appointed and removed by the

[10] Zhang Qianfan, 'May the Media "Slander" Officials?' *China Economic Times* (18 January 2008).
[11] Huang Xiuli and Kou Aizhe, 'Who Saved Xie Chaoping?' *Southern Weekend* (22 September 2010).

government. Contemporary forms of media are much more pluralistic than those of the revolutionary heyday. Many more books, newspapers and magazines are published today, and TV and radio have many more channels, but none of them are allowed to go beyond the political base-line, and the government can easily turn any media outlet upside down by simply replacing its major leaders.

To begin with, the 'press' (出版, *chuban*) is an ambivalent term in Chinese. In its broad sense, the word in Article 35 of the Constitution stands for television, radio and the publication of books, journals and newspapers; in a narrower sense, it merely stands for print publications, as exemplified by the Regulation on Administration of Publications, which does not cover film, television and radio. These are regulated by a separate State Administration for Radio, Film and Television (国家广电总局, *guojia guangdian zongju*). Since both regulatory schemes are similar, the discussion here is limited to the Regulation on Administration of Publications.

Enacted by the State Council in 2001, the Regulation provides for freedom of the press but predicates such freedom on the observance of 'the cardinal principles ascertained in the Constitution' and 'state, social and collective interests' (Article 5). Article 11 states that to establish a press, an application must be made to the provincial administration of publications and be approved before it is submitted to the State Administration of Press and Publications (SAPP) (国家新闻出版署, *guojia xinwen chubanshu*) for approval. In practice, this process is extremely difficult, usually accompanied by heavy bribery; any publication will be deemed illegal and its publisher will be heavily punished if a permit is not first obtained. The publisher is also required to submit an annual publication plan with book titles to both the provincial administration and the SAPP for approval (Article 19); it must also provide free copies to the SAPP and the State Library.

Article 25 sets out eight categories of prohibited content, eg, 'incite-ment to secession', 'sabotage of national solidarity', 'disclosure of state secrets', 'promotion of obscenity, superstition or violence' and 'harm to social morality and the excellent cultural tradition of the nation'. While ordinary violations are subject to fines, serious violations may lead to 'closure of business for rectification' (停业整顿, *tingye zhengdun*) or revo-cation of the publication permit.

The press may also be limited by other laws that restrict the disclosure of information. Prime examples are the State Security Law, enacted by the National People's Congress Standing Committee (NPCSC) in 1993, and the Law on Guarding State Secrets, enacted by the NPCSC in 1988 and revised in 2010, after the State Council promulgated the Regulation on the Disclosure of Government Information in 2007. While the State Security Law is primarily directed at harmful acts, its Rule for Implementation adds several categories of acts endangering state security, eg, 'manufacturing ethnic conflict and incitement to secession' through 'fabrication or distortion of facts' or 'publication or spreading of words or speeches' (Article 8). These provisions are prone to expanded interpretations that criminalise speech and publication.

The State Secrets Law broadly defines a state secret as anything that relates to 'state security and interest, the disclosure of which may damage the state security and interest in political, economic, defence, diplomacy and other areas' (Article 9), including: 'secret matters in the major decisions of state affairs' (clause 1); 'secret matters in national economy and social development' (clause 4); and 'secret matters of political parties'. More disturbing is the fact that numerous bodies are authorised to decide that particular information constitutes a state secret. While the State Secrecy Bureau is in charge of deciding the scope and level of a state secret, and the Central Military Commission (CMC) is in charge of deciding military secrets (Article 11), every department is authorised to decide whether a matter within its jurisdiction should be classified as a state secret and when it should be declassified (Article 12). It used to be that local governments at all levels had the authority to identify their own 'state secrets', making it possible for any information to be classified as 'state secret' in China. 2010 revisions limit such authority to the governments of cities that are divided into districts and the levels above (Article 13), but such limitation falls far short of the mission stated in the Regulation on the Disclosure of Government Information – ie, to 'enhance the transparency of government works' and 'promote administration according to law' (Article 1).

Under these laws, China's press has been effectively suppressed, and Chinese society has paid dearly for the lack of information that is so essential to rational living. The Tangshan earthquake in 1976, for example, took 240,000 lives in mere seconds, but the death toll was revealed only three years later because 'the numbers of those who flee from famine, beg for food or die in natural disasters' had long been considered a 'state secret'. This classification was reinforced by the State Secrecy Bureau and the Civil Affairs Bureau in 2000, when they jointly issued Guidelines for

State Secrets and the Specific Scope of Secrecy Levels in Civil Affairs. It was not until 2005 when the revision to the Guidelines deleted the words 'or die' from the text that the death toll was allowed to be revealed. Although concealing the death toll of an earthquake may seem harmless, the habit of withholding information from the public can lead to monstrous consequences. Indeed, the Tangshan earthquake itself may have been predicted and some casualties avoided. But Tangshan was close to Beijing, the political centre of the nation, which was fraught with political unrest at that time, Premier Zhou Enlai having just died and the death of the 'Great Leader' Mao Zedong imminent. Primarily out of concern for political stability, the local government suppressed many forecast reports that indicated the possibility of an earthquake, and the suppression of such crucial information disposed a totally unprepared people to sound sleep that fateful night when calamity arrived.[12]

The same suppressive habit persists today. When Guangzhou was struck by the severe acute respiratory syndrome (SARS) in early 2003, the epidemic could have been controlled by allowing the press to report the events and by cautioning ordinary people to take self-protective measures. By suppressing the early SARS report of the *South Metropolitan Daily*, the Chinese authorities deprived their people of information that was essential to their own protection, until the epidemic had spread nationwide. In fact, suppression of the press is not unique to local newspapers; it has even happened to the orthodox national Party newspaper, the *People's Daily*. On 28 August 2003, the newspaper's fifth section published a criticism of the local government of Dingnan county (Jiangxi province) for engaging in illegal land-taking. The next day, two county officials managed to take away the fifth section from all copies of the *People's Daily*, making that section mysteriously 'vaporise', as it were, from the locality.[13]

Despite recent intensification of official restrictions, correspondents in China have been consistently gaining in courage, strength and profes-

---

[12] A counter example is found in Qinglong (青龙), a county in the vicinity of Tangshan, where its chief and party secretary Ran Guangqi (冉广岐) risked his own post by leaking the news about a potentially imminent earthquake to his people on the eve before it arrived. As a result the county suffered only minor personal injury and property loss, without a single death toll. See Zhang Qingzhou, *The Lesson of Tangshan: The Beginning and End of the Omitted Report of the Great Earthquake on July 28, 1976* (Shanghai, Shanghai People's Press, 2006).

[13] Cheng Gong and Tao Dabin, 'The Consequences and Causes of the "People's Daily Incident" in Dingnan', *Southern Weekend* (18 September 2003).

sional competence. Even though the *South Metropolitan Daily* was punished after it published reports of the SARS epidemic and the Sun Zhigang incident, it has by and large maintained its spirit and character. With courageous correspondents and editors, the burgeoning news media has contributed a great deal to the information and knowledge that are essential for the rational governance of contemporary Chinese society. And in an age when people crave information, it will be on the winning side of the battle between public disclosure and state secrecy.

C. Freedom of Assembly and Its Regulation

The June 2007 'collective walk' (集体散步, *jiti sanbu*) that took place to protest a PX factory in Xiamen opened a promising new chapter in China's constitutionalism, although it did not erase a nearly six-decade record: since 1949, the People's Republic has not officially sanctioned a single demonstration, except an assembly of dubious origin in front the United States Embassy in 1999 following the American bombing of the Chinese embassy in the former Yugoslavia. In March 2004, more than 100 villagers dared to hold a demonstration in Jinhua city (Zhejiang province) to protest insufficient compensation for the public taking of village land. Although the compensation was promptly raised after the protest, its major organisers were punished under Article 296 of the Criminal Law for 'illegal assembly' and sentenced to 18 months' imprisonment.[14] The district court decided that the procession had 'seriously damaged the good image' of the district and city governments and Party committees and was likely to result in illegal mass petitions, thereby seriously undermining public order, which is prohibited by the Law on Assemblies, Processions and Demonstrations (hereafter 'Law on Assemblies').

The Law on Assemblies was enacted by the NPCSC in 1989, partly to tighten regulation of popular assemblies in the aftermath of the Tiananmen protests. It requires applicants to obtain permission from the local PSB, which shall inform the applicants in writing whether permission is granted or not two days prior to the date of the proposed assembly, and failure to serve notice within the time limit shall be construed as the granting of permission (Articles 7 and 9). Rejection of an application must be accompanied by reasons; applicants may appeal an

[14] Xu Nan, 'First Illegal Demonstration Case in Zhejiang', *Southern Weekend* (9 September 2004).

decision to the government at the same level for reconsideration within three days of receiving notice of the decision (Articles 9 and 13). An application will be rejected if the proposed assembly falls within the four categories of situations defined in Article 12, the most frequently invoked one being that there is 'sufficient ground' to suspect that the assembly or demonstration 'will directly endanger public security or seriously undermine public order' (clause 4).[15] When an application for assembly is almost invariably rejected on the ground that it would 'seriously undermine public order', the legal avenue of appeal is rarely used, since it is practically foreclosed. As a result, the applicants are usually obliged to hold an unapproved assembly at their own risk (as illustrated in the Jinhua demonstration case), to keep silent (as the vast majority chooses to do) or to invent ingenious ways to express their demands such that the law cannot reach.

Four years after the Sun Zhigang incident, a historic event occurred in Xiamen, the capitol of the southern coastal province of Fujian, when the latter option was chosen. Thousands of Xiamen residents, coordinating through mobile phones, gathered in June 2007 before the city government to protest its decision to construct a plant for producing PX chemical, a toxic and potentially carcinogenic substance, less than seven kilometres from the densely populated central city area.[16] A few months earlier, over 100 members of the National Political Consultative Committee (NPCC),[17] led by a senior toxicologist, Professor Zhao Yufen of Xiamen University, petitioned to stop the project during the highly publicised annual NPC and NPCC conventions. Their efforts, however, were in vain, and they were advised to renounce their negative statements and keep silent. The project went on to receive favourable

---

[15] Dr Xu Zhiyong, one of the petitioners in the Sun Zhigang case, applied several times to hold a six-person demonstration against the nonfeasance of the Public Security Bureau and Supreme Court, but all applications were rejected on the ground that the demonstration might 'seriously disturb public order': Decision No 56 of Beijing Public Security Bureau for Disallowing Assembly and Demonstration (2005).

[16] See reports in *South Metropolitan Daily* (31 May 2007) and (9 June 2007). Whether exposure to the PX chemical will produce cancer is a subject of dispute. While the city government claimed that its investigation showed no positive carcinogenic effects, experts and city residents disagreed, insisting that the project met safety standards only if it was relocated at least 100 kilometres from residential areas. See, eg, 'Xiamen's Chemical Project Worth 10 Billion [Yuan] Invoked Safety Disputes, 105 Committee Members Petitioned for Relocation', *China Management Daily* (16 March 2007).

[17] See further below ch 9.

evaluation for its environmental impact and was approved by the National Environmental Protection Agency. Having witnessed the failure of these elite efforts as organised by academics and specialists through official channels and foreseeing the fate of any assembly application, Xiamen residents decided to take the matter into their own hands. They bypassed the procedural niceties legally required for a 'demonstration', instead coordinating themselves to take a 'collective walk' to the city hall. The large turn-out eventually succeeded in pressuring the city government to give up the project.[18] It was the first successful event organised by the spontaneous efforts of local grassroots bodies in the history of the People's Republic.

Other local decisions with environmental impacts have since sparked civil protests and participation nationwide. Several months after the Xiamen 'walk', for example, Shanghai residents resorted to similar action against a maglev train project that would generate electromagnet pollution for nearby residents, some residing within 3 kilometres from the site. The residents succeeded in pressuring the city government to suspend the project.[19] In 2009, when the city government in Guangzhou decided to construct a garbage treatment plant in the Fanyu district, many local residents worried about the deterioration of their living environment. They debated alternative approaches to garbage treatment and held massive protests before the city government. After some hesitation, the Guangzhou government openly expressed their willingness to consider alternative plans if they gained wider public support.[20] These successful efforts point to the possibility of a more positive and promising approach than that offered by the official system of arbitrary decision-making by local governments. Moreover, these grassroots events illustrate that whenever the vital interest of an identifiable group is seriously injured, that group is likely to take positive action to protect its members' own interest, and might successfully use new technologies as well as traditional media to make its voice heard.[21]

[18] See report in *South Metropolitan News* (9 June 2007).

[19] Cai Huiqun, 'State Yet to Define Standard for Electromagnetic Pollution of Maglev Trains, Shanghai Residents Walked to Express Concerns', *Southern Weekend* (18 January 2008).

[20] See Liu Gang and Zhou Hualei, 'The Guangzhou "Walk" in Name of Environmental Protection', *China Newsweek* (26 November 2009).

[21] For example, Yirenping basically rely on Internet news distributions and informal publication (as formal publications are tightly restricted) of their monthly gazette to propagate anti-discrimination appeals.

Yet even these instances of civic activism share many of the same limitations demonstrated by the Sun Zhigang model. Indeed, the Xiamen event came about only after the failure of other efforts, and its ultimate success remains somewhat unexplained. Fundamentally, since there is nothing in the current institutional framework that guarantees success for spontaneous demonstrations, the Xiamen model inevitably lacks predictability and reproducibility. The approach has so far been replicated only in similarly 'civilised' cities like Shanghai and Guangzhou, where the local governments already exhibit more respect for residents' freedom of expression and exercise more restraint in using force against them. It goes without saying that even such limited respect and restraint are not guaranteed elsewhere. In fact, the PX chemical project was driven out of Xiamen city, but the Fujian provincial government only relocated it to another city, Zhangzhou, where the local government repackaged the project and took deliberate precautions to prevent similar popular gatherings.[22] A year later, a similar PX chemical plant was to be installed at a location upstream to the even more densely populated city of Chengdu, the capital of Sichuan province, where the residents imitated their Xiamen compatriots by organising a 'collective walk' to the city government. The result, however, was exactly the opposite: the organisers not only failed to persuade the Chengdu government to reverse its decision but were arrested and convicted.[23] Hence, the Xiamen line of events did not follow the Sun Zhigang model; but it was nevertheless limited by the same institutional impediments.

The most recent advent of public assembly in China was an event in Wukan village (Guangdong province), where villagers gathered before the Lufeng city government building, originally to protest the allegedly unlawful land-taking abetted by the villagers' committee. Unsatisfied with the official resolution of the problem, the Wukan villagers voted to establish a 'temporary representative council' and 'women's federation' and organised another protest before the city government on 21 November 2011. The government increased their control efforts and retaliated by detaining several protest organisers, one of whom died in police custody. The event provoked tens of thousands of the Wukan villagers to protest and demand the investigation of the true cause of

[22] Chan Shibing, 'The "Tangerine in North Becomes Orange in South" Game at the Zhangzhou PX Chemical Project, *Huashang Daily* (6 February 2009).
[23] 'Six Activists Were Punished in Chengdu Walk Event', *New Beijing Daily* (12 May 2008).

the victim's death, and even established barracks against the work groups sent by the government. The stand-off was resolved only after the Guangdong Party Secretary, Wang Yang (汪洋), dispatched a high-profile delegation to visit the village and satisfy the villagers' demands by removing several village officials who had been dubiously elected and committed illegal acts in land-taking and village finance.[24] Showing appreciation and good will to the Party, the villagers triumphantly returned to regular life. On 3 March 2012, they successfully elected their own villagers' committee, to be headed by one of the chief organisers of the protests.[25]

D. Freedom of Association and Its Regulation

Like freedom of the press, freedom of association is regulated not by any law but by the Regulation on the Registration and Administration of Social Organisations, enacted by the State Council in 1998. And like the conditions for establishing the legal status of a publisher, the conditions for establishing a non-profitable 'social organisation' (社会团体, *shehui tuanti*), as opposed to an 'economic organisation', are extremely strict, leading to the ingenious if not bizarre strategies for circumventing the strict requirements. While new journals in China are often published as 'books' because registering a new journal is next to impossible for ordinary people without 'special background' (ie, connections with the very top of the central government), nongovernment organisations (NGOs) in China are often registered as 'companies' for the same reason. Such a tactic may invite retribution, however, if not used with sufficient care. In

---

[24] M Patience, 'China's Wukan Village Stands Up for Land Rights', *BBC News* (15 December 2011), http://www.bbc.co.uk/news/world-asia-china-16205654; and Li Qiang, 'Deputy Party Secretary of Guangdong Province Visited Wukan Village, Claimed to Resolve the Issues by Relying on the Mass', *Southern Daily* (23 December 2011). Any public comment of the event was strictly prohibited in China, however. When I approached one of the most outspoken newspapers in China to write a positive comment, in part to praise the way in which the Guangdong government handled the conflict, I was told that the newspaper was forbidden to publish anything about the event other than the news releases provided by the official Xinhua News Agency (新华社, *Xinhua she*).

[25] 'Lin Zulian was Elected the Chief of the Villagers' Committee in Wukan, Guangdong', *Tencent News* (3 March 2012), http://news.qq.com/a/20120303/001453.htm?pgv_ref=aio.

2009, the Public Alliance, an NGO registered as a 'company' by Dr Xu Zhiyong (许志永) and other public interest lawyers, was investigated and closed by the State Administration of Taxation for failing to pay 'tax' on the donations it received.[26]

To register a 'social organisation', an applicant must obtain approval both from the 'unit in charge of the business' (业务主管单位, *yewu zhuguan danwei*) and from the registration authority, which is the local civil affairs department (Regulation on the Registration and Administration of Social Organisations, Articles 3 and 6). An association must meet the substantive requirements of membership (at least 50 individual members or 30 unit members or 50 mixed members) and finance (activity funds of at least RMB¥100,000 for a national society and RMB¥30,000 for a local society), as well as have full-time recruitment dedicated to the professional activities of the association (Article 10). An application will not be approved if the proposed association is opposed to the 'cardinal principles' of the Constitution, 'damages state unity and security and ethnic solidarity', 'damages the state and public interest' or 'contravenes social morality' (Article 4), or if 'the establishment is unnecessary because there are social organisations covering the same or similar professional scope within the same administrative jurisdiction' or if the initiators or persons proposed to be in charge 'are or once were deprived of political rights' (Article 13).

The application procedure is extremely cumbersome. Applicants must first obtain approval for 'preparation for the establishment' of the organisation and adopt a charter for the proposed association before they may formally apply for the establishment of the association (Article 14). And the story is not over once it is established and registered, since the organisation is to be annually reviewed: a 'preliminary review' conducted by the 'unit in charge of the business' and a formal review conducted by the local civil affairs bureau. The association is obligated to submit a detailed report describing the activities, the personnel and institutional changes, and financial management of the past year (Article 27). Activities found inconsistent with the charter of the association will lead to such censures as warning, reprimand for correction, order to cease activities, order to replace the directly responsible person in charge or even revocation of the registration (Articles 33 and 34).

---

[26] B Demick, 'Beijing Frees Legal Activist Xu Zhiyong', *Los Angeles Times* (24 August 2009).

Falling outside the Regulation are 'people's organisations' (人民团体, *renmin tuanti*) participating in the Political Consultative Committees and those organisations exempted by the State Council. An example of the people's organisations is the All-China Federation of Trade Unions (ACFTU) (中华全国总工会, *zhonghua quanguo zonggonghui*), an umbrella organisation for all trade unions in China. Since unions are given very limited power and their leaders are not genuinely elected, the functions they perform are restricted to insubstantial ones, such as delivery of holiday gifts, and they have no role to play in protecting workers from abusive employment practices and poor management. Although the right to organise independent unions is provided for in Article 8 of the International Covenant for Economic, Social, and Cultural Rights, which was ratified by the NPCSC in 2001, a specific reservation was made with respect to the role of leadership performed by ACFTU. Indeed, foreign enterprises flock to China from all over the world partly to make the most of this 'low human rights advantage'.[27]

The right to form unions is fundamental in many other countries, where they are equipped with a full range of legally protected strategies for advocating on behalf of workers, above all the right to strike. While employers must take union demands seriously in these countries, in China they need not even allow unions at all. Even if unions are formed, they are so easily manipulated that they usually turn out to be more like the bosses' henchmen than the workers' comrades. Even if a union leader dutifully vindicates the rights of the workers (which is rare), he can simply be laid off and replaced.[28] The right to strike, which was provided for in the 1975 and 1978 Constitutions but deleted in the 1982 Constitution, has never been recognised in practice. In 2003, a few foreign enterprises in coastal provinces started allowing employees to elect their union leaders directly, which produced phenomenal effects on the employees' benefits,[29] but this practice has not been expanded to most enterprises, foreign or domestic. Moreover, in the vast rural areas, peasants, who once could form 'peasant associations' (农会, *nonghui*), which

---

[27] For the origin of this phrase, see Xiong Peiyun, 'Qin Hui on the Surprising Competitive Strength of the Low Human Rights Advantage', *South Wind Weekly* (15 July 2009).

[28] 'Fired Union Chair Wins Arbitration', *New Beijing Daily* (15 September 2006).

[29] 'Direct Election of Labour Union Chair in Foreign Invested Enterprises', *Xinhua Daily* (29 January 2003).

were deployed by the Chinese Communist Party (CCP) against the land-lords and their Nationalist protectors, have not been granted any right of association since 1949.

The absence of active unions and associations has long left Chinese society without the self-protective capacity to oppose abuses of public or private powers, and as a result, the Chinese people are entirely dependent on an unfortunately undependable government. It used to be common practice, for example, for 'peasant workers' who sojourn to the cities for work to receive salaries only once a year, right before they return to their rural homes for the Spring Festival. As payday approaches, however, some employers escape and disappear with their employees' salaries for the whole year, leaving them desperate. A few victims have jumped off buildings to attract public attention to the problem. At one point, Premier Wen Jiabao (温家宝) stepped forward to help peasant workers get their salaries back[30] – but without giving them the right to association, which would have enabled them to fight for their own sala-ries, a Premier cannot possibly save 200 million peasant workers. In 2004, the central government listed peasant worker salaries as a top pri-ority on its agenda and designed special judicial procedures for their protection, yet the problem appeared to be unresolved by the Spring Festival in 2011.[31]

Without effective unions that are protected by a constitutional right to association, it is not only the lower classes such as peasant workers who are vulnerable; elite, white-collar workers such as pilots fare no bet-ter. In late March 2008, 18 pilots of passenger airplanes from Eastern Airlines refused to land and took the passengers back to their points of departure. The pilots, dissatisfied with their salaries and welfare but una-ble to switch airlines without breaking their lifetime contracts, succeeded in attracting national attention. Had they been allowed to exercise the right to association or to strike while on land, they would not have had to 'strike' in the air.

---

[30] 'Five Million Salaries Have Not Being Received', *New Beijing Daily* (5 December 2003).

[31] Ren Guoyong, 'Peasant Workers Demanding Pay Clash with Armed Security Guards, Many Wounded', *Yangtze Evening News* (16 December 2010).

III. FREEDOM OF RELIGION

Freedom of expression and religious freedom join hands to safeguard peace, harmony and unity in a culturally diverse nation. Religious tolerance enables members of a community to peacefully resolve sectarian disputes, while freedom of expression enables different religions and cultures to communicate and understand each other, thereby inculcating mutual sympathy and reducing animosity. For contemporary China, these matters have been of cardinal importance because the population is composed of the dominant Han and many minority cultures, which often have their own distinctive religions. Official interference with or intolerance of religious beliefs is the surest road to religious and social unrest, disrupting the unity and peace of the nation.

Ironically, in an era when orthodox Marxist ideology has lost its popular appeal, the government today fears religion less as a rival faith and more as a form of civic association that is capable of organising independent social action. As the large-scale persecution of the Falun Gong (法轮功) sect in 1999 illustrates, however, the more harshly a government cracks down on religious activities in the name of social order, the more disorder and unrest will it bring to society. Official control of expression and of the exchange of ideas further disposes different peoples to misunderstanding and intensifies animosity among them, turning political disputes between the government and ethnic minorities into potentially violent clashes between angry groups of people on a national scale. Unfortunately, such is precisely the situation with Tibet and Xinjiang today, where past religious suppression has created ethnic hatred and separatist tendencies. The prohibition of free expression and the deliberate distortion of official media reports on ethnic conflict have meant that the dominant Han population in the rest of China is entirely blind to the true causes of the ethnic tensions in these regions and is willing to do anything to defend national unity. The ethnic hostilities expressed on the Internet with regard to the unrest in these areas are reminiscent of the racist hysteria in Nazi Germany during the 1930s.[32] The free exchange of ideas and religious tolerance are precisely the institutional prerequisites of the peaceful unity of China.

[32] See Wang Lixiong, *My West Territory, Your East Land* (Taipei, Mass Culture Press, 2007) 56.

The significance of religious freedom is even harder for China to appreciate, however, precisely because religious conflicts have been few and far between in its history. While the Western principles of religious freedom and separation of church and state were developed through centuries of religious persecution and crusades, China hardly witnessed a single religious war; indeed, many even question whether traditional Chinese civilisation had a 'religion' in the Western sense at all outside of the debatable case of Daoism.[33] Since 1949, China has been dominated by Marxist ideology, which treats religion as 'superstition' and the 'opium of the people' for soothing the pain of individual souls.[34] The atheist animosity for religion reached its climax during the Cultural Revolution (1966–76), when religious sites were defaced by mobs and taken by government on a massive scale.

Since the economic reform movement began in the late 1970s, China's attitude toward religion has been considerably softened, yet its religious policies are still influenced by the remnants of the atheist mind-set and the fear of the organisational capacity of churches and sects. Religion thus remains a sensitive political issue and is prone to pervasive control by the government. Yet as the recent riots in Tibet and Xinjiang demonstrate, failure to take religious freedom seriously has produced and will continue to produce violent consequences for Chinese society.

A. Constitutional Protection, Legal Restrictions

Unlike the freedom of speech, which is expressed in rather categorical language in Article 35, the freedom of religion is protected in the 1982 Constitution only within carefully circumscribed limits. Article 36 does provide for religious freedom and a secular state as basic principles:

> Citizens enjoy freedom of religious belief. No state organ, public organisation or individual may compel citizens to believe in or not to believe in any religion; nor may they discriminate against citizens who believe in or do not believe in any religion.

[33] M Weber, *The Religion of China*, HH Gerth (trans) (New York, Free Press, 1951) 235.
[34] K Marx, 'Contribution to Critique of Hegel's Philosophy of Right' in RC Tucker (ed), *The Marx–Engels Reader*, 2nd edn (New York, Norton, 1978) 54.

But it is quick to add:

> The state protects normal religious activities. No one may make use of religion to engage in activities that disrupt public order, impair the health of citizens or interfere with the educational system of the state. Religious bodies and religious affairs are not subject to any foreign domination.

The crux of the issue is the scope of 'normal' religious activities and the extent of restrictions that the state may legitimately impose without violating the principle of religious freedom. In practice, China's religious freedom is carefully restricted by laws and regulations that have substantially reduced the scope and effectiveness of the constitutional protection of religious freedom. The major legislation that sets forth the restrictions on religious rights is the Religious Affairs Regulation, enacted by the State Council in 2005. First, Article 6 of the Regulation requires religious groups to follow provisions of the Regulation on the Registration and Administration of Social Organisations (discussed above) whenever they are founded, changed or disbanded. Since the latter Regulation sets forth strict conditions for establishing a 'social organisation', applying the same to religious groups obviously imposes serious restrictions on religious establishment and practice. To begin with, China recognises only five legitimate religions: Catholicism, Protestantism, Islam, Buddhism and Daoism. Limiting official recognition to only 'three-self patriotic churches' (三自爱国教会, *sanzi aiguo jiaohui*)[35] has created many 'underground', illegal 'house churches' (家庭教会, *jiating jiaohui*), whose religious practices used to be severely prosecuted by the government.

Second, the Religious Affairs Regulation also imposes strict restrictions on religious publications: 'Published materials that contain religious information shall comply with the Regulations Governing Publication' and must not contain any material that would 'upset harmonious relations' between believers and non-believers or 'between different religions or within a religion', 'propagate religious extremism' or 'violate the principle of religious autonomy and independence'. Furthermore, a religious society must obtain a certificate of approval from the State before printing and circulating religious materials. These restrictions set onerous conditions on the freedom of religious speech.

---

[35] The 'three-self' churches refer to those Protestant and Catholic churches that accept the CCP leadership and operate on the principles of 'self-governance', 'self-support' and 'self-propagation' (ie, without interference from foreign churches).

Last but by no means least, the Religious Affairs Regulation specifically provides for several legal consequences for violations of its prohibitions. Article 40 authorises religious affairs departments to 'order the halt of large-scale religious activities that are held without authorisation'. In such a case, the registering authority can even 'order' the religious group to 'replace the personnel directly responsible for the activities'; and if such activities 'harm public security or seriously upset the social order', the registering authority may rescind the registration of the responsible organising group, church or temple (Article 40). If a religious instructor violates a law, regulation or rule while engaged in a religious educational activity, 'the religious affairs department shall recommend that the relevant religious group rescind his instructor status' (Article 45). These provisions are enacted to facilitate official control over religion and constitute direct interference with the right to religious practice, education and autonomy.

More fundamentally, China's legislation provides no effective legal remedy to address the legal disputes arising from religious issues. Once religious freedom is violated, a victim can at best lodge a complaint to the local government via an application for administrative reconsideration, thus placing religious matters in the hands of bureaucrats. The Religious Affairs Regulation does provide for judicial remedy if a religious believer or group disagrees with official sanctions but limits such remedy by requiring the exhaustion of administrative remedies as a precondition. According to Article 46, an applicant must go through administrative reconsideration before bringing any administrative litigation, while ordinary administrative litigation has no such requirement (Administrative Litigation Law, Article 37). Religious freedom in itself is not effectively protected, however, given the absence of legal remedy for official violation of religious freedom, since administrative litigation is strictly limited to the scope of 'legal interests' defined explicitly in laws (Administrative Litigation Law, Articles 2 and 11) – not including the religious rights provided in the Constitution. At any rate, the courts in practice decline to review religious cases for fear for their 'sensitivity', as illustrated in the following case.

In September 2004, Qiu Jiandong (邱建东), an attorney in Fujian province, filed a civil action against the Network Education School of Sichuan University with the Wuhou District Court (Chengdu), claiming that his right to religious freedom was infringed by a passage in a textbook used by the University. The passage, from *The Philosophical Principles of Marxism*, asserts that 'religion is in nature spiritual opium for the working people.'[36] Qiu Jiandong alleged that the description violated Article 36 of the Constitution, which prohibits discrimination against religious believers, and demanded both correction of the offending text and symbolic compensation of RMB¥1 for spiritual damage. The court declined to review the case and rejected the claims. Qiu Jiandong appealed the decision to a superior court, which sustained the original ruling; he then turned to the Ministry of Education for administrative reconsideration, but without success.

B. How to Distinguish 'Normal Religion' from 'Evil Religion'?

Article 36 of the 1982 Constitution limits state protection to 'normal religious activities', implying that religions or religious activities outside the scope of 'normal' will be not protected and may be restricted by law. Responding to the rise of active sects like Falun Gong, the NPCSC in 1999 amended the Criminal Law and reasserted its resolve to punish 'evil religious organisations' (邪教组织, *xiejiao zuzhi*),[37] but the introduction of this cryptic criminal term raises more questions than it answers. How is 'evil religion' to be defined and distinguished from 'normal religion', which is to be protected according to the Constitution? Who is authorised to define this abstract notion? How should abuses of power be prevented in the processes of defining and prosecuting 'evil religion'?

The Supreme People's Court (SPC) and the Supreme People's Procuratorate (SPP) jointly promulgated two judicial interpretations in October 1999 and June 2001 for the purpose of setting up judicial guidelines for trying religious cases.[38] Article 1 of the 1999 document defines

---

[36] Wang, Yi, 'The First Textbook Litigation Case in China and the Right to Education', *China Law Info* (15 April 2005), http://article.chinalawinfo.com/article/user/article_display.asp?ArticleID=30025.

[37] Decision of the Standing Committee of the National People's Congress on Banning Heretic Cult Organisations and Preventing and Punishing Cult Activities, adopted at the 12th Session of the Standing Committee of the Ninth National People's Congress, 30 October 1999.

[38] Explanations of the Supreme People's Court and Supreme People's Procuratorate Concerning Laws Applicable to Handling Cases of Organisations and Employing Heretic Cult Organisations to Commit Crimes [hereafter 'Explanations'], adopted at the 1079th Meeting of the Judicial Committee of the Supreme People's Court, 9 October 1999, and at the 47th Meeting of the Ninth Procuratorial Committee of the Supreme People's Procuratorate.

'evil religious organisations' as 'illegal organisations established under the guise of religion, qigong or other forms that deify their leading members, enchant and deceive others by concocting and spreading superstitious fallacies, recruit and control their members, and endanger society'. Articles 2 and 3 of the interpretive document also delineate circumstances that shall be regarded as 'particularly serious' in the meaning of Article 300 of the Criminal Law. Punishment in such cases shall be determined, according to Article 300 (clause 1) of the Criminal Law, for the organisers and employers of evil religious organisations and the participants of the harmful activities that violate state law and regulations. These 'special punishments' fail to clearly distinguish innate beliefs from overt activities that may cause tangible harm to society, and they therefore run the risk of violating the equality principle outlined in Article 33 of the Constitution. Article 33 requires that crimes of similar social impact should be similarly treated, irrespective of the beliefs, if any, in the minds of those who committed the crimes: a murderer shall receive the same criminal punishment whether he is a Muslim, a Christian, a Falun Gong member or, for that matter, a Communist atheist.

Although the judicial guidelines regarding 'evil religious organisations' may narrow down the problematic term and somewhat reduce abuses of public power, the texts of the judicial interpretations are themselves full of vague, broad and loaded terms, such as 'superstitious fallacies', 'control members' and 'endanger society', which may be easily manipulated to serve the purpose of suppressing any targeted and otherwise 'normal' religion. The prolonged persecution of the Falun Gong sect since 1999 is a natural consequence of the Constitution failing to provide meaningful protection to any religion, whether 'evil' or 'normal'.

No less important is the fact that by providing for special procedures for religious activities, the Chinese government projects itself into religious affairs, which leads to excessive entanglement between religion and the state. Indeed, by providing funds to religious schools, approving the construction of religious buildings, registering religious associations and evaluating religious personnel, government at various levels is deeply involved in matters that properly belong to the religious organisations themselves.

C. The State–Religion Relationship

Although Article 36 of the Constitution does not explicitly express the separation of religion and the state, both the government and the academic community agree that this principle is implicit in the Constitution. At the Central Ethnicity Work Conference in 1999, the General Secretary of the CCP and State President, Jiang Zemin, seemed to endorse the separation principle by stating that religion shall neither have any privilege over the Constitution and laws, nor interfere with the State in the course of its administrative, judicial and educative functions.[39] Yet the separation principle, properly understood, not only keeps religion out of secular affairs but also prohibits the secular state from interfering with religious practice, lest the state creates the appearance of favouring or disfavouring any particular sect. State practice has been very much the opposite, however, and the Goddess of Mercy Statute in the city of Sanya provides a window through which to view just how the state is entangled with religion in China.

The southwestern part of Sanya City (Hainan Province) is traditionally believed to be the starting point for a visit by the Goddess of Mercy (观音菩萨, Buddha Guanyin) to the South China Sea. In order to exploit the tourist appeal of the region and to spread Buddhist culture, a construction company invested in the building of a religious statue, the Icon of South Mount Goddess of Mercy. During the six years of construction, it was reported that 'every leader from the central government who came to this place paid a visit to the construction site, where they were briefed about the progress of the construction and expressed their support.'[40] At the press conference for the opening ceremony in 2004, a group of officials from Sanya city government even stated, 'The completion of the project owes a great deal to the support and effort of the State Administration of Religious Affairs, the Hainan Provincial government and the Party Committees of Hainan province and Sanya City.' Hence a religious facility had essentially turned into a government project; in fact, the company was eventually obliged to assign 100 per cent

---

[39] Guo Yanjun, 'The Principle of Handling Church–State Relations' (2005) 6 *Legal Science Monthly* 11; and Han Dayuan, 'Tentative Discussion on the Constitutional Value of the Separation of Church and State Principle' (2005) 10 *Legal Science Monthly* 3.

[40] See Tong Zhiwei (ed), 'Legal Issues Involved in the Religious Projects Invested by Local Governments' (2005) 11 *Legal Science Monthly* 13.

of the property rights of the statute to the municipal government, which would directly run and derive tourist income from the site.[41] Although the government may have been interested in the income alone, it was apparently heedless of the religious aspect of the project.

A more serious entanglement is the systematic appraisal systems that local governments have set up for evaluating religious personnel. For example, the United Front Work Department of the Party Committee in Liangpin county (Chongqing municipality) formulated an 'Implementation Method for the Performance Evaluation of Religious Personnel'. This 'quantitative appraisal method' evaluates legally registered religious personnel using seven criteria, including 'patriotism and religious love', 'religious activity', 'service to the believers', 'observance of laws', 'contribution to society', 'political life' and 'personal work summary'. Yearly assessment is meant to 'enhance the moral and political education of the religious personnel, continuously improve their personal qualities, implement orderly management of the religious activity places'.[42] Someone who scores 85 or above is classed as 'excellent' and praised by the county's religious administrative department; someone who scores below 60 is regarded as a failure and is subject to remonstration by his or her associates according to the command of the county's religious affairs department; and anyone who fails the appraisal for two consecutive years is deprived of his or her religious status by relevant religious groups under the recommendation of the county religious affair department. Such a practice, intended to make believers docile to the Party and government, injects secular standards into religious evaluation and constitutes appalling state interference into religious activities.

Such a practice also makes religious associations assume quasi-official power and thereby become channels through which the government can administer and restrict religious activities. The inevitable result is excessive entanglements between the state and religion bodies, as well as religious reliance on government appointments. Official control over the appointments of Catholic bishops, for example, has long created serious conflict between the Chinese authorities and the Vatican. Moreover, the official control over the appointment of Banchan Lama (班禅喇嘛) led to the bizarre co-existence of two Banchan, one

---

[41] Ibid.

[42] Zhang Qianfan and Zhu Yingping, 'Religious Freedom and Its Legal Restrictions in China' (2011) 6 *Brigham Young University Law Review* 101–36.

appointed by the government but unrecognised by most Tibetan Buddhists, another appointed by the Dalai Lama (达赖喇嘛) but unrecognised by the Chinese government. The feud over appointment powers ultimately disposed the CCP to cut ties with the Dalai Lama, the supreme leader of Tibetan Buddhism, and seriously escalated anti-government animosity among Tibetans.[43]

In recent years, religious associations in China have become increasingly like quasi-state functionaries, continually declining in independence. The tell-tale signs of official management are unmistakable in the Articles of Association of most organisations, and the obvious political characteristics of the documents make them almost identical to the charters of satellite political parties or political consultative committees. The Articles of the Chinese Buddhist Association, for example, state that the Association aims 'to assist the people's government with implementing the policy on religious freedom, to uphold the legal rights and interests of the Buddhist societies, [and] to actively participate in the construction of socialist material and spiritual civilisation' (Article 2). The Articles of the Chinese Islamic Association, passed at the Sixth National Congress of Islamic Association in 2006, reads almost identically to a Party or government document, with Article 3 declaring the Association's basic objective to 'uphold the banner of patriotism', 'actively direct Islam in order to adapt to socialist society', 'support the leadership of the CCP and the socialist system', 'follow the guidance of Deng Xiaoping Theory and the important thought of "three represents" ', 'uphold ideals of scientific development', 'abide by socialist moral standards', 'enhance ethnic solidification', 'maintain social stability' and 'promote and uphold the unity of China'.

Such non-religious declarations by religious associations are not surprising given their explicitly subordinate status to state administrative organs. Article 3 of the Daoist Articles declares, 'The superior organ of the association is the State Administration of Religious Affairs.' Similarly, Article 4 of the Islamic Articles also explicitly states, 'This association is subject to the guidance and supervision of the State Administration of Religious Affairs and the Ministry of Civil Affairs.' Furthermore, the tenure of the religious associations is affected deeply by state administration. For some associations, the qualifications of the religious personnel even

---

[43] Wang Lixiong, *Celestial Burial: The Fate of Tibet* (Taipei, Mass Culture Press, 2007) 546–47.

include a state position as prerequisite. For example, Article 16 of the Islamic Articles stipulates that the Chairman, Vice Chairman and Secretary General of the Association must 'uphold the leadership of the CCP, uphold the socialist system and excel in political quality'.

Finally, funds appropriated by the government have become a significant part of the expenses of religious associations in China. As religious associations become increasingly identified with the State in terms of tenets, missions, appointment of leaders and even minimum qualifications for practitioners, they also become more reliant on the government provision of funds, without which the religions would find it increasingly difficult to sustain their activities.

IV. THE RIGHT TO ELECTION

The Sun Zhigang incident initiated reforms to dismantle official discrimination policies based on the urban–rural distinction, but it did not immediately bring about the end of overt political discrimination against peasants. It was not until March 2010 that the NPC deleted the 'quarter vote' clause and declared that 'the population represented by each deputy should be equal for urban and rural areas' (Election Law, Articles 14 and 16). This is no doubt a victory for peasants' political rights, but its substantive effect remains to be seen. Indeed, electoral improvements would fail to produce any consequences if elections are meaningless to begin with. Even for China's urban residents, who were *not* the victims of the earlier discriminatory policy, elections are made largely meaningless by heavy top-down manipulation and partisan control, and it is the very absence of genuine elections that makes the Sun Zhigang model indispensable – yet ultimately limits its effectiveness.

A. The Making of the People's Congresses: Election or Selection?

For ordinary Chinese citizens, 'political rights' mean primarily the rights to elect deputies and to stand for elections as deputy candidates of the People's Congresses at the township and county levels.[44] As provided in

---

[44] For discussion of central and local government structures, see above chs 3 and 4.

Article 34 of the 1982 Constitution, the right to election is to be generally enjoyed by citizens above the age of 18. More than 97 per cent of this group is entitled to vote, the rest being restricted by law. The major legal restriction to voting right is the Criminal Law, which provides that the penalties for serious crimes may be supplemented by deprivation of 'political rights'. For crimes that endanger state security, normal penalties '*shall* be' so supplemented. According to Article 54 of the Criminal Law, these 'political rights' include not only the rights to vote and to stand for election but also freedom of speech, which is otherwise provided for in Article 35 of the Constitution. Although Article 34 of the Constitution authorises exclusion of 'persons deprived of political rights according to law', such an exclusory clause is absent from Article 35, and the constitutionality of expanding the scope of rights deprived by the Criminal Law is in serious doubt. While criminals sentenced to death or imprisonment for life shall be deprived of their political rights for life, the period of the deprivation is reduced to between three and ten years if the sentence is reduced to a limited term; otherwise, the period of the deprivation shall last from one to five years (Criminal Law, Article 55). Such supplemental penalties are severe because such persons will be deprived political rights during the time they serve their sentences *and* for a period *after* they have served their sentences.

A key step in any election is the selection of candidates. Although any citizen above the age of 18 may stand for election (Constitution, Article 34), a candidate for deputy is to be nominated either by political parties and 'people's organisations' or by recommendation signed jointly by more than 10 voters (Election Law, Article 29); but the final candidate list will be decided after 'repeated deliberation, discussion and consultation' by the voter group of the electoral district and will be published at least 15 days before the election day (Election Law, Article 31). This cryptic 'deliberation' process is usually enough to filter out any undesirable candidates and fix any candidate structure desired by the county LPC Standing Committee in charge of deciding the deputies' seat distribution among the electoral districts. In 2002, for example, the deputy structure of the 15th electoral district of Yixing city (Jiangsu province) consisted of 'a cadre at the bureau level, a technical person without CCP membership and a female candidate without CCP membership', and that of the Dagang district in Tianjin municipality consisted of a local police chief, a non-CCP member candidate in charge of the urban resident committee and an unemployed female candidate without CCP membership. In fact, remarkably, the voters were already informed of such a structure at the candidate recommendation stage. In most cases, the candidates determined in such a closed process are unknown to the voters, who are obliged to vote for them with little knowledge about their views, competence, personal character or goals to be pursued once elected.

Such a closed process necessarily invites electoral fraud and corruption, which are positively promoted by political control that diminishes both the value of elections and voters' enthusiasm in genuine participation. In recent years, bribery in elections, a phenomenon first made known to China by Cao Kun (曹锟) in the 1920s,[45] has returned and expanded into LPC elections. A rising number of entrepreneurs have bought themselves deputy status primarily to establish even closer relations with the government.[46] Since these deputies seldom spend any time with their constituents, an overwhelming majority of voters do not even know the names of their deputies.

On the other hand, candidates widely supported by voters and truly dedicated to community service have been repeatedly intimidated and impeded in electoral campaigns.[47] In 1990, for example, Yao Lifa (姚立法) printed 2000 copies of his personal résumé and distributed them among voters at his own expense, but he was ordered by the local authority to cease and withdraw from the election. In 1993, he wrote several letters introducing both himself and the Election Law to voters and was censured by local officials for being 'very dangerous'. In 1998, he failed again to become the formal candidate but still managed to win the second highest poll in the election and won by edging out the formal candidates fixed by internal appointment. In 2011, a record number of activists spontaneously stood as 'independent candidates' (独立参选人, *duli canxuanren*) for LPC elections in contrast to those appointed by official organisations, but they were overtly discouraged by the NPCSC, and a female activist was disqualified for having 'illegally petitioned' the government in the past.[48]

---

[45] See above ch 1.

[46] 'Big Shot Fulfilled Election Bribery Wishes', *Yangtze Evening News* (1 August 2001).

[47] Huang Guangming, 'The Reality of a Plebeian Deputy', *Southern Weekend* (16 January 2003).

[48] The Legal Affairs Committee of the NPCSC, 'Independent Candidate Lacks Legal Ground', *China News* (8 June 2011), http://www.chinanews.com/fz/2011/

Improving the candidate selection process can substantially enhance the quality of China's elections. In August 2002, for example, Jingshan county (Hubei province) experimented with direct election of candidates for the Party Secretary and the chief administrator of Yangji town.[49] Although the incumbents were eventually re-elected by the majority of voters, the electoral competition produced more than enough pressure on the candidates to improve their administrative efficiency once they resumed office. This kind of salutary experiment seemed to lack sustainability, however, and most independent candidates were subsequently excluded from the ballot list in the closed selection processes.

Unlike in Western countries where representatives are normally expected to serve fixed terms until re-election, a deputy in China may be removed during his term. The Election Law provides that a minimum of 30 voters may present to a county LPCSC a jointly signed petition to remove a county or township deputy, who can then be removed by referendum of a majority of voters in the electoral district (Article 44). Deputies to a People's Congress above the county level are elected by the LPC at one level below and may be removed by a majority vote of the deputies in that LPC; the motion to remove may be proposed by the presidium of that LPC or over one tenth of its deputies during the session. When the LPC is not in session, more than half of the component members of the LPC standing committee may remove a deputy at the next higher level (Article 45). The power to unseat officials has occasionally been used by voters, but instances of success are rare. Most removals occur at the People's Congresses above the county level when the deputies in question have been convicted for corruption.

B. The NPCSC Violation of the 'One-person One-vote' Principle

As the People's Congresses above the county level are not directly elected by voters, their elections are even more prone to corruption and political control. A less notorious but no less serious problem is the fact

06-08/3098230.shtml; and Li Xingwen, 'Jiangxi Female Worker Failed to Obtain Qualification for Participating in LPC Election', *Tencent News* (14 May 2011), http://news.qq.com/a/20110515/000132.htm?pgv_ref=aio.

[49] Deng Ke, 'The Yangji Experiment: Electing Candidates for Town Chief and Party Secretary', *Southern Weekend* (19 September 2002).

that the selection of the standing committees for the People's Congresses above the county level are not regulated by the Election Law. Moreover, while the elections of the People's Congresses themselves generally adhere to the 'one person, one vote' principle by rather evenly apportioning deputies' seats among electoral districts (with the exception of special privileges to military deputies), the apportionment of their standing committee members is not bound by the same principle. The disproportionate distribution of the standing committee seats amounts to a serious violation of the democratic principle of equal representation implied in Article 33 of the Constitution since, no less than the People's Congresses themselves, the standing committees are independent legislatures capable of enacting legally binding norms in China.[50]

The NPCSC provides the most glaring example of electoral malapportionment in China. The 'one person, one vote' principle in theory means that the number of Standing Committee members from each province should be roughly proportional to its population; in other words, the proportion of seats in the Standing Committee allotted to a particular province should roughly equal the proportion of that province's voters out of the total eligible voters nationwide. But if one calculates the ratio, for example, for the tenth NPCSC, which was constituted in 2003, one finds serious deviations from the expected numbers.[51] The proportion of seats allotted to Shanghai, Beijing and Tianjin, for instance, was respectively 2.5, 3.5 and 4.8 times greater than the proportion of total voters from those municipalities. In contrast, the proportion of seats allotted to Shanxi, Shandong, Guangdong and Sichuan was respectively 0.2, 0.4, 0.4 and 0.5 times the proportion of the total voters from those provinces. In other words, voters in Shanghai, Beijing and Tianjin enjoyed 12, 17 and 24 times greater representation, respectively, than Shanxi voters did in the NPCSC – which is supposed to evenly represent the entire nation in major policymaking.

Since the members from the large municipalities have dominated the NPC Standing Committee, it is no wonder that discriminatory policies such as the university admission regime, which is heavily preferential in favour of municipalities and affluent provinces,[52] are so difficult to dis-

---

[50] See above ch 4.

[51] Election data can be found at the NPC website: http://www.npc.gov.cn/npc/xinwen/index.htm. See also the data provided by Xinhua News: http://news.xinhuanet.com/ziliao/2004-10/25/content_2136303.htm.

[52] For discussion of university admissions policies, see above ch 7, s II.

mantle. The formal abolition of the 'quarter vote clause' in the Election Law, which pertains only to the election of deputies to the People's Congresses, thus hardly bears on the substantive discrimination still practiced against the vast rural population.

C. Elections of the Villagers' Committees: China's Grassroots Democracy?

The election of villagers' committees used to be seen as China's experiment with 'grassroots democracy' and the only hope for genuine electoral democracy After two decades of practice, however, the experiment has largely failed. Article 13 of the Organic Law on the Villagers' Committees (OLVC) does provide villagers with rights similar to those provided in Article 34 of the Constitution. Moreover, in contrast to the elections of the People's Congresses, the ballots of village elections are counted and announced on the scene, thereby reducing opportunities for electoral fraud (OLVC, Article 15). Like the deputies to the People's Congresses, a member of a villagers' committee may be removed by the majority of the villagers' votes; one fifth of the villagers or one third of the villagers' representatives may propose to remove a committee member (Article 16). Village elections won by violence, threat, deception, bribery, ballot forgery or false report of ballot numbers are invalid (Article 17). Despite these provisions, violence, bribery and political interference are commonplace.[53]

The top-down political interference in township governments, discussed earlier, also seeps into villages, not only through direct and illegal appointment or replacement of villagers' committees[54] but also through more covert means (eg, by instigating villagers to remove elected committee members). Such practices notwithstanding, political interference is prohibited by Article 5 of the OLVC.[55] A local government may exert

[53] Zhang Wenyu, 'Village Election Invoked Gun Shooting', *Southern Weekend* (22 August 2002).

[54] Between September 1999 and May 2002, for example, the township governments in Yao Lifa's Qianjiang city (Hubei province) replaced over half of the 329 elected villagers' committee chairmen for failing to collect agricultural taxes. (For discussion of Yao Lifa, see above ch 4.) Huang Guangming and He Hongwei, '187 Village Officials Fired During 3 Years', *Southern Weekend* (12 September 2002.

[55] See Yi Ying, 'A Village Chief's Confusion for Losing Post', *Southern Weekend* (1 January 2003).

its influence even more easily through the village Party branch, which is directly subordinate to the leadership of the township Party committee. Ever since the village experiments were initiated, conflict between the 'two committees' (两委, *liangwei*) – the villagers' committee and the village Party branch – has been a topic of perennial debate. The matter has now largely been resolved in the favour of local Party branches as a result of efforts by the CCP to tighten its control over the villages.[56]

The village committee and the local Party branch of a village are supposed to be elected by different constituencies: the villagers' committee is elected by voters above the age of 18; the Party branch is elected by the village Party members, who constitute only a small proportion of village voters – even smaller than the average proportion (seven per cent) of Party members nationwide. Different models have been implemented to bring consistency between the two committees. While some provinces require that a villagers' committee chairman and the Secretary of the local Party branch be the same person, others require the local Party secretary to acquire the majority consent of the villagers. In both cases, the uneasy relationship between the state, society and the ruling party has been translated into the conflicts between the two committees at the very grassroots level of Chinese politics. Unsurprisingly, such conflicts tend to be resolved in ways that further tighten Party control.

This is hardly a 'resolution' of the social conflicts in any real sense, however, since political control necessarily diminishes the value of village elections, which can be measured in a sense by the 'cost' of electoral bribery. Since the villagers' choices do not count, and even a properly elected committee has no choice but to follow the 'direction' and 'support' of the township government anyway, why bother to vote? Why not simply 'sell' one's ballot to someone who is willing to pay? As the ballots become 'cheap', bribery becomes rampant in the village elections,[57] and true 'grassroots democracy' gets trampled underfoot. And when, as a consequence, the villagers' committees end up maintaining the status quo rather than protecting the interests of peasants, rural social conflict only multiplies, as tragically demonstrated by the case of Tang Fuzhen.[58]

[56] For more on the ruling party's efforts to tighten control over villages, see above ch 5.

[57] 'Why Village Grassroots Democracy Worth Little', *China Youth Daily*, 16 December 2002.

[58] See above ch 7, s IV.

D. A One-Party-Dominant-Multiparty System?

Finally, since everything has been connected to the ruling party in China since at least1949, a word needs be said about the structure and role of the CCP. Perhaps the single largest party in the world, the CCP claimed its 2010 membership was over 70 million – obviously a huge size , but in actuality a small minority of China's nearly 1.4 billion population. If the CCP is a small, elite group – a mere five per cent of the population – its daily decision-making is monopolised by a still smaller group, estimated to be about 100,000 members, a little over 0.1 per cent of the Party size. This is the result of implementing the 'chief takes responsibility' system in every local government, just as the presidential responsibility scheme is implemented in every court.[59] Ultimate decisions are made by the nine members of the Politburo Standing Committee, assisted by the 24 Politburo members.

Unlike the Nationalist one-party monopoly, however, the CCP is not the only legitimate party in China. With parallels to the state-sanctioned religions, eight satellite 'democratic parties' are recognised, constituting, together with the dominant CCP, a system of supposed 'multi-party cooperation' (多党合作, *duodang hezuo*). These parties are 'satellites' around the CCP centre precisely because their role is limited to friendly cooperation rather than opposition to or competition with the ruling party. An Opinion published by the CCP Central Committee in 1989 made it clear that the legitimacy of these 'participatory parties' (参政党, *canzheng dang*) is conditional on their acceptance of the CCP leadership, and their role is primarily to make suggestions and recommendations in policymaking and to provide criticism and supervision during policy implementation.[60] Membership of the eight satellite parties roughly 300,000 in total – less than 0.5 per cent of that of the CCP.

Any political party beyond the eight sanctioned satellite parties is illegal and will be prosecuted. In 1998, for example, Xu Wenli (徐文立) and Wang Youcai (王有才) were convicted of the charge of subverting state power for establishing the Chinese Democratic Party. It is impossible to lawfully register a political party, since the right to association provided

---

[59] See above ch 6.

[60] Opinion on Insisting on and Perfecting the Multi-Party Cooperation and Political Consultation Led by the CCP, issued by the CCP Central Committee in 1989.

in Article 35 of the Constitution has been limited by interpretation to mean 'social organisations' of non-economic, non-political nature. In fact, the CCP and the eight satellite parties themselves are not registered and are technically without legal status. Legally undefined and unregulated, they essentially operate above the Constitution and other laws, even though the CCP Charter declares in its 'General Principles' that 'the Party must operate within the scope of the Constitution and laws' without giving substance to such promise. The ruling party commands the state machine and may take from the state treasury at will. The central government made attempts to 'separate the party from the state' (党政分离, *dangzheng fenli*), but the effort halted after June 1989, leaving China with a Constitution but without constitutionalism.

FURTHER READING

Carlson, ER, 'China's New Regulations on Religion: A Small Step, Not a Great Leap, Forward' (2005) *Brigham Young University Law Review* 747.

Cheung, ASY, 'In Search of a Theory of Cult and Freedom of Religion in China: The Case of Falun Gong' (2004) 13 *Pacific Rim Law and Policy Journal* 1.

Liebman, BL, 'Watchdog or Demagogue? The Media in the Chinese Legal System' (2005) *Columbia Law Review* 1.

Stevenson, C, 'Breaching the Great Firewall: China's Internet Censorship and the Quest for Freedom of Expression in a Connected World' (2007) 30 *Boston College International and Comparative Law Review* 531.

Wong, KC, 'Law of Assembly in the People's Republic of China' (2006) 12 *Washington and Lee Journal of Civil Rights and Social Justice* 155.

9

Conclusion: The Future of China's Constitutionalism

BACK TO 1911? THE ONGOING SAGA OF CHINA'S CONSTITUTIONAL JOURNEY – TOWARD THE THIRD REPUBLIC? THE FUTURE OF CHINA'S CONSTITUTION-ALISM

AFTER MORE THAN a century of reforms and revolutions, China seems to be back to square one with its constitutional development. In fact, the situation in some ways can be seen as even worse than it was in 1908, when the Empress Dowager promulgated the first Constitutional Outline, since the current ruling Communist Party seems even more resistant to the fundamental changes that are essential to China's constitutionalism. This final chapter will discuss the state of China's constitutionalism after a century of steps forward and backward, as well as the political roadblocks ahead. I will end the book with some conjectural remarks about possible reforms that might bring about a brighter future for China's constitutionalism.

I. BACK TO 1911? THE ON-GOING SAGA OF CHINA'S CONSTITUTIONAL JOURNEY

Viewed a century after the 1911 Revolution, the constitutional history of China is full of unfortunate coincidences. Had China's success in constitutional reform and revolution not depended so critically on such an opportunist as Yuan Shikai, who first allegedly betrayed the Hundred Day reformers under the auspice of Emperor Guangxu, then turned his back against the Qing regime and finally broke with the Nationalist revolutionaries; had the Soviets not succeeded in Russia and actively engaged their eastern neighbour in order to gain international support for Communism, a critical doctrine that the Chinese at the time must have felt too appealing to reject after they were betrayed by the Western powers; had the American President, Woodrow Wilson, not yielded to Australia and Japan at the expense of China with regard to the Treaty of Versailles, thus reawakening massive patriotic anger against the hypocrisy of Western liberal democracies; had the Japanese military not invaded China and critically undermined the Nationalist control over the country and its strength vis-à-vis the Communists . . . China's constitutional journey may well have taken a completely different course. Each event seemed innocuous enough, but they all contributed in their own ways to the continuous failure to establish constitutionalism in China – a process that was always going to hang on a delicate balance in a country with such a long tradition of political despotism.

The Tiananmen Protests were but the latest footnote to a conundrum that has defeated every Chinese constitutional reform at key historical turning points. By 1989, a decade of reform had nurtured a fledging civil society, but it was not yet developed enough to significantly influence the political struggles within the new Forbidden City (中南海, *zhongnanhai*). As a result, the outcome of the Tiananmen Protests was dictated by the outcome of the struggle within the central power circle. As such, it was both the reverse and the replica of another notable power struggle, namely the Cultural Revolution.

In outward appearance, the political struggle that occurred in the aftermath of the Tiananmen Protests was the reverse of the Cultural Revolution: it reinforced the ruling status of the CCP mainstream against a mass opposition, while the campaign against the Gang of Four in 1976 had put an end to a political disaster that ultimately devastated both the country and the Party. At the root, however, the Tiananmen Protests were triggered by the same sort of circumstances that preceded the Cultural Revolution. If the Cultural Revolution was in essence a coup that Mao Zedong plotted against Deng Xiaoping and Liu Shaoqi, then the State President and the nominal highest leader, to protect Mao's de facto supremacy, the crackdown on the Tiananmen Protests was in a sense but another coup, both to maintain Deng's status in the face of a potential challenger, Zhao Ziyang, then the party Secretary-General, and more broadly, to maintain the CCP's ruling status over the nation.

Like all the court struggles since the Hundred Days' Reform, the progressive reformists lost to the more powerful conservatives, despite mounting popular support outside the Forbidden City.

China's constitutional misfortune is not merely a problem for the mainland Chinese population; it may be exported beyond its borders. If a regime is not accountable to its own people, how can it be held accountable to the rest of the world? The salience of this question is demonstrated by China's publically disclosed military expenditure, which exceeds total expenditure for national education and has been increasing annually by double-digit percentages. With a constitution but without constitutionalism, China today is prone to many crises of worldwide impact due to its sheer size and ever-growing economic power. The mixed success of recent economic reforms illustrate, disturbingly, that national strength and economic development are not necessarily felicitous harbingers of institutional reform.

China's increasing economic power has reduced the weight of international pressure that can be used to force the improvement of domestic human rights. China's rise on the international stage has moreover consolidated the supposed legitimacy of the ruling party, inflated the national pride of ordinary Chinese people, whose history textbooks constantly remind them of the humiliations they suffered during the Opium Wars and after, and disposed them to rank territorial integrity as the top national priority above all else. Any secessionist sparks in Taiwan, Tibet or Xinjiang are likely to foment patriotic hysteria and inevitably prompt conspiracy theories that link such events to 'foreign intervention' and to 'Western imperialism', to the detriment of the domestic reception of Western-style liberal democracy.

China today is in the same nationalistic mood as it was in during the May Fourth Movement (1919), only now the country is apparently more united and powerful than ever, and is capable of inflicting revenge. The People's Republic is very much a product of the two World Wars, and now – without constitutional mechanisms to keep its powers in check – it surely has the capacity to initiate another war.

II. TOWARD THE THIRD REPUBLIC? THE FUTURE OF CHINA'S CONSTITUTIONALISM

It remains to be seen whether past tragedies have taught China and the rest of the world enough lessons to divert a future crisis. Past experiences point to the negative, however. Despite active intervention, the Americans failed to prevent the Communist takeover of China and other parts of Asia. And even though international pressure may play a critical role in pushing for democracy and human rights in China, the country is perhaps simply too large to be moved by external force. The contrasting fates of the protesters in Tiananmen Square and in Tahrir Square, Cairo, are telling. While conditions in Egypt in early 2011 no doubt differed from China in June 1989, it is easy enough to conclude that American President Barack Obama's consistent pressure on Egyptian President Hosni Mubarak played a crucial part in the success of the Egyptian domestic democratic movement. The same can be said about the NATO military intervention in Libya later that year, which helped opposition forces to overthrow the dictator Muammar Kaddafi. But moving the scene back to Tiananmen Square, one can see that were the 1989 protests to happen again today, they would be destined to fail, just as they did over two decades ago. Although international pressure and support play an important role in promoting domestic progress, China is simply too massive to be moved by external forces alone, and its constitutional progress ultimately depends on changes coming from within.

The Sun Zhigang Incident and, even more promisingly, the Xiamen 'collective walk' do suggest that the people are on the rise in China. What is missing, however, is a critical link – a way for the people's voices to be effectively translated into policymaking. After all, a People's Republic can be nothing but a fake if it fails to provide the people with meaningful opportunity to participate in the republic. It is at this point that the age-old reform-versus-revolution dilemma returns and haunts China. More than in 1895, 1908, 1911 or even 1989, China in 2011 is more firmly than ever caught in this dilemma. The ruling regime, having lost moral legitimacy in the Tiananmen Protests, is now decidedly entrenched in order to protect the status quo. If it took the 1911 Revolution to remove the obstinate Qing regime and to establish the First Republic, it appears that another revolution is the only means powerful enough to remove the institutional impediments to contemporary constitutional reform. But the experiences of the first revolution and, in particular, of the second revolution, which established the Second Republic in 1949, recommend the very opposite. The Communist revolution, accomplished through 'the forcible overthrow of all existing social conditions',[1] has not only failed to bring about sustainable constitutionalism to China but permanently derailed China from the constitutional course by establishing a more centralised and less accountable regime.

With violent revolution a dead end and progressive reform stalled by the status quo, China's constitutionalism is truly at a crossroads today. It desperately calls for a new, Third Republic to fulfil the very promise indicated by the name. This Third Republic is not to be forcibly established by any revolutionary vanguards who see themselves as morally and intellectually superior to ordinary Chinese people but rather to be brought about precisely by the common people themselves, through their daily actions in defending rights and giving substance to existing constitutional provisions. Exactly how such a movement will take place in a less than friendly institutional environment is a challenging question that confronts the Chinese people today even more than it did over a century ago.[2]

Looking ahead, China's constitutional reform has many difficult missions to accomplish before it becomes a true people's republic. Since the ultimate impediment to constitutionalism is the status quo protected by the ruling party, the CCP must somehow 'return power to the people' (还权于民, *huanquan yu min*), a challenge that has perplexed China ever since the revolutionary Nationalists established 'tutelage politics'.[3] To be sure, there has been an increase in power-sharing among key Party figures, but on the whole, power struggles among various Party factions are as opaque, unregulated and unaccountable as they were between the reformist Emperor Guangxu and the conservative Empress Dowager in 1898, and as between the reformist General-Secretary Zhao Ziyang and the conservative mainstream led by Deng Xiaoping in 1989. Even worse, the Party seems to be unanimous in suppressing the electoral campaigns of 'independent candidates', whose active political participation would

---

[1] K Marx and F Engels, *The Communist Manifesto* (1948) (New York, International Publishers, 1998) 44.

[2] Zhang Qianfan, 'China's Mission for Constitutional Transformation and Personality Reformation' (2011) 10 *Leaders* 66–83.

[3] See above ch 1.

revitalise the dormant 'supreme' power of the People's Congresses, which are required by the Constitution to exercise the state power that properly 'belongs to the people' (Article 2). And Premier Wen Jiabao has been the lonely exception among the nine Politburo Standing Committee members in persistently calling for political reform, just as the Party Secretary of Guangdong province has been quite alone in promoting the active model of civic participation undertaken in Wukan village.[4]

More fundamentally, though the constitutional consciousness of the general populace has risen continuously since 1978, the vast majority remains politically passive under a regime that effectively discourages political participation and makes elections into meaningless performances. This dormant majority has been shocked by the tragedies of Sun Zhigang and Tang Fuzhen and in those instances unhesitatingly expressed its moral disapproval, but it has yet to learn the necessity of stepping out and casting votes to prevent like tragedies from reoccurring. To make their country a new republic, the Chinese people need to transform themselves from subjects of a despotic regime – whether under an emperor or a monopolistic ruling party – into citizens with a republican spirit.

FURTHER READING

Cai, D, 'The Development of Constitutionalism in the Transition of Chinese Society' (2005) 19 *Columbia Journal of Asian Law* 1.

Chen, HA, *An Introduction to Legal System of the People's Republic of China*, 4th edn (Hong Kong, LexisNexis Butterworths, 2011) ch 5.

Zhang, Q, 'A Constitution without Constitutionalism? The Paths of Constitutional Developments in China' (2010) 8 *International Journal of Constitutional Law* 950–76.

---

[4] See above ch 8; and 'Wang Yang: Reform should Begin with Ruling Party, Emphasise to Stand By the People and Spread Wukan Experience throughout Province', *Ming Pao Daily* (6 March 2012).

Index